"Rachel Ehrenfeld has undertaken an ambitious project—to sketch the sprawling agenda of a billionaire who has called the United States "the main obstacle to a stable and just world." She shows how he has used his resources to undermine this country's justice system, its sovereignty, and its social cohesion. The only other country on which George Soros arguably has inflicted comparable damage is Israel. Although Soros was born Jewish, he has done more to spread anti-Israel propaganda than anyone on the face of the earth, according to a former U.S. ambassador to Israel, and has cynically used his Jewish birth to hurl promiscuous accusations of anti-Semitism at anyone who dares to criticize him. In this wide-ranging description of what Soros does through the ironically named Open Society Foundation, Ehrenfeld describes not only the multi-faceted malign conduct of George Soros but also the obstacles he puts in the way of anyone who would expose the financial underpinnings of his various organizations. Rachel Ehrenfeld brings skill and passion to presenting a damning indictment of a dangerous man."

–MICHAEL B. MUKASEY, U.S. ATTORNEY GENERAL
(2007 TO 2009), AND U.S. DISTRICT JUDGE (1988 -2006).

ALSO BY RACHEL EHRENFELD

Narco-terrorism: How Governments Around The World Have Used The Drug Trade To Finance And Further

Evil Money: Encounters Along the Money Trail

Funding Evil: How Terrorism is Financed—and How to Stop it.

RACHEL EHRENFELD

THE SOROS AGENDA

REPUBLIC

BOOK PUBLISHERS

THE SOROS AGENDA

Copyright 2023 Rachel Ehrenfeld

FIRST EDITION

The information included in this book is based on official and public documents and statements and the author's interviews, views, and analysis.

This book was written before the 2022 midterm elections.

ISBN Paperback: 978-1-64572-047-8   Ebook: 978-1-64572-048-5

For inquiries about volume orders, please contact:

Republic Book Publishers

editor@republicbookpublishers.com

Published in the United States by Republic Book Publishers

Distributed by Independent Publishers Group

www.ipgbook.com

Book designed by Mark Karis

Printed in the United States of America

IN MEMORY OF HOUSTON T. "TERRY" HAWKINS,
the insightful, brilliant futurist, strategist, innovator,
and always attentive and encouraging friend and
true American patriot (1941-2021)*

*At the time of his passing, Terry was a Los Alamos National Laboratory (LANL) Fellow assigned to the Principal Associate Directorate for Global Security and concurrently served on the Advisory Board of the American Center for Democracy.

CONTENTS

INTRODUCTION

SHORTLY AFTER "BLACK WEDNESDAY" IN 1992, when the British pound was devaluated, I was listening to the animated discussion of my acquaintances from the Metropolitan Police's Serious Fraud Office on the sudden termination of their routine investigation of the events that hit them in their pockets. They also mentioned a rumor (not reported by the media) that George Soros, known for his activities in the former Soviet Union and Russia, may have received some of the collateral he needed to bet against the pound from Russian accounts in Swiss banks.

I was investigating international drug and terrorist money laundering operations at the time and did not follow up on the conversation.

But in 1994, when George Soros declared war on U.S. drug laws and invested some $15 million in organizations and campaigns for drug legalization, I began paying attention.

As an expert on drug addiction and drug trafficking, with three published books on this topic, I knew that drug legalization would cause a massive increase in the number of drug addicts. Moreover, I recalled that enabling easy access to narcotics was mentioned in the *Soviet Military Encyclopedia* as an important weapon during so-called peacetime. It was recommended because when easily accessible, narcotic use spreads like fire, undermining the targeted country's society, economy, and political integrity.

In February 1995, I was at a dinner at Soros's home in New York City and took some notes, which were published in *Insight Magazine* (which no longer exists). "An Evening at Soros's" help illustrates the early days of his drug-legalization campaign:

> "Cocaine is as good a stimulant as coffee with less harmful effects on the body," said a drug legalization advocate in New York. A colleague from Duke University chimed in, "And it fills a spiritual vacuum in the deep void left by our shallow, materialistic society."
>
> Caricature? Not at all: These are some of the comments made by the respected guests of billionaire financier George Soros at a gathering at his opulent Upper East Side Manhattan duplex. Having spent hundreds of millions of dollars to foster the democratic values of an "open society" and claiming credit for bringing down Communist rule in Eastern Europe, Soros began mobilizing some of his vast resources to fight against the evils and misguided policy of the drug war,[1] one which he often claimed, was "doing more harm than good."[2]

Ethan Nadelmann, director of Soros's Lindesmith Center, was present and told us how, during the Gorbachev Foundation's "State of the World Forum" meeting in San Francisco, he "introduced those ideas as part of the New World Order while moderating the session on 'creative approaches to the international drug crisis.'"[3]

Nadelmann recalled that Soros told him, "'We are basically in agreement . . . [I] empower you to accomplish our common objectives.' Nadelmann's objective is to 'legalize the personal use of drugs by adult Americans. . . .' And Soros 'is comfortable with that,'" he said.[4] *He must be because he is paying for it*, I thought.

> Other guests were equally unrestrained on this memorable evening at Soros's. New York district judge Robert Sweet, who favors decriminalization, remarked, "This [drugs] is a phony issue. People want to change their state of mind because they don't have jobs, they are deprived . . .

And it is a lie that violence is caused by drug addicts . . . The harm comes from the drug laws, not from drugs." "And let's not forget that drugs are fun," added a well-known pro-legalization jazz musician."[5]

That evening, Soros posed as open-minded on the drug issue and said he was interested in debating it. He loudly praised the Swiss experiment of supplying addicts with heroin, morphine, and free needles to inject the drug of their choice and methadone.

However, I was just back from Switzerland, where I had visited the government-sponsored injection facilities and extensively interviewed the experts and government officials involved in the project since it started in 1986. The sad consensus was that the experiment failed terribly. It produced tens of thousands of new addicts.

So, politely, I interrupted Soros, pointing out that he was ill-informed. He seemed stunned that I dared contradict him and forcefully repeated his praise of the Swiss. When I insisted he was wrong, the angry Soros turned around and left the big living room. The other guests, who until then stood around us, listening, moved very fast away from me. The scene reminded me of something Woody Allen would have created.

On Feb. 7, 1996, as Soros increased his drug legalization campaign, I noted in The *Wall Street Journal* how Soros' "sponsorship unified the movement to legalize drugs and gave it the respectability and credibility it lacked." I also opined that unchallenged Soros would change the political landscape in America.[6]

My article did not go unnoticed. Shortly after it was published, I received a warning letter from Soros's lawyer, Bernard Nussbaum, who previously served as President Clinton's White House's legal counsel. Soros did not like my criticism.

I kept wondering why Soros wished to intimidate me into silence. I had merely criticized his drug legalization efforts. (Early on, Soros suggested the legalization of *all* drugs. "I firmly believe that the war on drugs is doing more harm to our society than drug abuse itself," he stated.[7] Encountering opposition, he modified his campaign, first to legalize the use of marijuana for "medical" purposes, although no scientifically approved medical use of the drug was then available. Achieving that, he progressed to campaign for universal legalization of marijuana.) I asked why Soros, who claims to advance an "open society," is promoting the biggest slavery ever: drug addiction. I did not think that this warranted any reaction from Soros.

It took a few more years—and billions of dollars of Soros's investments in reshaping America by changing its criminal justice system to fit his perverted vision of an "open society"—to comprehend why or what in my article upset him.

It seems it was my observation that "unchallenged, Soros would change the political landscape in America." Indeed, I identified that drug legalization was merely his opening gambit to reshape America. But Soros needn't worry about my prognosis of his agenda. It took twenty-six years for Americans to catch up with the profound changes Soros has set out to achieve—and has achieved—in America.

Many reports, articles, and books have been published about Soros's "political philanthropy" (an oxymoron). That's not what this book is about. This book is about the skillful craftiness with which he advanced his plans to change America.

Most of what we know about Soros the person is what he has told us repeatedly in books, articles, and speeches. Curiously, there is no thorough, independent, objective, investigative book about him. Such work would require an intrepid, curious, dedicated, multilingual team, connections, and lots of money. But as long as Soros is alive, legal obstacles will prevent access to some privileged information.

Over years of examining Soros's activities, his political philanthropy, and the way it is used—which served me as an excellent study of corruption—I encountered many who refused to talk about him, even though they initially agreed to do so. When asked, many in positions to know responded, "Soros, who?" Quite a few admitted they feared him. Why? This arrogant central European man didn't frighten me.

An indication of his power is the difficulty of finding out how many billions of dollars Soros has invested in past elections, progressive Left organizations, causes advancing his political agenda, and his direct and indirect links that influence domestic and international affairs all over the world. It is a byzantine task.

In 2016, *Tranparify* rated Soros's OSF (Open Society Foundations), which serves his global network, as highly opaque,[8] and the least transparent of "200 think tanks . . . in 47 countries" worldwide that were ranked.[9]

Soros once described the influence of large cash donations in politics as "a fundamental crisis in democratic self-government."[10] This, however, did not stop him from channeling his "political philanthropy" through an intricate, multilayered web that would put to shame the elusive "Darwin's bark spider" (*Caerostris darwini*), creator of the largest known orb webs.[11]

This book explores several important topics in Soros's general agenda to change the U.S. by funding Left-oriented individual public figures, groups, and politicians. It highlights his methods, meddling, influence, and contradictory statements and actions. It also shows the gradual progression of his funding of increasingly radical causes and the changes he has effected, mainly in the U.S. political landscape. His successes have only increased violence and division in the country, weakening it from within while decreasing its influence in the world, no doubt bringing the ninety-two-year-old billionaire some *naches* (Yiddish for "proud pleasure, special joy—particularly from achievements"[12]).

Portraying Soros's agenda with a broad brush required focusing on the impact of his activities that have already left their mark on America. Identifying his modus operandi and the direction he charted for the future should help develop a new, sophisticated application that could identify even his tenuous links to prevent them from carrying out Soros's full-scale revolution.

1

THE ONE-EYED KING

*I have developed a conceptual framework that
puts me slightly ahead of the crowd*

−GEORGE SOROS, AUGUST 11, 2020.

IN MY 1996 op-ed in the *Wall Street Journal,* I remarked on how Soros's "sponsorship unified the movement to legalize drugs and gave it the respectability and credibility it lacked."[1] I also opined that unchallenged, Soros would change the political landscape of America. I did not need a crystal ball to foresee his plan. Carefully listening to Soros's megalomanic dissing of, and implicit threat to, the U.S. was enough.

Yet, Soros, who once described himself as the "one-eyed king among the blind,"[2] remains unchallenged. And feared.

Much has been written about Soros's past as a survivor of the German occupation of Hungary during World War II and the Soviet occupation that followed. He uses those experiences as his leading credential to justify meddling in political and social affairs as he sees fit. And for the past four decades, Soros has been using his multibillion-dollar political-philanthropic global network to impose his Weltanschauung around the world.

Early on, the megalomaniac savvy currency manipulator understood he needed to mask his intentions and schemes to spread his made-up, wily, neo-Marxist, globalist ideas. So he took a page from Orwell's doublespeak and borrowed Austrian philosopher Karl Popper's term "open society" to name his foundations.[3]

Popper's idea of an "open society" specified that individual freedom is essential to maintaining an open society. "Freedom is more important than equality . . . The attempt to realize equality endangers freedom; and . . . if freedom is lost, there will not even be equality among the unfree," he argued in his *Unended Quest*.[4]

Soros, however, abhors individual freedom—except his own. He has devoted decades of his life and much of his fortune to promoting the opposite: sociopolitical collectivism and globalism. As the late journalist Stefan Kanfer put it, Soros's goal is to liberate America "from the restraints of constitutionalism, American exceptionalism, free-market capitalism, and other obsolete isms."[5]

"I fancied myself as some kind of god, the creator of everything," Soros once wrote. "I carried some rather potent messianic fantasies."[6] In 1993, Soros told the *Independent*, "It is a sort of disease when you consider yourself some kind of god, the creator of everything, but I feel comfortable about it now since I began to live it out."[7] However, the imperious and vainglorious Soros, who has been living out his fantasies, is barred by the U.S. Constitution from becoming president, the most coveted, influential position a man like him could have wanted. But Soros is not known for giving up. So he used his money and celebrity to change the U.S. from the most prosperous, democratic, and powerful nation into a crime-ridden, racially divided, anarchic , and confused nation with rising inflation and a floundering economy that had lost its superpower status.

To grasp Soros's success, look no further than the rise of the progressive neo-Marxist Democrat party and the utterly corrupt Biden

administration's policies to remake America, which have already destabilized the U.S. and the rest of the world. The proof of his success can
be found in the Oval Office, where the president rules by fiat, in courts
around the country that facilitate spiking crime rates in big and small
cities alike,[8] illegal and undocumented migrants flooding into the country
through illegally open borders, in growing racial divide, in the indoctrination of children from kindergarten[9] to adults in the military,[10] and the
overwhelming stench of marijuana and trash arising from the homeless
tents in cities and towns across America—mostly those led by Democrats.[11]

A fawning media invariably refers to George Soros as a "philanthropist,"[12]
but his actions defy the term. Soros's lofty, compassion-laced reasons for
launching specific initiatives contradict everything he ultimately does.

A skilled agitator, Soros routinely masquerades as a compassionate
liberal. He told Politico his money would go to support "causes and
candidates, regardless of political party" who would be "strengthening
the infrastructure of American democracy: voting rights and civic participation, civil rights and liberties, and the rule of law."[13]

However, Soros's idea of what constitutes America's democracy is
different than that of the Constitution. In 2006, Soros declared: "Our
Founding Fathers were children of the Enlightenment, and thus believed
the division of powers was sufficient to protect our democracy. But
they did not fully recognize how imperfectly we understand the world,
how our own perceptions of reality actually change that reality. On the
contrary, the preamble to the Declaration of Independence says: "We
hold these truths self-evident." After 200 years, we have discovered that
when it comes to human affairs, truth can be manipulated."[14]

Indeed, the enormous sums of money he gives personally and
through his various tax-exempt foundations and other entities go only
to progressive Left groups and candidates who, when elected, do their
best to follow the Soros doctrine: to change America's "imperfect" constitutional framework.[15] And worse. With friends in high places, discreet
accountants, and a few remaining tax havens, such as Curaçao, a tax-
free haven in the Caribbean, Soros has managed to avoid accountability

for decades.

Anyone looking to George Soros as a moral compass should recall his infamous 1994 interview with Steve Kroft on CBS's *60 Minutes*. When Kroft called him on the carpet for his currency manipulations, Soros replied, "I don't feel guilty because I'm engaged in an amoral activity which is not meant to have anything to do with guilt."[16]

According to Soros, his character was shaped during the Nazi occupation when he was fourteen, including the time he had accompanied a Nazi Hungarian official at the Ministry of Agriculture named Baumbach, who was bribed by George's father to keep the teen at his apartment and present him as his godson.[17] Soros accompanied Baumbach as the official identified Jewish property for confiscation by the Nazis. "I was only a spectator," Soros told Kroft, "I had no role in taking away that property. So I had no sense of guilt."[18] Notably, however, Soros failed to use the opportunity to convey his regret.

In interviews, books, and public appearances, Soros has revealed that he was trained to recognize vulnerabilities and use them to his advantage from a young age. Soros "knows how to identify and exploit his prey's point of greatest vulnerability," noted RealClear Politics.[19]

Soros's blasé attitude toward social mores has not stopped him from declaring moral outrage. He criticized Republican presidents Ronald Reagan, George W. Bush,[20] and Donald Trump, along with his economic plans and political agendas that favored American hegemony. "If I abstain from certain actions because of moral scruples, then I cease to be an effective speculator," Soros told the London *Guardian*.[21]

He has certainly proved to have no moral scruples about anything. Unfortunately for America, his speculations on advancing the destruction of its Western political, economic, and social systems are proving very effective.

Soros has described himself as both "brilliant" and "clever."[22] We have already seen that he considers himself a deity. His close friend, Byron Wien, explained, "You must understand he thinks he's been anointed by God to solve insoluble problems." But how does Soros *know* he was chosen? "The proof is that he has been so successful at making so much," Wien said.[23]

* * *

In early April 2022, a Google search listed more than 18,500,000 results for George Soros.

A major funder of the Democrat Party in the U.S., Soros has been constantly in the news since October 1992, when he advertised that it was he who had devalued the British pound a month earlier. "'I had no platform,' Soros said, 'So I deliberately [did] the sterling thing to create a platform.' Obviously, people care about the man who made a lot of money," noted author Noreena Hertz.[24] Since then, his influence has only grown. "I . . . have access to most people I want to have access to," he bragged.[25]

According to the *Telegraph*, "Then a little-known financier whose fame stretched no further than the City [of London], he was soon to become a household name as 'The man who broke the Bank of England.'"[26] Soros has been milking his celebrity ever since to advance his business interests and mostly to gain access to heads of state, directors of international organizations, politicians, and intellectuals, and, more importantly, to cultivate influential journalists all over the world.

The more famous he became, the more influence he gained, which he used to advance his political agenda under the guise of promoting an "open society" with an investment of at least $32 billion. The more successful he became, the more cash he had on hand. The more cash he had on hand, the more influence he had over events.

At a certain point, Soros stopped merely reacting to situations and began instigating them. His consolidated financial power has always benefited him, of course. But does he personally benefit from legalizing marijuana? Why does he fund Palestinian and BDS groups advocating eliminating the Jewish State of Israel? (See Chapter 6.) Why did he invest millions in groups[27] lobbying for Obama's terrible Iran deal that helped facilitate Iran's nuclear weapons program and those supporting

Biden's efforts to sign a new disastrous deal with the mullahs?[28] Why is he funding groups calling for the removal of Iran's major terrorist group, the Islamic Revolutionary Guard Corps (IRGC)—which has the blood of thousands, including Americans, on their hands—from the U.S. sanctions list?[29] How did he benefit from funding color revolutions in former Soviet republics and Communist European countries? Or changing regimes in the Balkans? And how does he profit from funding reactionary neo-Marxist and progressive Left groups in the United States? What does he gain from destroying the richest, freest, and most powerful country in the world?

Perhaps the real question should be: on whose behalf has Soros done all this?

CAPITALISM FOR ME–NOT FOR THEE

"George Soros is trying to change the system that made him rich," read the headline of a *Washington Post* article on July 6, 2020.[30]

Since communism failed in Russia and Eastern Europe, Soros's writings have certainly had a neo-Marxist flavor, condemning market fundamentalism "as a false and dangerous doctrine."[31]

Soros implied that his 1997 *Atlantic* article, "The Capitalist Threat,"[32] was misunderstood. Misunderstood how?

He has declared himself, for example, "at odds with the latter-day apostles of laissez-faire" and further doubted the markets' ability to allocate goods properly.[33] "I now fear that the untrammeled intensification of laissez-faire capitalism and the spread of market values into all areas of life is endangering our open and democratic society," Soros, then the thirty-eighth-richest man in the world, wrote in the *Atlantic*. "The main enemy of the open society, I believe, is no longer the communist but the capitalist threat." Later in the same article, Soros added, "Laissez-faire ideology . . . is just as much a perversion of supposedly scientific verities as Marxism-Leninism is."[34]

In 2003, in *The Bubble of American Supremacy,* Soros asserted that the Communist doctrine failed "only because the free enterprise model has been pursued in a less dogmatic, extremist way than the Communist one."[35]

In the same book, Soros laments that "international income distribution is practically nonexistent."[36] Haughty words from a man with a bank account larger than the GNP of some Third World countries. But it followed his statement to Charlie Rose in 1998: "I am not opposed to capitalism. I want to improve it to make it more viable."[37]

Indeed, Silicon Valley's progressive Left billionaires have been singing the same tune. And, like him, they are funding the Democrat Party's radical Left.

If the rich getting richer pains them, why not go ahead and share their colossal fortunes with the poor? Indeed, they could fund erecting a fence on the U.S. southern border to protect all Americans from invading predators, increase the public's health and security by financing the police and other law enforcement agencies, pay all student loans, reduce the country's national debt, open manufacturing facilities around the country, and on and on. And they'll have enough money left to maintain the lifestyle they have gotten adjusted to. That is if they really hate the system that makes them so rich.

"It is exactly because I have been successful in the marketplace that I can afford to advocate these values," Soros said candidly in *Soros on Soros*. "I am the classic limousine liberal."[38]

Nevertheless, Soros blames capitalism for the coarsening of American culture. He is the only one able to handle wealth properly. The rest of us savages couldn't be trusted with money: "Unsure of what they stand for, people increasingly rely on money as the criterion of value," Soros writes in "The Capitalist Threat." "What is more expensive is considered better. The value of a work of art can be judged by the price it fetches. People deserve respect and admiration because they are rich. [Why does Soros think people respect him?] What used to be a medium of exchange has usurped the place of fundamental values, reversing the relationship postulated by economic theory. What used to be professions have turned into businesses. The cult of success has replaced a belief in principles.

Society has lost its anchor."[39]

Tough talk for the man who also has boasted, "I cannot and do not look at the social consequences of what I do."[40] The word *hypocrisy* doesn't even begin to describe Soros's involvement. Deeply ingrained *deceitfulness* comes closer.

Although widely credited as the quintessential anti-communist, Soros has chafed at the term in the past. Soros told the *New York Times* in 1990, "I feel more comfortable with Soviet intellectuals than I do with American businessmen."[41]

Soros also complained to the *New Yorker* in 1995 about a newspaper that had had the gall to call him an anti-communist in the late 1980s. "It was highly embarrassing and damaging to me, because I had a foundation in China, where I said I was a supporter of the Open Door Policy," Soros said. "'I'm not an anti-Communist,' I said to them. So you would have to say different things in different countries."[42]

Not surprisingly, in 1987, he named his first foundation in the Soviet Union the Soviet American Foundation Cultural Initiative. He refrained from using the phrase "open society" in Communist-run countries. His goal, as he explained in the case of South Africa, was to create an elite that would subvert the governing system from within. He proved his skills as an excellent agitator by succeeding. But he was not doing it alone. His foundations overseas have been closely linked with U.S. government agencies and representatives of the European Council.

Soros has also maintained close ties with Germany. Or vice versa. In September 1985, when James Baker, then secretary of the Treasury, held a top-secret meeting at the Plaza in New York with other finance ministers, orchestrating the largest one-day drop of the dollar against the Japanese yen in history, Soros made the "killing of a lifetime" and cleared $150 million in profits. As Soros tells the tale, this move resulted from months of careful analysis. However, in 1996, Robert Slater, in his unauthorized biography of Soros, implied that Soros might have had connections in Germany.[43] And in *The Soros Connection*, Robert E. Kaplan extensively documented Soros's German links, which he claims were behind Soros's devaluation of the British pound in 1992, which netted him at least $2 billion and made him famous.[44] Be that as it may, there are no other independent sources for this claim. Soros, however, used this opportunity to begin his life as a celebrity.

The August 23, 1993, cover story of *Business Week*, "The Man Who Moves Markets," painted the picture of an investor whose manipulation of the press is matched only by his ability to manipulate his financial empire.[45]

"All told, Soros made $2 billion in profits on the trade, tripling the value of his fund, at the expense of the British taxpayer and the government. Without a global network and precise timing to rely on, Soros could never have pulled such an extreme trade."[46]

Another instance of cooperation is the 2007 German Foreign Office invitation to Soros presidential candidate Barack Obama to speak at the Brandenburg Gate in Berlin. This turned Obama, who until then had no known foreign policy experience, into an international superstar. Soros, Obama's major funder, also became his impresario. He expected a handsome return. But the pompous, publicity-hounding Soros has again decided to keep his working relationship with Obama secret. Or was it the other way around?

To deceive the public about his influence on the new administration, Soros used the same tactic he had used to hide his close connections with the Clinton White House. "It's remarkable how the White House doesn't use one of the few resources it's got, which is me," he complained.[47]

There was nothing further from the truth. Soros's extensive involvement in Clinton's foreign policy earned him the title of "a national resource—indeed, a national treasure, " as Strobe Talbott, then Clinton's deputy secretary of state, told the *New Yorker*.[48]

Moreover, Soros was so close to the Clintons that when the Monica Lewinsky scandal broke in January 1998 and Hillary Clinton withdrew from the public, one of only two outside visitors Hillary saw that first week was George Soros, with whom she discussed Ukraine. What was so urgent about Ukraine?

They kept close. In January 2002, Soros flew Hillary to Davos. Her speech was so influenced by his "Open Society" thinking that observers expected her to take over the Soros Foundation. Instead, she ran for Senate with Soros's help. He initially supported her attempt to run for president in the 2008 elections but dropped her in favor of Barack Obama, whom he backed with millions of dollars.

But not long after Obama settled into the White House, Soros made it known he was disappointed that Obama was not accessible, saying he regretted not supporting Hillary, who served as state secretary.[49] Hillary's emails, which were exposed by DCLeaks, document Soros's influence on her decisions, which resulted in promoting Soros's interests in countries big and small. As for Obama, he may have met Soros infrequently, but his staff, which included many former Soros beneficiaries, had close links with him and his Open Society Policy Center (OSPC),[50] a seven-minute walk from the White House.

While Obama's policies to destroy U.S. government credibility and curtail Washington's critical international role may not have originated with Soros, these undoubtedly served the billionaire's ambition to reduce America's power in the world.

Donald Trump's ability to reverse the trend threatened Soros and the globalist cabal. Soros's experience instigating several color revolutions, meddling in the national elections of many countries, and using the well-kept Leftist media to misinform the public helped place the feeble and corrupt Joe Biden in the White House. This guaranteed the reintroduction of Obama's plans to change America from within and reduce its power from without.

To fight climate change, as Soros and the globalists decreed, Biden, like Obama before him, has limited the exploitation of natural gas resources, blocked Canadian oil and gas exports through Texas refineries, and stopped the Keystone XL pipeline, reversing America's energy independence, and causing huge price increases of oil, gas, and the "petrochemicals that derived from oil and natural gas [that] make the manufacturing of over 6,000 everyday products and high-tech devices possible," as stated on Department of Energy's website.[51] The byproducts are essential to our lives. Indeed, "Modern life relies on the availability of these products." It is President Biden's policies that led to fast-growing inflation, price increases, and limited supplies of most everything, including fertilizers, aspirin, cortisone, electric devices, detergents, cell phones, tennis rackets, TVs, computer parts, space-suits, batteries, solar panels, and wind turbine blades, which the Biden administration is now buying from its major hostile competitor, China.

The Biden administration's frenzied guidelines on racial and depraved gender identity, transgenderism, "gender-affirming care,"[52] and other sexual mores, and its soft-on-crime policies, evoked a warning from the judicious social critic Patrick Moynihan in an article titled "Defining Deviancy Down": "The amount of deviant behavior in American society has increased beyond the levels the community can 'afford' to recognize . . . Accordingly, we have been re-defining deviancy so as to exempt much conduct previously stigmatized, and also quietly raising the 'normal' level in categories where behavior is now abnormal by any earlier standard."[53] Moynihan wrote this in 1993, just as Soros, with his inflated ego and his motto, "If I spend enough, I will make it right,"[54] began his efforts to change America from within, to reflect better the ever-changing principles of his fictitious "open society" dream. He skillfully exploited the trend Moynihan warned about, to which he found willing accomplices more than ready to join saving America from the "excessive individualism" of its capitalist mentality.[55]

At that time, he wasn't that rich but felt strong enough with the $2 billion he had pocketed betting on the British pound. The richer he got, the more problems—some real, most invented—he chose to take on. Over time, his foundations have funded and promoted abnormal and depraved behaviors and deviant standards that are surely causing Moynihan and the Founding Fathers to roll in their graves.

While Soros was not the principal founder of the neo-Marxist, pro-gressive, radical, globalist, racist, anti-woman, anti-children, anti-family, anti-Christian, anti-Semitic, climate doomsday clans, he served as their prime agitator and used his OSF as prime brokerage to fund them.

"Though his causes have evolved over time, they continue to hew closely to his ideals of an open society," says his portrayal on the OSF's web page.[56]

THE STATELESS, ANTI-CAPITALISM CAPITALIST STATEMAN

Soros was no fan of the Reagan administration's hardline stance against communism. "Anti-Communism as it is professed and practiced by the Reagan administration runs a great risk," Soros wrote in the *Financial Times* in 1984. "If we interfere in the internal politics of countries within our orbit in order to prevent them from falling into the Communist orbit, we must deny them the privilege of choosing their own form of government."[57]

This is interesting in hindsight, with Soros proudly taking credit for overthrowing regimes and—in his own words—"meddling in the affairs" of other nations.[58] Soros went on in 1984 to try and foment fear and mistrust in the economy, writing that the only "alternative to economic and political calamity in 1985" would require "a thorough revision of U.S. economic and foreign policy."[59] Soros went so far as to repeat the age-old mantra of the Far Left that communist nations failed economically not because of ideology but because of American hegemonic ambitions, and accused the Reagan administration of developing "a new form of economic imperialism" to the detriment of the rest of the world. "Under the present arrangements we are . . . denying them [communist countries] economic prosperity," Soros wrote.[60]

His statement is eerily similar to what Osama bin Laden alleged and what the rest of the Islamist, anti-American lobby still claims today. For example, in bin Laden's so-called open letter to America, he wrote, "You steal our wealth and oil at paltry prices because of your international influence and military threats. This theft is indeed the biggest theft ever witnessed by mankind in the history of the world."[61] These two men, bin Laden and Soros, who have used their vast wealth to influence world events—are not so far apart in thought.

Thank God George Soros didn't get his way in the 1980s; otherwise, we might still be waiting for communism to collapse.

We now know that strength brought us peace, and tax cuts and deregulation brought us hitherto unknown prosperity before the dawn of the 1990s. But according to Soros, capitalism stings. In early 1997, the *Atlantic* published Soros's warning of "The Capitalist Threat": "Insofar as there is a dominant belief in our society today, it is the belief in the magic of the marketplace."[62]

Not so fast, warns Robert Samuelson in the *Washington Post*. What Soros has written is "powerful stuff," wrote Samuelson, then added, "Also rubbish. Soros's essay is rambling and incoherent. In some ways, it resembles the Unabomber Manifesto in its sweeping, unsupported, and disconnected generalizations."[63]

"As a seer [Soros is] a crackpot," Samuelson wrote in *Newsweek*. "The truth is that if Soros weren't the author, this gibberish wouldn't have made it into print. Its only appeal is its shock value: capitalist condemns capitalism. 'There was a man-bites-dog quality to this,' says *Atlantic* editor William Whitworth. The result is that we get assertion instead of analysis."[64]

Soros has claimed that "the spread of market values into all areas of life" endangers "open and democratic society."[65]

"Really?" Samuelson challenged. "If that were so, governments everywhere would be shrinking radically.

"They aren't," argues Samuelson, "in most rich democracies, the central problem of the political economy now is the reverse of what Soros says. It is not how to curb rampaging markets. It is how to maintain a large welfare state without suffocating a productive economy."[66]

Of course, we'll have to take Soros's word for whatever he's doing since, for most of their existence, his hedge funds operated overseas outside the purview of the Securities and Exchange Commission. And why are they not registered with the Securities and Exchange Commission?" As Soros acknowledged on *60 Minutes* in 1998, "We find it more convenient to operate without it."

"So, in some ways, it's to escape regulation?" reporter Steve Kroft asked. Soros brazenly replied, "Yeah, that's right."[67]

As an American citizen, Soros could not even join the board of his own Quantum Fund. If he ran the fund, it would have been subject to U.S. insider trading and tax laws. As an offshore fund, Quantum avoided the Investment Company Act, which at that time, according to economics writer Andrew Tobias, "severely restrict[ed] the ability of funds to sell short or to make big undiversified bets—betting half the fund's assets on the collapse of some foreign currency, say. Offshore fund shareholders are not subject to U.S. taxation, though their American fund managers are.

"Some Americans do invest in offshore funds," Tobias noted, "but they must perjure themselves to do so. Many use foreign trusts, with non-U.S. in-laws or non-U.S. institutions as administrators."[68]

Since then, the laws have changed, and Soros claims to fight corruption everywhere, as his foundations have invested in creating anti-corruption NGOs in several countries.

Investment lore says Soros started offshore because, in the beginning, only people outside the United States would invest in his fund, but that did not quite jibe with today's reality. It was clear Soros was strictly attempting to avoid American investment law with his funds. Take Quantum Realty, his one attempt at a U.S.-based investment house, for which Soros "was given assurances 'at high levels' that non-U.S. investors would be exempt from U.S. taxes. Politics then demanded this decision be reversed after the fund had been operating for over a year," Tobias wrote. "It had to be disbanded to protect the non-U.S. investors."[69]

The offshore fund faced little serious regulation, leading one of Soros's colleagues to explain to the *New Yorker* that "George has his own rules—they're different, larger. He is unencumbered." The same article described Soros as "a consummate gamesman, adept at finding tax loopholes and operating in gray areas where oversight is scant and maneuverability wide. Indeed, the sums of money he managed *not* to pay the I.R.S. for many years put his present gift giving in a slightly different light."[70]

The irony of that insight is that Soros would probably make no bones about it. Deception, smoke, and mirrors are all acknowledged parts of his personality and business. "I am sort of a deus ex machina," Soros told the *New York Times* in 1994. "I am something unnatural. I'm very comfortable with my public persona because it is one I have created for myself. It represents what I like to be as distinct from what I really am. You know, in my personal capacity I'm not actually a selfless philanthropic person. I've very much self-centered."[71]

In 2002, even Soros's semi-authorized biographer Michael Kaufman couldn't get a grip on exactly what was going on over at the Quantum Fund: All Gary Gladstein, the managing director of Soros Fund Management, could say was that the total number of investors in Quantum and the other five funds Soros established "probably" never exceeded a thousand. "They are very rich individuals . . . and many have interests in several or even all of the Soros funds," Kaufman wrote.[72]

Curacao's laws had changed by 2012 to align with current international standards. But at that time, "under the laws of Curacao, where the fund is legally chartered, it [was] illegal for any of its directors or representatives to identify any shareholder by name, even to the people at Soros Fund Management, the New York part of the operation that determines and carries out investment decisions as the fund's adviser." Many of these investors are known only by "coded Swiss bank accounts or by financial advisers serving as their nominees. It is quite likely that Soros does not know or, for that matter, care to know all of his shareholders," Kaufman noted.[73]

The general idea was that Soros didn't have to care because he was the primary investor. But for Americans, this setup posed an interesting quandary. Since Soros has been dumping so much money into social causes and political campaigns in the United States, was this done to prevent us from knowing who the nameless, faceless investors in America's future were?

And were their agendas tied in with Soros's agendas? Was there a wealthy investor with a specific interest in drug legalization, or open borders, for example? Were there investors who had a vested monetary interest in seeing the currencies of certain countries crash—which, notably, Soros was able to precipitate in the late '90s with a single letter to a newspaper?

Soros has spent a lot of time discussing the need for "transparency" and "openness" while running one of the world's most secretive and powerful investing firms. And it has affected everybody.

Occasionally, even with all his deceptions, hidden agendas, and personas, Soros has still gotten nailed. In 1979 he was charged with stock manipulation for buying a large amount of a computer company's stock, selling it off quickly to drive down prices, then buying a greater amount at an "artificially low price," the *New Yorker* reported.[74] Soros had signed a consent decree in which he neither admitted nor denied complicity in the act. Then in 1986, he was fined $75,000 by the Commodity Futures Trading Commission for using several private accounts to hold positions well above speculative limits.[75]

Soros's most infamous brush with the law was in France in 2002, where a court convicted him of insider trading and fined him 2.2 million euros ($2.3 million). Two other defendants in the case, Jean-Charles Naouri, a former aide to France's then finance minister Pierre Beregovoy, and Lebanese businessman Samir Traboulsi, were acquitted.

Soros met the decision with predictable bluster: "I have been in business all my life, and I think I know what insider trading is and what isn't."[76]

Nevertheless, there has yet to be a political will to put Soros in his place stateside. When pulled in front of the House Banking Committee, ostensibly to testify on hedge funds and the fatal danger international currency speculators like him posed to the economy, House Democrats were all too willing to let any serious questions fall by the wayside. "The members of the Banking Committee led by their chairman, Henry Gonzales, were ready to blame the hedge funds for kicking the markets downhill and risking the banks with their heavy borrowing,' business writer Irv Chapman said on Lou Dobbs' *Moneyline* after the hearing.

'But they wound up treating George Soros as an expert witness on world markets and currencies instead of a man whose heavy high-risk trading keeps them awake at night.'"[77]

Why? Because right off the bat, Soros was willing to tell them what they wanted to hear. After Soros's opening statement, which was but a cruder, shorter rehashing of his *Atlantic* article, Minnesota Democrat Bruce Vento praised Soros for the "heresy [he] may have committed here by admitting that Adam Smith's invisible hand has some fingerprints."[78]

Typical anti-capitalist, pseudo-populist rhetoric was all it took to throw Congress off Soros's scent. Committee members inexplicably took Soros at his word, even in the face of all the evidence, when he assured them that his unregulated Quantum Fund was not a "destabilizing" force. "I see no imminent danger of a market meltdown or crash," Soros breezily told the committee, later adding, "Frankly, I don't think that hedge funds are a natural concern to you or the regulators. . . . There is nothing to be regulated about hedge funds."[79]

However, Soros is smooth enough to know that there had to be some red meat, too, so he sent the committee off in another, more vague direction: derivatives traders. "There are so many of them, and some of them are so esoteric that the risks involved may not be properly understood even by the most sophisticated investors, and I'm supposed to be one," Soros said. "Some of those instruments appear to be specifically designed to enable institutional investors to take gambles which they would not otherwise be permitted to take."[80]

No one seemed to pick up the irony of that last bit: Soros was essentially describing what he did every day. But because he was willing to say capitalism was bad, the Dems let him slide. Perhaps his newfound distaste for laissez-faire is more thought-out and self-interested than most suppose.

In the love fest, everyone forgot the part where they were supposed to fact-check what the billionaire was telling them. For example, Soros told the committee, "The only thing [my type of hedge fund and others] have in common is that the managers are compensated on the basis of performance and not as a fixed percentage of assets under management."[81]

Soros forgot to add that whether they perform or not, most hedge funds also get paid a fee based on assets under management. However, Soros forgot to mention that the fund managers were also paid. According to a 2006 Congressional Research Service (CRS) paper, "In addition to the return on his or her own capital, the typical hedge fund manager takes 15%–25% of all profits earned by the fund *plus* an annual management fee of 1%–2% of total fund assets."

In a story for the Republican *Ripon Forum*, Jeffrey Kuhner suggested that Soros's anti-capitalism went hand in hand with his "ideological kookiness":

> The 20th century is littered with examples of messianic visionaries—Lenin, Hitler, and Castro—whose megalomania and absolute desire for power have wreaked unimaginable havoc . . . Mr. Soros' brand of neo-Marxism is no different. His one-world globalism and hostility to capitalism are part of the radical Left's long-term ambitions to alter human reality through social engineering. . . . If implemented, Mr. Soros' utopianism would eventually lead to a form of one-world authoritarianism and economic collectivism.[82]

Later, Kuhner also opined in the *Washington Times*, "The fact that Mr. Soros is the power behind the Obama regime reveals its moral and intellectual bankruptcy—and the depths to which liberalism has fallen. Rather than being a hero and benefactor, he should be an embarrassment to liberals everywhere. Moreover, he poses a clear and present danger to the republic and its founding values."[83]

In "The Capitalist Threat," Soros stressed, "Laissez-faire ideology does not prepare us to cope with this challenge [Soros's perceived period of post–Cold War disorder]. It does not recognize the need for new world order. An order is supposed to emerge from states' pursuit of their self-interest. But, guided by the principle of survival of the fittest, states are increasingly preoccupied with their competitiveness and unwilling to make any sacrifices for the common good."[84]

Soros's proof of this was the supposed failure of Western nations to lend a hand to Russia after the fall of communism. "The combination of laissez-faire ideas, social Darwinism, and geopolitical realism that prevailed in the United States and the United Kingdom stood in the way of any hope for an open society in Russia," he wrote. "If the leaders of these countries had had a different view of the world, they could have established firm foundations for a global open society."[85] Faster than you can say, "New World Order," there it is.

Soros's eccentricities became more nefarious as his fortunes grew. Bringing about global order and smashing sovereignty based on national borders has become a major focus of the Open Society Institute and later the OSF, primarily through the so-called Justice Initiative,[86] which, as their 2004, no longer available website, said, was seeking to give "local meaning to global norms."[87] What exactly does that mean? Who knows?

Since the collapse of the Soviet Union, which the West mistakenly saw as the end of communism, Soros and his organizations have been introducing, calling for, and supporting actions against Judeo-Christian values and Western political traditions, capitalism, national sovereignty, and America's supremacy.

The constant theme in Soros's writing is the need for an end to America as the world's preeminent power. During a September 2003 State Department Open Forum speech, Soros proposed a "modification of the concept of sovereignty, because" he opined, "sovereignty is basically somewhat anachronistic."[88] In his book *Soros on Soros, he wrote*, "An open society transcends national sovereignty."[89] That's no American patriot talking. That's the internationalist Soros, a liberal elitist determined to lay the foundation for a one-world government, and it is nothing new.

The end of American sovereignty has long been a part of the "Soros Doctrine," as he likes to call it. He is coveting the day when a weakened United States can be at the mercy of international institutions. "Our attachment to superpower status is understandable," Soros droned in his *Underwriting Democracy*, "but it is nonetheless regrettable because it prevents the resolution of a simmering crisis."[90] Soros hasn't given up.

His attacks on capitalism similarly lead to the same conclusion: a one-world government is the only thing to bring balance to the world's economies. And his foundations have gradually advanced radical progressive ideas, such as global warming, climate change, and "global climate justice."

THE CONSCIENCE OF THE WORLD

The rhetoric of OSF's Justice Initiative makes it sound like there is an egalitarian global order already, and it is only being held up by selfish, "stable" countries like the United States. Early on, a major goal of the Justice Initiative was to give the International Criminal Court, established in 2002, jurisdiction over every nation in the world.

The OSF website's postings inform us that the Justice Initiative has been contributing to the application, enforcement, and dissemination of international legal principles at the local level—whether helping judges apply international due process rules to pretrial detention decisions, building community capacity to secure police accountability consistent with international standards, or collaborating with lawyers to ensure local court enforcement of regional nondiscrimination norms.[91] In 2004, the OS website, at that time, elaborated, "The financial and jurisdictional limits of the ICC, as well as the frequent unwillingness or inability to prosecute on the part of the states most concerned, makes necessary investigation and prosecution by other states, notably through the exercise of universal jurisdiction."[92] Therefore, "legislation, institutional reform, and the preparation and promotion of cases will all be needed to ensure that national systems fulfill their role in ending impunity."[93]

At the time of this writing, the United States, Israel, Russia, and China have been resisting this "universal jurisdiction" for good reasons. There is no element of fairness built into the ICC and other bodies of international law, but plenty of bias.

One of many examples proving such bias and injustice was the 2004 World Court ruling attempting to end the construction of a barrier between Israel and the West Bank, which has been one of the most effective apparatuses in weakening the Palestinian suicide bombers' reign of terror.[94]

When Jews must be made to die to satisfy the Arab/Muslim, and lately, the Biden administration's plans, joined by the anti-Israelism and anti-Semitism of Europeans who have long romanticized the terrorist thugs running the Palestinian Authority, it is exceedingly clear that the world is not ready for open borders, despite the efforts of Biden, international organizations, and George Soros. Most Americans, like Israelis, do not want to see a day when they cannot set their border policy. Most Americans, Israelis, Hungarian, Poles, Czech, and Slovaks say no to open borders. George Soros says yes, as does the current U.S. president, Joe Biden, whose election was heavily backed by the billionaire who, as he told the *Washington Post*, considers himself a "citizen of the world."[95]

The ninety-two-year old Soros has invested tens of billions of dollars in his various "open society" networks; increased funds to "progressive" NGOs, politicians, and national and international propaganda campaigns; and lobbied legislators and international bodies promoting his "open borders" and his kind of global justice policies. Who will prevail?

Soros sees himself as the ultimate arbitrator of climate justice, social justice, and racial justice, as well as in promoting transgenderism, population control, and free abortion. His OSF website lists these and boasts the billions he has been spending to advance these ideas. He regularly increased funding to such groups to influence local and national elections. According to *Forbes*, Soros gave $17.3 million to Planned Parenthood and makes "regular contributions to the group's "political advocacy arm."[96]

In advance of the 2020 elections, Soros's various PACs funded organizations promoting people of color and transgender activists. For example, his Justice & Public Safety PAC contributed "$75,000 [to] New Virginia Majority group, which organized "Latinx, African

American, Asian American Pacific Islander, and youth communities, centering the leadership and demands of working-class women of color." A donation of $50,000 went to United for Progress PAC, to "build community-based political power and influence in the growing Puerto Rican and Latino constituencies in Florida."[97]

The billions Soros spent have already made deep inroads into predisposed academic institutions and led to modifications in our economic and social discourse and political conventions. If the past and the present are any indications, the billions he has invested in his neo-Marxism-touting foundations and other NGOs guarantee his radical socialist agendas will continue fueling political, economic, and social turmoil.

Soros's investments have paid off, probably beyond his expectation. Since 2020, the government he helped establish in the United States has, as the discerning Ruth S. King has noted, stopped recognizing dissidents, calling them instead "domestic terrorists"; limited their speech; controlled the media; altered the language; denied legitimate history; trashed tradition and culture; erased national borders; blurred the role of the military; destroyed the canons of education, science, and medicine; and used the powers of government to spy on its citizens.[98]

THE FRUSTRATED PHILOSOPHER

Another factor that sheds light on Soros's behavior is his misrepresentation of Karl Popper's concept of an "open society"—a society that would "maximize the freedom of individuals to live as they wish."[99]

Popper, the Austrian philosopher who moved to England in 1945, is considered one of the greatest philosophers of science of the whole of the twentieth century. While studying at the London School of Economics, Soros attended Popper's lectures but had little contact with him. This did not stop Soros from borrowing the term *Open Society* as the umbrella for his massive political philanthropic/investment endeavors. He also borrowed the term for titles of his books, such as *Open Society: Reforming Global Capitalism* and *The Crisis of Global*

Capitalism: Open Society Endangered, and many articles.

In practice, then, anything Soros endorses becomes a boon for "open society," while anything he disagrees with—Trump, Bush, immigration policy, the war on drugs, incarcerating criminals, even the United States itself—becomes its greatest enemy. Hence, the war in Kosovo was a justified defense of an "open society," while the war in Iraq was a tyrannical plot devised by George W. Bush. Soros even compared the United States to Nazi Germany. According to Floyd Norris, during a lunch with reporters in Davos, on January 27, 2007, Soros declared, "We [America] have to go through a certain de-Nazification process."[100] Elsewhere, Soros also repeatedly stressed that the U.S. war against Saddam Hussein was influenced by Israel and the American Israel Public Affairs Committee (AIPAC).[101]

Earlier, in 2004, in a speech at the Yivo Institute for Jewish Research, Soros actually "likened the behavior of Israel [in *defending* itself against Arab terrorist attacks] to that of the Nazis, invoking some psychological jargon about victims becoming victimizers."[102]

Not surprisingly, he funds organizations that make similar claims, accusing Israel—where all citizens have equal rights—of apartheid, claiming it commits war crimes and violates human rights and international laws.[103] (More on this later). Soros is "an outsider with a huge amount of money who has no hesitation about getting involved and trying to shape other people's societies, countries and in our [Israel's] case, democracy," commented Gerald Steinberg, founder, and president of NGO Monitor, a pro-Israel watchdog group.[104]

Soros has been jabbering on about "open societies" for decades now, but he is still unable to give a reasonable explanation of what one is. When he tries to define it, it comes out as the sort of pseudo-sociology one would expect from a starry-eyed college freshman. An "open society," to George Soros, is "a different conception of how society ought to be organized," and it is "really more sophisticated than the democracy or Communistic systems." His tone suggests that the "little people" would be hard-pressed to understand Soros's genius. We should collectively hand the keys over to the Soros godhead and his neo-Marxist buddies and let them drive us where they will.

Soros's heroes have always been philosophers and intellectuals, not businessmen. He's been known to pay graduate students in philosophy to just wander around with him, discussing "ideas." He puts on busy weekends at his home, inviting prominent intellectuals and philosophers to debate the philosophical tracts he has toiled on, writing and rewriting them throughout his life.

Biographer Michael Kaufman spoke to Jonathan Wolff, from University College, London, who had attended one of Soros's philosophy discussion parties. "He had apparently read no philosophy since the fifties and had made clear that he did not think that much of significance has occurred in the field since then," Wolff told Kaufman, adding, "He did not think any of us really understood his ideas. He had some of the typical features of an autodidact—an impatience with anyone who mentioned a text he had not read and a tendency to change the track of discussion when things got hard."[105]

Soros noticed this tendency in his work, writing in his unpublished essay, "The Burden of Consciousness," "I have tried to be concise, but occasionally I have slipped into verbosity—especially when I did not have anything original to say."[106]

At points, "The Burden of Consciousness" could get downright weird: "I have very definite ideas about the relationship between my mind and the outside world," Soros writes. "I realize that there is a world of which I am a part. That world has existed before I became a part of it and will continue to exist after I have ceased to exist. I can influence the outside world through my actions and of course the outside world impinges on my existence in an infinity of ways."[107] Huh? What nonsense.

"I have had these illusions, or perhaps delusions, of grandeur and they have driven me," Soros told biographer Michael Kaufman. Far from making light of these delusions, Soros embraced them. Explaining his self-proclaimed role as a "stateless statesman," Soros told Kaufman,

"My goal is to become the conscience of the world."[108] A tall call from the man who expressed "no sense of guilt" for accompanying a Nazi Hungarian official (Baumbach) who identified Jewish property for confiscation by the Nazis. Responding to Steve Kroft's question about his feelings at that time, Soros said: "There was no sense that I shouldn't be there, because…, in a funny way, it's just like in markets—that if I weren't there—of course, I wasn't doing it, but somebody else would be taking it away anyhow. I was only a spectator; the property was being taken away. So I had no role in taking away that property. So, I had no sense of guilt."[109, 110]

Moreover, he told Michael Kaufman, "Being in command of the situation, even though you are in danger, but basically maneuvering successfully… this was the most exciting time of my life," he said of his World War II experiences.[111]

In a 1995 speech, Soros hinted at his ultimate hope of philosophical vindication:

> "There is more to my existence than money," he explained. "I focused on it in my career mainly because I recognized that there is a tendency in our society to exaggerate the importance of money and to define values in terms of money. We appraise artists by how much their creations fetch." [Indeed, Hunter Biden's much sought-after paintings attest to that.] He added that we judge politicians not by their ideas or goals but "by the amount of money they can raise." Soros concluded that since he made a lot of money, he "may yet come to be recognized as a great philosopher, which would give me more satisfaction than the fortune I have made."[112]

Many have caught the scent of something other than philosophy in the air around Soros. His son Robert told Kaufman, "My father will sit down and give you theories to explain why he does this or that. But I remember seeing it as a kid and thinking, Jesus Christ, at least half of this is bullshit." Robert said his father is driven more by "temperament" than anything else. "He is always trying to rationalize what are basically his emotions. And he is living in a constant state of not exactly denial, but rationalization of his emotional state."[113] Is it possible Soros's confused emotional state was exploited early on by elements hostile to capitalist America?

In the end, Soros's philosophy is a kind of non-philosophical gibberish. He wants the world to follow him based on his discovery that he is probably wrong about everything.

"We have now had 200 years of experience with the Age of Reason, and as reasonable people, we ought to recognize that reason has its limitations," Soros wrote in his article "The Capitalist Threat." "The time is ripe for developing a conceptual framework based on our fallibility. Where reason has failed, fallibility may yet succeed."[114]

Yeah, right. According to this madman, failure is not only an option; it's our only option.

But do not expect any apologies, ever, from George Soros. After all, he once said, "I have no regrets."[115]

"When it comes to protecting your own life or saving the system, I know which one I would do first," Soros told the *Guardian*. "It's much better to be a successful speculator and then apply your moral priorities elsewhere."[116]

But at what cost? And what would Karl Popper think of that?

"One of the main arguments of the Open Society is directed against moral relativism," Popper wrote in his philosophical autobiography, *Unended Quest*. "The fact that moral values of principles may clash does not invalidate them. Moral values or principles may be discovered and even invented. They may be relevant to a certain situation and irrelevant to other situations. They may be accessible to some people and inaccessible to others."

However, Popper stressed, "all this is quite distinct from relativism; that is, from the doctrine that any set of values can be defended."[117]

Soros's incessant utopianism, his lack of respect for any opinion other than his own, and the way he drowns out other voices with a flood of cash would likely not have sat very well with Popper. Once again, from *Unended Quest*: "There can be no human society without conflict: such a society would be a society not of friends but ants. Even if it were attainable, there are human values of the greatest importance that would be destroyed by its attainment and which, therefore, should prevent us from attempting to bring it about. On the other hand, we certainly ought to bring about a reduction of conflict."[118]

The message is clear: we can and should work to alleviate conflict, but it cannot be eliminated, and utopian schemes usually destroy the human spirit rather than set it free. Therefore, Popper referred to the Open Society as his "war effort." It was openly influenced by his fears that "freedom might become a central problem again, especially under the renewed influence of Marxism and the idea of large-scale 'planning.'"[119]

If "large-scale planning" without the consent of the general population isn't Soros's shtick, what is?

Although Popper met with Soros once or twice while Soros was a student at the London School of Economics and even sent him a note with short comments on "The Burden of Consciousness," Soros failed to make much of an impression on the old philosopher. According to Kaufman's biography, when Soros contacted Popper in 1982 to let him know he'd been naming funds, foundations, and other entities after the concepts enshrined in the Open Society, Popper wrote back, "Let me first thank you for not having forgotten me. I am afraid I forgot you completely; even your name created at first only the most minute resonance. But I made some effort, and now, I think, I just remember you, though I do not think I should recognize you."[120]

In *Unended Quest*, Popper's "intellectual autobiography," remember, he stated that "freedom is more important than equality."[121] To Soros, "equality" and "collectivism" trump individualism. "An open society is a society which allows its members the greatest possible degree of freedom in pursuing their interests compatible with the interests of others," he said in 2002.[122]

Believing that no existing "philosophy or worldview is in possession of the truth,"[123] Soros developed his open society theory. An important clue to his thinking is his statement to the *New York Times*: "The arc of history doesn't follow its own course. It needs to be bent," he said. "I am really engaged in trying to bend it in the right direction."[124] (Not to be left behind, his son and heir, Alexander, has been doing his own bending by establishing Bend the Arc, a progressive-Leftist Jewish group that vigorously resisted former U.S. President Donald Trump's anti-socialist Make America Great Again plan, as well as Israel's former prime minister, Benjamin Netanyahu's, Zionist agenda of the Jewish State of Israel.)

Soros needed an excuse to explain why he was right and Popper was wrong—and it was his unrecognized "concept of reflexivity." He suddenly realized that was the very tool he needed to question Popper's concept of an open society. "I discovered a flaw in it," he said. [125]

Soros went on to criticize "Popper's hidden assumption that freedom of speech and thought will produce a better understanding of reality . . . what I have called the 'Enlightenment fallacy.'" Thus, Soros concludes," it is not necessary to gain a better understanding of reality to obtain the laws one wants." Instead, the ever-pragmatic Soros offered "a shortcut: 'spinning arguments' and manipulating public opinion to get the desired results."[126]

He went on driveling for page after page, which characterizes much of his writing. Where was his editor?

Though Soros does not say it, his "improvement" of Popper's philosophy was apparently also influenced by Antonio Gramsci's advocacy of undermining and disrupting the cultural, ideological, religious, and other traditional values prevailing in the targeted state/region.

Gramsci argued that "Socialism is precisely the religion that must overwhelm Christianity. . . . In the new order, Socialism will triumph by first capturing the culture via infiltration of schools, universities, churches and the media by transforming the consciousness of society." Soros has been doing his best to achieve that goal.[127]

Walter Adamson studied Gramsci's *Prison Notebooks* and is the author of *Hegemony and Revolution: Antonio Gramsci's Political and Cultural Theory*. The publisher notes:

> For Gramsci, revolution meant the steady ascension of a mass-based, educated, and organized "collective will," in which the final seizure of power would be the climax of a broader educative process. Success depended on countering not just the coercive power of the existing economic and political order but also the cultural hegemony of the state." He noted that to Gramsci, "counter-hegemony" required the leadership of an organized political party, but at its core lay his conviction that the common people were capable of self-enlightenment and could produce an alternative conception of the world that challenged the prevailing hegemonic culture.[128]

Soros found in Gramsci a kindred spirit. In *The Modern Prince and Other Writings*, Gramsci wrote, "Man can affect his own development and that of his surroundings only so far as he has a clear view of what the possibilities of action are open to him. To do this, he has to understand the historical situation in which he finds himself: and once he does this, then he can play an active part in modifying that situation. The man of action is the true philosopher: and the philosopher must be a man of action."[129] This description surely spoke to Soros's heart more than anything Popper had written. Indeed, Soros portrays himself as a man who puts his philosophy into action, à la Gramsci.

Moreover, he must have taken Gramsci's teaching to heart, especially on managing a successful revolution, with his plot of changing the U.S. from within. For the revolution to succeed, "a frank and loyal collaboration between two political forces, . . . [the] socialists and anarchists is necessary," Gramsci wrote in his April 1920 address to anarchists in Turin, Italy.[130] Soros's direct and indirect assistance (often through the San Francisco–based Tides Center[131]) helped transform the once-centrist Democrats into the progressive socialist Party and promote anarchist groups, such as Dream Defenders,[132] Black Lives Matter, the Defund the Police movement, and the like. Their "loyal collaboration" is well on its way to turning what was the beacon of democracy and capitalism not long ago into a debt-ridden, cash-strapped, lawless, despotic society.

In 1995, Soros declared, "I do not accept the rules imposed by others . . . I recognize that there are regimes that need to be opposed rather than accepted. And in periods of regime change, the normal rules don't apply."[133] Of course, he considers himself uniquely qualified to determine when the "normal rules" should and shouldn't apply. His preferences are the policies his well-funded various Open Society organization networks promote. These are neither independent nor nonpartisan causes or policies. Instead, they promote uniformity of thought,[134] speech, standards, and ways of life. And not just any uniformity, but only the kind that advances his woke global progressive-socialist agendas.

Soros's goal, as the British daily *Guardian* sees it, is to push the world "in a cosmopolitan direction in which racism, income inequality, American empire, and the alienations of contemporary capitalism would be things of the past."[135] In his late eighties at the time, Soros was hurrying to leave an even grander legacy behind.

It is conceivable that Soros's observation of the spread of Marxist/ Socialist ideology, especially among the intelligentsia, highlighted the usefulness of establishing an international educational system to guarantee the promotion of a "critical" mode of thinking;[136] his progressive revolutionary doctrine of "open society" will continue to impregnate the minds of the young everywhere, long after he's gone. So, after decades of developing a web of political philanthropic and semi-philanthropic organizations, he established the Open Society University Network (OSUN) as a feeder and overseer of the global network of academic institutions that distribute, expand, and ingrain his Open Society doctrine.

In January 2020, Soros chose the World Economic Forum in Davos as the site where he would announce his most ambitious initiative, the "most important and enduring project" of his life, the Open Society University Network (OSUN).[137] He pledged $1 billion to create what "the world really needs," an international platform for teaching and research that existing universities all over the world would be able to join, among other things, "to fight dictators and would-be dictators."[138]

How would the scholars at the OSUN identify "would-be dictators"? Easily. Soros says, "A perfect way to tell a dictator or a would-be dictator is if he identifies me as an enemy."[139]

Soros's latest global self-styled academic venture comes on top of his OSF's $407,790,344 in gifts and commitments to higher education since the year 2000, as reported by the Media Research Center in January 2020.[140]

Soros created the OSUN, a "new kind of global educational network,"[141] to serve as a global indoctrination organ for training and fighting against "climate change"—the Left's hottest crusade, plan, and proliferate teaching "against nationalism"[142]—and support other opportune themes that advance his progressive Left diversionist agenda, all under the guise of his distorted "Open Society" doctrine. Soros established the OSUN to guarantee that radical socialist political activism endures and spreads after he's gone.

The OSF's press release announced that the OSUN would join forces with other Soros-funded universities: his Vienna-based Central European University (CEU); Bard College in upstate New York—with campuses in New York City, Boston, California, Germany, and Russia (which was later banned by the Putin government) Arizona State University, the American University of Central Asia in Kyrgyzstan, and BRAC University in Bangladesh.[143] Bard College also partners with the Palestinian al-Quds university.[144]

The OSUN, like the OSF, OSI, and other Soros-funded organizations, operates as both a teaching and an advanced finishing school that recalls not the Swiss Brillantmont International School for the offspring of the well-to-do[145] but Soviet's Moscow-based Peoples' Friendship University of Russia (RUDN), aka the Patrice Lumumba University.[146]

In 1960, RUDN was founded in Moscow as "an integral part of the Soviet cultural offensive in nonaligned countries." It provided higher education with large doses of indoctrination to "young people from

Asia, Africa, and Latin America,"[147] who propagated the Communist ideology worldwide. And while the collapse of the Soviet Union duped the West into concluding that the Communist ideology died with it, they were soon proven wrong. Thousands of thoroughly indoctrinated international students continued spreading the Marxist, anti-capitalist, anti-West, globalist, socialist utopia.

Man of the world that he is, Soros surely noted the madrassas' (Islamic religious schools') effectiveness in spreading radical Islamic revolutionary principles around the world. Their efforts resulted in the 9/11 attacks on the United States and unending terrorist attacks everywhere, making the world a much more dangerous place.[148] Not surprisingly, OSUN's global structure is not unlike the successful multibillion dollars worldwide Islamist propagation efforts of Saudi Arabia, Iran, Qatar, Turkey, and the Muslim Brotherhood.

Soros's Open Society doctrine is a clarion call for resistance and revolutions. It evokes some of Karl Marx's and Leon Trotsky's ideas on permanent revolutions. Indeed, Soros's activities recall the strategies and methods used by the German Communist Willi Münzenberg[149] (known as the Red Millionaire[150]), a follower of Vladimir Lenin. He designed and brilliantly executed the Soviets' propaganda tactics from 1921 to 1936.

Speaking of Lenin, Kent Clizbe, a former CIA spy, has detailed in his book *Willing Accomplices* how Lenin's ideas to change the United States were designed "to instill a reflexive loathing of the United States and its people as a prime tropism of Left-wing enlightenment…The U.S. had to be depicted as an almost *insanely xenophobic place, murderously hostile to foreigners.*"[151] Ironic, isn't it, that Soros has made "changing" the U.S. his "top priority" because the idea of the war-on-terror, which the U.S. declared after the 9/11 attacks on the homeland, "undermines the principles of an open society"[152] and that he uses his celebrity status and media access to vilify U.S. domestic and foreign policies repeatedly? But I digress.

Back to Münzenberg. In his excellent book *Double Lives,* Stephen

Koch described Münzenberg's role in the Soviets' propaganda machine.[153] He formed international front organizations to support the Soviets' agenda. He established the World League Against Imperialism and Workers' International Relief."[154] He was behind the establishment of the League of American Writers, "an association of American novelists, playwrights, poets, journalists, and literary critics,"[155] which, in addition to Communist Party members, also included many "fellow travelers."[156]

Münzenberg used the front organizations "to enlist the support of liberals and moderate socialists in defending the Bolshevik revolution," all the while insisting, "These people have the belief they are actually doing this themselves. This belief must be preserved at any price."[157]

Münzenberg, like Lenin and the Bolshevik comrades,[158] efficaciously used the tools available at that time, including publishing, media, radio, and film, to create an effective network of global organizations that spread Communist propaganda. In addition to using similar methods with advanced communication systems, Soros took advantage of the NGOs scheme created in 1945 when the United Nations was established.

By April 2020, there were 197 countries and 10 million NGOs worldwide. Many operate in collaboration with thousands of international nongovernmental organizations (INGOs). The last available data, from 2013, said there were more than 40,000 INGOs.[159]

It is important to note that "INGOs are not elected bodies, are not founded on the principle of representation, and are not accountable to the public," as pointed out by Dr. Raphael Ben-Ari, an expert on NGOs and international law. INGOs have no legal recognition and guidelines; their often biased "fact-finding" reports are rarely questioned by the media or "national courts and international tribunals and institutions."[160]

NGOs and the INGOs that often fund them claim to advance civil society, democracy, education, free speech, justice reform, and public health and to protect human rights and similar noble causes. Funding for such groups comes from wealthy individuals, charities, intergovernmental organizations, and international organizations and from national wealth funds and individual governments that use NGOs and INGOs as satellites to extend their policies and interests. Anyone can establish a domestic NGO in compliance with local and national laws. Similarly, anyone can launch an INGO "and start issuing human rights fact-finding reports that would then be relied on by the media, or worse—by national courts and international tribunals."[161] But of course, the wealthier the INGO, the more significant its influence. Soros's OSF is a good example.

Soros's "political charities," such as the OSF and OSI, have been funding and training NGOs and individuals to employ proven practices that advance political dissent and resistance. The training focus on how to take advantage of local cultural, social, and political disputes, flare them up and publicize them by using traditional print, online and social media, radio, TV, documentaries, films, and art exhibits, and organize small- and large-scale demonstrations—as the Bolsheviks, and à la Saul Alinsky's 1971 handbook *Rules for Radicals*[162]

In a 2007 article titled "From Karl Popper to Karl Rove—and Back," Soros wrote, "In his novel *1984*, George Orwell chillingly described a totalitarian regime in which all communication is controlled by a Ministry of Truth and dissidents are persecuted by political police." Then he added, "The United States remains a democracy governed by a constitution and the rule of law, with pluralistic media, yet there are disturbing signs that the propaganda methods Orwell described have taken root here."[163]

Soros opined that since 1949, when Orwell's book was published, "techniques of deception have undergone enormous improvements," many of which were developed in connection with the advertising and marketing of commercial products and services and then adapted to politics. Their distinguishing feature," he said, "is that they can be bought for money." Indeed, Soros should know.

Soros then pointed out that "more recently, cognitive science has helped to make the techniques of deception even more effective, giving rise to political professionals who concentrate only on 'getting results.'" He blamed Popper for failing "to recognize that in democratic politics, gathering public support takes precedence over the pursuit of truth."

The article was published by Project Syndicate, which Soros himself funds. He argued that "politicians will respect, rather than manipulate, reality only if the public cares about the truth and punishes politicians when it catches them in deliberate deception."

But how would the public recognize the "truth" when political professionals are distorting reality?

Here Soros laid out his plan to brainwash the public by using "the media, the political elite [and] the educational system, which must all act as watchdogs. In addition, the public needs to be inoculated against the various techniques of deception . . . and false arguments . . . by arousing resentment against Orwellian Newspeak," said Soros, using Orwell's Doublespeak. "What is needed is a concerted effort to identify the techniques of manipulation—and to name and shame those who use them. Now [just before the campaign for the 2008 presidential election] is an ideal time to begin that effort."[164]

His efforts are continuing to pay off with dividends.

"The main obstacle to a stable and just world order is the United States," Soros wrote in 2006 in his introduction to *The Age of Fallibility.* Therefore, "changing the attitude and policies of the United States remains my top priority," he said.[165]

There is little doubt Soros would be delighted to be held responsible for decreasing America's image at home and abroad. Unsurprisingly, he has done his best to destabilize the country by advancing anti-American ideas and anti-capitalist "philosophies" and founding and financing organizations to propagate his ideas. His celebrity status and readiness to put money behind his causes have brought many socialists, Marxists, and other haters of American and Western ideals, including sharia-loving Muslims, to his door.

Victor Davis Hanson, the brilliant political observer, laments in his latest book, "how [America's] elites" have degraded the concept of citizenship to the point that "tribalism and globalism are destroying the idea of America."[166]

How did all this affect the perception of democracy in America?

In November 2021, David P. Goldman bemoaned the stunning change in the perception of America. In an article titled "The World No Longer Believes in American Democracy, and Neither Do We," citing an October 29, 2021, Pew Research Institute survey about American democracy, Goldman reported that "only 17% of the world's major countries said the U.S. 'is a good example for other countries to follow,' while 57% said it used to be. Twenty-three percent said it never was." Even worse, "only 19% of *Americans* think our democracy is a good model for others to follow, while 72% said it used to be and 8% said it never was."[167]

As much as Soros would like to claim responsibility for this drastic change, he was only an expediter, though an influential one. As a leading figure of the U.S. radical-Left elite, Soros has successfully corrupted America's democracy. The Pew results prove it.

2

SOROS'S DRUG LEGACY

"The war on drugs is doing more harm to our
society than drug abuse itself,"[1]

—GEORGE SOROS, 1998

IT TOOK TWENTY-EIGHT YEARS and untold millions of dollars, but on April 1, 2022, the U.S. House of Representatives voted "to federally legalize marijuana."[2] Soros should have celebrated the occasion by lighting a joint if he didn't.

In 1993, when Soros debuted on the American domestic political scene, he intended to remake the United States according to his vision of an "open society." Recently famous as "the man who broke the Bank of England,"[3] which made him $2 billion, Soros used his newly acquired celebrity and influence in the financial circles to advance his agenda.

To test the American public's resolve to keep long-held moral values and attitudes, and especially the resilience of his adoptive country's legal system, he needed an illegal and unwelcomed behavior he thought could be successfully challenged and chose laws controlling the use of illicit drugs. It offered him the opportunity to sway the rule of law in the U.S.

The savvy international currency speculator chose well. If he speculated that once marijuana was legalized, many Americans would be willing to use illicit drugs, he was right.

In 1994, under the pretext of compassion to right the wrong caused by the ban on drug use, he declared, "The war on drugs is doing more harm to our society than drug abuse itself,"[4] and proceeded to give $15 million to establish and support the development of pro-drug organizations. He gave $6 million to the Drug Policy Foundation (DPF), at least $4 million to the Lindesmith Center, and $3 million to Drug Strategies, to promote "more effective approaches to the nation's drug problem."[5]

In 1995, he "provided $450,000 to Human Rights Watch for their first-ever project on the abuses of the war on drugs worldwide."[6] Other, non-American organizations that have benefited indirectly from Soros's largesse include the Canadian Foundation for Drug Policy, which was formed in 1993; the International Anti-Prohibitionist League, which is based in Montreal and has offices in Europe; and the Australian Drug Law Reform Foundation.

In October 1995, interviewed by Bill Weinberg in *High Times*,[7] a magazine published by the pro marijuana group NORML, Ethan Nadelmann, then director of Soros's Lindesmith Center, declared, "It is important to see drugs as a human rights issue, because it is typically the same sorts of people who mount major wars on Communists and major wars on drugs." He added that "from a scientific perspective, cocaine is not a dangerous drug for the large majority of the people who use it," and as for legalization, "take the chance and come out of the closet . . . the way homosexuals . . . came out. . . When all of a sudden, your cousin or your childhood friend or your daughter comes out, your whole view of it begins to get normalized."

On several occasions, as I've noted elsewhere,[8] Nadelmann

passionately argued that "millions of Americans have to lie to their kids because they think if their kids know they smoke pot, they'll report them . . . That's a tremendous travesty. The fear that children will put loyalty to the state ahead of loyalty to the family is a lot more like Stalinist Russia or Nazi Germany than traditional American values."[9]

Comments of this kind were also made that evening at Soros's, as he aimed to establish a new intellectual climate. Those who make such assertions think people who oppose drugs are also opposed to sex, rock 'n' roll, good times, freedom, and love.

At that time, the notion of abolishing laws restricting the use of drugs with a high potential for abuse, as defined by the Controlled Substances Act, was unthinkable and unacceptable.[10] Or so it seemed. The voices to legalize drugs in the United States were marginal and not in sync.

As I noted in 1996 in the *Wall Street Journal,* a national Gallup Poll when Soros began his efforts to legalize drugs in America revealed that "85 percent of Americans rejected drug legalization. The public views the issue through the lens of common sense. It realized that being under the influence of mind-altering substances is the problem—not the drug laws."[11]

But Soros's sponsorship unified the pro-drug groups, created a movement, and, more important, gave the "drug-legalization" campaign a veneer of respectability and credibility.

Moreover, he has utilized the 1960s and 1970s counterculture that still lives on. When Soros began his drug legalization campaigns in 1994, he was joined by the influential, well-to-do, and well-connected at receptions and conferences he attended. His steady campaign misled well-intentioned people who began as firm opponents of drugs to mistakenly conclude, "If you can't beat 'em, join 'em."

Soros has been paying the pro-drug legalization pipers at various nonprofits to broadcast his tune. He chose Arizona and California to test his plan to legalize ALL drugs in America. When that was rejected in Arizona, he adjusted his approach.

The Soros-funded Drug Policy Alliance facilitated massive media campaigns to legalize all drugs. In May 2021, the DPA called on the U.S. House of Representatives to end the war on drugs and demilitarize law enforcement. It has also asserted that allowing the sick to use marijuana and other drugs for "medical purposes" is not only right but also compassionate."[12]

HOW "COMPASSIONATE" IS SOROS?

According to the *New Yorker*, [13]Soros's terminally ill father had agreed to an operation, "but he didn't want to live after the operation if his personal integrity was invaded. And, unfortunately, that was what happened. But then he wanted to live," Soros said. "I was kind of disappointed in him. I wrote him off," he told the *New Yorker*.[14]

A few weeks later, Soros admitted, "I was there when he died [in 1968], yet I let him die alone. I saw him, but I didn't touch him."[15]

Was this the behavior of a compassionate man?

Nonetheless, arguing "compassion" toward the sick—though there was no proven safe medicinal use of marijuana—worked. Soros-funded activists passed eighteen state laws permitting the prescription of "medical marijuana," which was widely abused. The evidence of the harm caused by marijuana was pushed under the rug, and laws approving "recreational marijuana" followed in thirty-eight states. The rest are expected to follow suit. Facing high inflation, economic difficulties, lost revenues, the influx of illegal immigrants, and homelessness, other states are now tempted to allow the new multibillion-dollar marijuana industry, which offers huge revenues and new jobs. But are there going to be enough sober workers to perform them?

At the same time that marijuana dispensaries were popping up everywhere, facilitating easy access to the drug, the illegal cannabis trade did not shrink as Soros and the drug legalizers claimed it would. On the contrary, it grew exponentially, with competing gangs of drug dealers roaming the streets of even rural towns in America, reeking marijuana stench. Violence and crime ensued, as have the incidents of overdoses caused by fentanyl-laced marijuana. The Soros-elected progressive Left, woke, "racial justice," prosecutors and mayors, and the anti-police movement allowed drug dealers and criminals, predominantly Blacks, to increase their illegal activities with impunity.

By the end of 2021, another national Gallup poll[16] found that 68 percent of Americans support marijuana legalization. "While most Democrats (83%) and political independents (71%) support legalization, Republicans are nearly evenly split on the question (50% in favor; 49% opposed)."[17] The poll also found that 54% of Democrats thought the U.S. had a drug problem, compared with 81% of Republicans who said it was extremely serious.[18] Yet, federal legalization was considered inevitable "due to overwhelming support among younger adults."[19] Soros must have been thrilled with the news.

In early February 2022, Soros was surely pleased when the Department of Health and Human Services (HHS) revealed a $30 million grant—paid for by taxpayers' money—to distribute "smoking kits/supplies" as part of its so-called Harm Reduction program.[20] In the *Washington Free Beacon*, Patrick Hauf argues that "these kits will provide pipes for users to smoke crack cocaine, crystal methamphetamine, and 'any illicit substance.'"[21]

The Biden administration argued that supplying "clean pipes" would "curb the injecting drugs with needles, which is far riskier." But the HHS grant will offer clean needles, too. But since it is illegal to sell or distribute drug paraphernalia—including such pipes as the HHS offers—unless authorized by state, local or federal law, such laws are likely to be adopted soon.[22]

According to Harm Reduction International, the "safer smoking kits . . . can include glass stems, rubber mouthpieces [which can be affixed to any pipe to prevent the spread of infection], brass screens, lip balm and disinfectant wipes."[23] The rubber mouthpieces will "prevent cuts and burns," and the brass screens will "filter contaminants," the *Daily Mail* reported.[24]

According to the HHS spokesperson, the crack pipes distribution targets "'underserved communities,' including African Americans and 'LGBTQ+ persons,' as established under President Joe Biden's executive order on 'advancing racial equity.'"[25]

In reaction to the outrage aroused as soon as the *Washington Free Beacon* exposed the details of this shocking plan, White House press secretary Jen Psaki declared, "Nope, we're going to leave out the crack pipes."[26] But they did not, as the *Free Beacon* reporters found out. The reporters discovered this when they visited five harm-reduction organizations and called more than two dozen others. "In fact, every organization we visited—facilities in Boston, New York City, Washington, D.C., Baltimore, and Richmond, Va.—included crack pipes in the kits," they reported.[27]

Baltimore, Maryland, according to an OSI website, is Soros's "most intriguing effort to improve a place . . . He began funding the Open Society Institute–Baltimore in 1998."[28] But after investing tens of millions of dollars, the city is riddled with corruption,[29] and its crime rate, drug addiction, and homelessness are among the highest in the nation. "On average, a crime occurs every twelve minutes in Baltimore City. And if you're not fortunate enough to have a home security system, "your home is 300% more likely to be robbed," says CrimeGrade.org.[30] Not surprisingly, Baltimore does not get hyped on the OSF website.

Patrick Hauf, a reporter for the *Free Beacon*, described his visit to Baltimore's Charm City Care Connection:[31] "a nonprofit that provides harm reduction services to combat 'oppression.'" There,

> an employee said that identification is not required to receive a smoking kit but did ask for initials, date of birth, and zip code before handing over two smoking kits containing glass crack pipes as well as Chore Boy copper mesh, a cleaning product used to hold the crack rock at the end of the pipe.
>
> The bag included directions for how to use the pipe,[32] heat-resistant mouthpieces, wooden sticks for packing the mesh into the pipe, and alcohol wipes. Most importantly, the organization provides all drug paraphernalia recipients an "Authorized Harm Reduction

Program Participant Card" that serves as a get-out-of-jail-free card to show to law enforcement because the paraphernalia is illegal in the state of Maryland.[33]

According to Hauf, "Charm City Care Connection receives funding from both the Baltimore city and Maryland state governments, as well as at least $200,000 from Left-wing billionaire George Soros's Open Society Foundations as part of the organization's 'Addiction and Health Equity Program.'"[34]

When the White House announced it would exclude pipes from the drug kits, the Drug Policy Alliance tweeted its objection, saying the decision to "remove pipes from safe smoking equipment is deeply disappointing."[35]

"This is a missed opportunity to be preventative of more deaths due to overdose," the group wrote on Twitter. "Giving clean drug-using equipment such as a pipe & syringe reduces transmission of disease including Hep. C & HIV."[36]

"Harm reduction works to meet people where they are at and keep people free of diseases and alive, so they have a chance of recovery and healing," the group added.[37]

But despite the White House and the HHS denials, Senator John Kennedy (R-LA) remarked, "They're still sending out kits, and these drug smoking kits that are designed to facilitate the smoking of crack cocaine and meth. And they say, 'If you use our kits, it's safer, and it promotes racial equity.' There's no safe way to use crack cocaine and meth."[38] He is right.

Still, on August 3, 2022, Hauf reported that two non-profit "harm reduction" organizations, which operate in Maine, with a $1.2 million grant from the Biden administration, handed him bags of a dozen crack pipes…along with foil and a smoking kit that contained a mouthpiece, copper scrubber, lip balm, and instructions on how to smoke crack cocaine. They also handed out three meth pipes, a snorting kit, naloxone, fentanyl test strips, and a condom." The White House refused to comment on why despite its "assurances that taxpayer funds would not underwrite the distribution of crack pipes," and despite the bipartisan bills passed by Congress "in June and July that bar the administration from funding it," the funding of such programs is continuing.[39]

Soros has been relentlessly funding marijuana-legalization propaganda campaigns through the OSF's numerous programs.[40] These have pushed for drug policy reforms—often led by the Soros-funded Drug Policy Alliance, as well as smaller pro-marijuana groups, such as NORML (norml.org)—holding local, national, and international conferences[41] and advertising online and via social media. It paid off. State after state has legalized marijuana.[42] Indeed, Soros's deep-pocketed perseverance, his well-funded Democrats in Congress, and President Joe Biden are eager to reward him with a law that will turn his vision of stoned America into a reality.[43] As of June 2022, Biden had still declined to sign a marijuana legalization law; however, in April 2022, his spokesperson, Jen Psaki, said the president "'remains committed' to honoring his campaign pledge to release 'everyone' in federal prison for marijuana."[44]

In January 2018, Soros attacked the social media cartels Google and Facebook at the World Economic Forum in Davos, Switzerland, for "deliberately engineer[ing] addiction to the services they provide." He warned that this addiction "can be very harmful, particularly for adolescents," and argued that there is a "similarity between internet platforms and gambling companies."[45]

Soros did not mention addiction to drugs, the most harmful and quick-addicting substances. It was not an oversight. Soros has invested untold fortunes in legalizing, hence facilitating drug addiction, which enslaves human bodies and minds. He has used both his money and his time lobbying for and successfully legalizing—or in his lingo, "decriminalizing"—their use.

Eager to convince, Soros went on to describe the symptoms of addiction to social media, saying that what is happening in "our digital age" is " very harmful and maybe irreversible . . . inducing people to give up their autonomy," making it difficult "to assert and defend what

John Stuart Mill called 'the freedom of mind' . . . [which] once lost," he warned, "will be difficult to regain."[46]

It sounds a lot like the symptoms of *drug* addiction, which, unfortunately, have become all too familiar due to his and his affiliates' relentless disinformation campaign about the horrific effects of regular drug use—addiction. Soros's conclusion that "people without the freedom of mind can be easily manipulated" was based on his decades-long practice of doing just that.[47]

Advancing the greatest slavery ever—drug addiction—sits well with Soros's and the Left's rejection of the notion of the unalienable Right of liberty in favor of a progressive ideology of equitable rights and entitlements.

Initially, Soros said his overarching goal was to promote informed discussion of drug policy. But debate and discussion are not his style and were not his objectives. Instead, he used his resources to fund think tanks, foundations, conferences, media campaigns, and public policy action groups that have successfully muddled public opinion enough to change the public's attitude toward drug use and focused on changing the criminal justice system concerning the use of all illegal drugs.

For now, he has succeeded in advancing the legalization of marijuana in the House. Still, it is unclear if the Senate would vote to approve it due to the overwhelming scientific evidence of long-term physical, psychological, social, and economic harm caused by using marijuana.

Earlier, Senator Cory Booker (D-NJ) proposed a bill that would legalize marijuana, delete the criminal records of those convicted for marijuana-related offenses, and invest the revenues from the marijuana business "in the communities most harmed by the War on Drugs." Booker stated, "The war on drugs has systematically targeted people of color and the poor, harmed job prospects and access to housing for our nation's most vulnerable communities, and destroyed countless lives. The House Judiciary Committee's decision to advance this bill is a significant step toward righting these wrongs and healing the wounds of decades of injustice."[48]

Ironically, Booker and other woke Democrats are plugging the allocation of marijuana businesses to the black communities that have already
been devastated by drug abuse—which most often begins with marijuana.

* * *

When asked for his motive for investing so much money and efforts
to legalize drugs, Soros claimed that since prohibitionist drug policies
contradict his vision of an Open Society, he resolved to change them.

"When I decided to extend the operations of my Open Society
Foundation to the United States, I chose drug policy as one of the first
fields of engagement. I felt that drug policy was the area in which the
United States was in the greatest danger of violating the principles of
open society," he stated.[49] He also claimed that "laws that make drugs
illegal" create a criminal problem and "to treat the drug problem as
primarily a criminal problem is a misconception."[50]

On different occasions, he claimed his intention was merely to
"start a conversation." He always spoke of "changing policy" to reduce
the harm caused by the unjust war on drugs but never about changing
the criminal laws on controlling and preventing drug abuse. "The war
on drugs has put millions behind bars, disrupted entire communities,
particularly in the inner cities, and destabilized entire countries," he said.
Soros did not claim he had all the correct answers. Still, he was sure
of one thing: enforcing laws prohibiting the abuse of dangerous drugs
caused "more harm than the drugs themselves."[51] He even declared,
"Some drugs are addictive; others like marijuana are not."[52]

Replacing "harm" with "compassion" required changes in the federal and state laws that ban the use of 116 dangerous drugs. Instead
of lobbying Congress to relax the law, Soros targeted California and
Arizona, each with a rich past of drug abuse and a substantial number
of drug users, to test his ability to change the local laws. He and his billionaire friends spent a few million dollars on propaganda (articles and
advertisements in local papers and on T.V., town hall meetings, ballot
organizing, etc.) and funding to local pro-drug "grassroots" groups to

collect signatures for referendums to modify the state laws to allow prescriptions for "medical marijuana."[53]

Soros's choice of drugs to exploit American society's weaknesses is akin to the Soviets' tactics to undermine the West. The *Soviet Military Encyclopedia*,[54] mentioned earlier, lists specific measures to be utilized in peacetime to advance Soviet foreign policy objectives. They include using "poisons and narcotics" as weapons against the West. The Soviets recognized that encouraging and endorsing drug abuse would destroy America's social and economic structure and erode its moral fiber. So, they instructed their surrogates to use this tactic.

As Nikita Khrushchev put it, "Anything that speeds the destruction of capitalism is moral."[55]

On May 1, 1983, Edward Codey, in the *Washington Post*, wrote that "according to the State Department, Fidel Castro decided in early 1979 to allow Cuba to be used as "a bridge and support base" for narcotics traffickers as a means to aid Cuba economically and contribute to the "deterioration of American society.[56]""

The Sandinistas in Nicaragua have done the same. On August 2, 1984, during the U.S. Senate's Committee hearing on Drug and Terrorism, Antonio Farach, the highest-ranking Nicaraguan defector at that time, said that the Sandinista official Humberto Ortega and the Nicaraguan Interior Minister Tomas Borge told him, "The drug trade produced a good economic benefit which we needed ... we wanted to provide food for our people with the suffering and death of the youth in the U.S.... the drugs were used as a political weapon because we were delivering a blow to our political enemy."

Soros used the same approach as he successfully made the once-unthinkable, unacceptable, and illegal in the U.S. a thing of the past. He set out to turn marijuana use in America into the "soma" that Aldous Huxley described nearly a century ago.

In his 1932 dystopian novel *Brave New World*, Huxley portrayed the global World State in the year A.F. 632 as a government that used "soma"—the "perfect drug . . . euphoric, narcotic, pleasantly hallucinant"—to calm and control its populace.[57] *Soma* was served with coffee, *soma* tablets were placed on the table during presidential meetings, and a "loving cup of strawberry ice cream *soma* was passed from hand to hand."[58]

This "soma" of which Huxley wrote was taken "to calm your anger, to reconcile you to your enemies, to make you patient and long-suffering. In the past, you could only accomplish these things by making a great effort and after years of hard moral training."

"Now, you swallow two or three half-gramme tablets, and there you are. Anybody can be virtuous now. You can carry at least half your morality about in a bottle. Christianity without tears—that's what soma is," said one of Huxley's characters. In time, "soma had raised a quite impenetrable wall between the actual universe and [society's] minds."[59]

A brief examination of the programs, causes, and policies Soros has been funding and promoting (such as open borders, critical race theory, the people's sovereignty, gender fluidity, gender-affirming care,[60] climate change initiatives, environmental justice, and on and on) lead to the inevitable conclusion that clearheaded Americans would reject his crazy woke initiatives. So, he did his best to dope them, raising his "impenetrable wall" between reality and the public's minds.

By 1996, the slogans of "medicalization" and "compassion" were fused with "legalization" and "decriminalization," as well as "nonviolent drug offender," began shaping the vocabulary of the public dialogue.

David Callahan, liberal founder and editor of the website Inside Philanthropy, noted in his 2017 book, *The Givers*, that "no philanthropist has done more than Soros to soften America's drug laws. Soros got behind that cause in the mid-1990s, funding a new drug policy think tank and bankrolling the push for medicinal marijuana, widely seen as a bridge to legalization."[61]

Soros's strategy of legalizing marijuana by lobbying to change state laws instead of the federal law—which still considers marijuana a dangerous drug—was apparently supported by President Obama, who once "suggested that the best way to get the attention of Congress is to legalize marijuana in as many states as possible at the state level. If a majority of states approve marijuana measures and public opinion continues to swell in favor of cannabis, Congress may have no choice but to consider decriminalization—or legalize the substance," journalist Sean Williams explained in 2016.[62]

Soros's crafty initiatives to legalize drugs in California and Arizona in 1996 led Joseph A. Califano Jr., Jimmy Carter's secretary of health, education, and welfare and a former president of the National Center on Addiction and Substance Abuse at Columbia University, to protest in the *Washington Post*: "The Anything Goes Emmy for Political Hoodwink in 1996 does not go to a candidate. It belongs to the campaigns in Arizona and California to pass pro-drug legalization propositions, sold to voters as getting tough on violent criminals and offering compassionate care for the dying.

"And the award for best supporting role," Califano went on, "goes to billionaire George Soros, the Daddy Warbucks of drug legalization. He does not reside in either state, but he bankrolled both efforts."[63] Indeed, Califano pointed out Soros's typical crafty modus operandi of interfering in local affairs.

Responding to the question, "Why should a New York millionaire be writing laws in Arizona?" Soros told the *Washington Post*, "I live in one place, but I consider myself a citizen of the world. I have foundations in 30 countries, and I believe certain universal principles apply everywhere—including Arizona."[64]

There you have it! This was not merely another of Soros's meaningless statements. It is his raison d'être.

Which universal principles was Soros referring to? The *Post* did not ask.

In Arizona, the 1996 initiative, also funded by Soros's fellow billionaires Peter B. Lewis and John Sperling, was misleadingly labeled "Drug Medicalization, Prevention and Control." It passed. But when Arizona legislators realized the law did not refer only to marijuana but "included 116 other Schedule One drugs, including LSD and heroin . . .

a new Bill was quickly passed to scrap the whole idea," Norman Aisbett reported in the *West Australian*.[65]

It took almost three decades and lots of money to achieve what he set out to get. Since regular use of marijuana leads to dependency and addiction that blurs the mind of its users, it causes people to "give up their autonomy,"[66] as Soros noted elsewhere. The increased number of users who get addicted leads to increased dependency on services provided by the state, which also regulates the industry. Once dependent, to quote Huxley, these addicts "can be easily manipulated." So, legalizing the drug seemed a critical steppingstone to growing the number of its users, thus reducing the number of potential opponents to his and the radical Left's Marxist-sounding policies in the U.S.

Soros, who claims to hate Marxism, developed his version of neo-Marxism.[67] He uses similar-sounding themes, such as race (and, more recently, gender), hatred, class conflict, anti-individualism, anti-capitalism, and pro-collectivism. He used the guise of "compassion" and advancing an "open society" to legalize the drug as part of criminal and racial justice reform.

The lack of serious pushback from the public, the states, and the federal government encouraged Soros to carry out his plans to change America. As he pushed for drug legalization, Soros repeatedly claimed that addiction to a substance would decline once it became legal, as though addiction is caused by laws that prohibit its use, not the drug consumed. Alas, he was wrong. While the profusion of drugs may reduce their price, unlike most other commodities, their excess and lower price increase their abuse. He also argued in the *Wall Street Journal*, "Legalizing marijuana may make it easier for adults to buy marijuana, but it can hardly make it any more accessible to young people."[68] He was wrong again.

Moreover, marijuana is a gateway drug; once legalized, its use increases significantly among the young. The National Institute on Drug Abuse's (NIDA) 2014 website warned, "Illicit drug use in the U.S. is on the rise," and "More than half of new illicit drug users begin with marijuana."[69]

A recent study published in the May 26, 2022, issue of *Addiction* found that cannabis use in states that legalized marijuana (medical and recreational) increased, especially among twelve- to twenty-year-olds (approximately 49.6 million people).[70] The principal investigator, Yuyan Shi, Ph.D., stated, "It's especially concerning that increased cannabis use occurs among young people because of the detrimental health effects associated with cannabis use at a young age, including impaired respiratory function, cardiovascular disease and adverse effects on mental health."[71]

Soros probably borrowed from his market experience when he opined in the *Wall Street Journal* that "criminal organizations in Mexico and elsewhere . . . would rapidly lose their competitive advantage if marijuana were a legal commodity" and weaken them.[72] He rejected the claim that this would lead the crime syndicates to move into other illicit enterprises. Not only was he wrong, again, but the booming market of marijuana in the U.S. have created an even larger illegal marijuana industry run in California, Oregon, Oklahoma, New Mexico, Colorado, and elsewhere.

Narcofornia[73], a documentary released in July 2022, documents millions of marijuana plants illegally cultivated by members of Mexican cartels and illegal Chinese migrants on public land or land stolen from farmers. "The illegal plantations steal public water, draining counties of their needed water while damaging the soil and polluting the ground-water permanently with fertilizers," says John Nores, the former game warden for the California Department of Fish and Wildlife. The illegal growers create "incredibly egregious environmental crime here," he says. The understaffed local police forces fear the violent cartels who continue to threaten "wildlife by killing and injuring animals and plants and leave parts of nature infertile."

So not only did the Mexican cartels get out of the marijuana business, but they've also expanded their involvement by moving it to the U.S., where, unlike the legal growers, they need no licenses and obey no regulation and most often, are left alone by law enforcement.

This evolving dangerous situation highlights the results of

implementing Soros's two major policies: marijuana legalization and open borders.

In 1996, Soros's investment paid off. California was the first state to modify its drug control law, known as the Compassionate Use Act of 1996 (Health & Safety Code, section 11362.5), permitting the cultivation, prescription, and use of "medical marijuana."[74] The Arizona referendum was also advertised and passed as a "medical marijuana" initiative. But when the state legislators realized it also included the distribution of clean needles to addicts injecting all illegal drugs, they immediately reversed it.

Soros and the other proponents of medical marijuana and drug legalization wrongly claimed that the price of government-approved "legal" drugs would significantly lower their cost, thus removing the necessity to commit crimes to secure the drugs. However, a black market will always supply groups prohibited by law from using drugs—adolescents, airline pilots, bus drivers, surgeons, and so on. Soros had to wait until 2009 for a government amiable to his idea.

In 2009, he found a kindred spirit in President Obama, who, while then did not publicly endorse the legalization of marijuana, eased the enforcement of federal laws concerning this drug. The chosen vehicle was Obamacare. The first indication of this came on August 5, 2009, when NIDA's little-noticed tender[75]for the production and distribution of large quantities of marijuana cigarettes, for purposes other than for research, clocked under the DEA control and supposedly in compliance with FDA (Food and Drug Administration) regulations.

Through Attorney General Eric Holder, the Obama administration pushed for reduced sentencing for "drug dealing" crimes and non-prosecution of "low-level" drug offenders.[76]

According to pro-legalization activist Sean Williams, and the Drug Policy Alliance, President Obama seemed to like Soros's idea of "rolling back the Drug War."[77] As noted earlier, Obama wanted to see marijuana legalized in as many states as possible at the state level. Not surprisingly, leaks from the DEA indicated the agency anticipated legalizing "medical marijuana" in all fifty states, even without FDA approval. Obama's move mainly went unnoticed, though *Forbes* published my warning of this development, British psychiatrist, thinker, and writer Anthony Malcolm Daniels (aka Theodore Dalrymple) observed that "the consumption of drugs has the effect of reducing men's freedom by circumscribing the range of their interests. It impairs their ability to pursue more important human aims, such as raising a family and fulfilling civic obligations. Very often, it impairs their ability to pursue gainful employment and promotes parasitism. Moreover, far from being expanders of consciousness, most drugs severely limit it."[78]

These characteristics suit the mindlessness requisite of recruits to the progressive Sorosian racial, social, equity, and climate justice and "America Last" policies of the Democrats and the Biden administration.

The overwhelming evidence of the short- and long-term harm caused by marijuana to the user and society should have stopped any attempt to legalize the drug. However, vast amounts of money spent on influencing politicians, medical professionals, psychologists, health care workers, and the like to ignore the horrible effects of drug addiction, including marijuana, that they encounter every day generated the desired social acceptance of the "compassionate drug," marijuana. So, why not recreational marijuana?

Recreational use of marijuana has nothing to do with medical marijuana. As with other drugs, the development of marijuana/cannabis as a medicine must follow modern medical rules—advancing with clinical trials of specific compounds, looking for side effects and interactions with other drugs, and so on.

But in November 2015, the DEA acting administrator, Chuck Rosenberg, said, "We can have an intellectually honest debate about whether or not we want to legalize something bad and dangerous but don't call it medicine. That's a joke."[79]

Rosenberg opined there was a need for "legitimate research into the efficacy of marijuana for its constituent parts as a medicine. "But," he added, "I think the notion that state legislatures just decree it so is ludicrous."[80] The pro-drug lobby called for his dismissal.

Memory loss is among the ill effects of marijuana use (whether obtained legally or not), as proven by researchers at Northwestern University. Their study also found "evidence of brain alterations . . . significant deterioration in the thalamus, a key structure for learning, memory, and communications between brain regions." The study concluded that if this were not enough, "chronic marijuana use could boost the underlying process driving schizophrenia."[81]

This study, like many others, documented the devastating long-term harm caused by marijuana use. The website MedicineNet noted that "marijuana smoke contains 50% to 70% more carcinogenic hydrocarbons than tobacco smoke . . . which further increases the lungs' exposure to carcinogenic smoke."[82] And according to one study, "marijuana users have a 4.8-fold increase in the risk of a heart attack in the first hour after smoking the drug. . . This risk may be greater in aging populations or those with cardiac vulnerabilities."[83, 84, 85]

Other studies documented distorted perceptions, impaired coordination, difficulty in thinking and problem-solving, and ongoing problems with learning and memory.[86] As a result, "someone who smokes marijuana every day may be functioning at a suboptimal intellectual level all the time."[87] In conclusion: "Research clearly demonstrates that marijuana has the potential to cause problems in daily life or make a person's existing problems worse. In fact, heavy marijuana users generally report lower life satisfaction, poorer mental and physical health, relationship problems, and less academic and career success compared to their peers who came from similar backgrounds. For example, marijuana use is associated with a higher likelihood of dropping out of school. Several studies also associate workers' marijuana smoking with increased absences, tardiness, accidents, workers' compensation claims, and job turnover." NIDA's survey from 2013 shows that drug users are exacting more than $700 billion annually in costs related to crime, lost work productivity, and health care.[88] Add to this the cost of newly hooked Americans on social welfare, including food stamps, Obamacare, public housing, free cell phones, and other entitlements.

Yet, the Obama administration moved to relax federal oversight on marijuana use on August 29, 2013, with a Department of Justice memo clarifying the government's prosecutorial priorities. It stated that the federal government would rely on state and local law enforcement to "address marijuana activity through enforcement of their own narcotics laws."[89]

By kicking the control and policing of marijuana abuse to the state authority, the Obama administration borrowed a page from Soros's strategy of changing the U.S. criminal justice system.

In 2018, the number of young adults who reported regular use of marijuana in the U.S. rose to 11.8 million, and the number of teens in eighth and tenth grades saying they used it every day had also increased because of their perception that regular marijuana use was risky had been altered. Their perception changed because Soros's funded pro-drug lobby and its successful legalization campaign disseminated misleading information on hazards caused by consuming "natural marijuana" and "medical marijuana." In 1995, In *Soros on Soros* (p. 198), he declared: "Some drugs are addictive; others like marijuana are not."[90] His statement and the legalization lobby's propaganda created the false perception that using marijuana is safe, "cool," and even therapeutic.

According to Dr. Carlton E. Turner, President Ronald Reagan's drug czar, marijuana "is a dirty drug with so many different side effects that it will never pass the required safety and efficacy testing for medicine. Marijuana can contain over 700 individual chemicals, and when smoked, the number of chemicals expands to the thousands. The smoke contains 50 to 70 percent more cancer-causing compounds than tobacco."[91]

By February 2020, marijuana was legal for medical use in 33 states, and 11 states allowed recreational marijuana use for adults over 21,[92] though the drug is readily available everywhere. Moreover, legalizing marijuana removed the social stigma of drug abuse. It drove more Americans to regularly use and get addicted to marijuana and other drugs that are often mixed with the joints they buy. The rising number of overdoses on fentanyl-laced marijuana and other drugs is a recent, more deadly example. Worse, the legalization of marijuana in the U.S. set a trend that encouraged other countries to do the same.

According to the CDC, 2021 saw an increase of 15 percent in overdose deaths.[93] Many of the 107,622 Americans who overdosed consumed dangerous drugs, such as heroin and other opioids, methamphetamines, and cocaine, often laced with fentanyl. Fentanyl[94] is a synthetic opioid, about 100 times more potent than morphine and 50 times more potent than heroin. It is highly addictive and frequently deadly; 2 milligrams are enough to kill a person.

China is the major exporter of fentanyl, and many other synthetic drugs, which are shipped in huge quantities to Mexican drug cartels who have developed a lucrative business of producing millions of counterfeit pills, either laced with fentanyl or, more frequently, containing only fentanyl. They flood the U.S. with millions of pills smuggled through the open southern border. Yet, Biden's administration keeps the border open and, instead of fighting the drug cartels, has been providing "Safe injection" sites for addicts and drug paraphernalia in what the Health and Human Services (HHS)[95] Department described as a "harm reduction" effort, just as Soros has been recommending and funding since 1997.[96] But there is nothing safe at such sites. Everywhere they open, they create an open drug market. "Safe injection sites have not delivered on their promises and have caused a significant increase in trash, crime, and disorder,"[97] so they were shut down.[98] But Democrat-run cities and the Biden administration are following Soros's plan, which instead of reducing harm, increases it to the users and the public.[99]

On July 22, 2022, the *Daily Mail* listed studies showing the increased danger caused by the legalization of marijuana:

- Rates of car crash injuries rise by 5.8 percent across Colorado, Washington, Oregon, and California after legalization.

- Colorado alone saw a shocking 17.8 percent jump in the number of crash injuries.

- Cannabis use grows markedly after legalization, and people are not aware of the health risks, says New York study.

- Children as young as nine are curious about trying cannabis— often due to signals from parents and peers.

- Teenagers are more than three times as likely as adults to get addicted to cannabis.

- Cannabis users are 22 percent more likely to end up in a hospital emergency room than others.[100]

- Users "misperceive" how well their romantic relationships are faring and are more critical, demanding, defensive, and negative when rowing with loved ones.

- The U.N. (World Drug Report 2022)[101] says cannabis legalization has "accelerated" its use and upped chances of depression and suicide."[102]

And on June 6, 2022, Erik Robinson from Oregon Health & Science University (OHSU) wrote, "A systematic review of scientific literature finds thin evidence that cannabis has clinical benefits."[103]

Unsurprisingly, the legalization of marijuana opened the door to the new multibillion-dollar cannabis industry, which has increased state revenues.

According to the website American Marijuana, "It is predicted that in 2025, legal marijuana sales will earn as much as 23 billion USD in the U.S. alone."[104]

Despite Soros's efforts, marijuana (cannabis) is still identified by the U.S. Drug Enforcement Administration (DEA), the U.S. National Institutes of Health (NIH), and the National Institute on Drug Abuse (NIDA), as a Schedule I drug "with no currently accepted medical use and a high potential for abuse."[105] Democrats in Congress, led by Sen. Chuck Schumer, are proposing new legislation to remove marijuana from the list of dangerous drugs, allowing it to be used freely. They are likely to succeed, since they won the majority of the Senate in the 2022 mid-term elections.

Meanwhile, Soros's success in legalizing marijuana use has put millions of Americans who have taken up smoking marijuana (because it's legal and widely advertised as "good for you"[106]) at higher risk of infection by COVID-19. Soon after the pandemic began in early 2020, NIDA warned, " Because it attacks the lungs, the coronavirus that causes COVID-19 could be an especially serious threat to those who smoke tobacco or marijuana or who vape," because, like the mice used in one medical study, they have "enhanced tissue damage and inflammation" in their lungs.[107]

The marijuana plant's primary component causing psychoactive effects, Delta-9-tetrahydrocannabinol (Δ^9-THC), was discovered and isolated by Professor Raphael Mechoulam[108] in Israel in 1964.[109] Since then, thousands of scientific papers identifying additional components have been published, focusing on the therapeutic aspects of the isolated chemicals found in the plant.

In his preface to the book on *Endocannabinoids[110]*, Prof. Mechoulam remarked: "There have been very few clinical trials with THC or with CBD or with cannabis extracts containing fixed ratios of the major constituents. Such trials on small numbers of patients have shown very positive results in epilepsy, post-trauma, Parkinson's disease, Crohn's disease, and a few other disorders. Somewhat larger clinical trials on schizophrenia and graft-versus-host disease (GVHD) have led to statistically significant therapeutic effects. But where are the clinical trials in various cancer diseases where anecdotal evidence points to possible therapeutic effects?"

Mechoulam went on to say, "We have made major advances in understanding the chemistry, biochemistry, and pharmacological effects of the plant cannabinoids and the endocannabinoids . . . I have no doubt that further research with endocannabinoids will throw additional light on the actions of these compounds. However, I believe that the most important future steps in the endocannabinoid area are to advance cannabinoid-based clinical trials in many disease states where strong anecdotal evidence already exists."

Had Soros, the speculator who prides himself on being a highbrow go-getter, genuinely considered marijuana such an important drug, he could have invested much less of his money in lobbying Congress to support scientific research to identify the medicinal properties found in cannabis, as well as in sponsoring the clinical trials necessary to develop effective treatments for a variety of diseases. Instead, he has been promoting the consumption of raw marijuana, which has many devastating adverse effects on the regular user and even their offspring.[111]

Meanwhile, under Soros's influence, Regina LaBelle, acting director of National Drug Control Policy, highlighted the Biden administration's true focus in the fight against drugs, as gathered from "The Biden-Harris Administration's Statement of Drug Policy Priorities for Year One": "Ensuring racial equity and promoting harm reduction efforts."[112]

In August 2021, the FDA commissioner Dr. Stephen M. Hahn [113] stated: "The FDA has approved one drug, Epidiolex, that contains a highly-purified form of CBD for the treatment of seizures associated with LennoxGastaut syndrome (LGS), Dravet syndrome (D.S.), or tuberous sclerosis complex (TSC) in people one year of age and older. However, we still have a limited understanding of the safety profile of CBD and many other cannabis-derived compounds, including potential safety risks for people and animals. . . . Better data in these areas are needed for the FDA and other public health agencies to make informed, science-based decisions that impact public health."[114]

Hahn is right. There is a lot unknown about marijuana, as noted by Professor Mechoulam. Then why the rush to legalize it? And why allow cannabidiol (CBD) in thousands of edible products?

According to the *Journal of Food Composition and Analysis*, "The 2018 Agricultural Improvement Act removed hemp (industrial cannabis) from Schedule I control, creating a market for hemp products, including cannabidiol-containing products. Due to the market's rapid growth, little is known about the presence and concentration of cannabinoids in commercial products."[115] Today, CBD is used in brownies, ice cream, soda, bottled water, coffee, candy, beer, gummies, chocolate, and even dairy products. While the level of THC in any edible is supposed to be limited to 0.3 percent, oversight is lacking.

Dr. Hahn, the U.S. Senate, and the White House should be interested in Reece and Hulse's recent paper, which provides epidemiological evidence that "prenatal cannabis exposure has been linked with several pediatric cancers, which together comprise the majority of pediatric cancer types." Moreover, "Cannabis-liberal jurisdictions were associated with higher TPCIR (cancer incidence rate) and a faster rate of TPCIR increase."[116]

A. Stuart Reece is a professor at the School of Psychiatry and Clinical Neurosciences at the University of Western Australia, specializing, among other things, in epidemiolocal studies of cannabis genotoxicity, epigenotoxicity, and chromosomal toxicity. In December 2021, Reece proved that "cannabis in all forms"—including smoking, eating, hemp products, and CBD in all forms—"takes a weed whacker to your chromosomes." He and his associates expressed grave concerns about "the heavy epigenomic footprint of cannabis as relates to . . . birth defects and . . . limblessness."[117]

On January 10, 2022, the *Times* published Reece's letter on the risks of cannabis.[118] Reece wrote:

> As appalling as the cannabis mental health data is, it is but a very small part of its public health risks, which now obviously include damage to both the genes and the complex system that regulates and controls genes. Cannabis genotoxicity is expressed clinically as elevated rates of many cancers (testicular, breast, pancreas, thyroid, and liver cancers), dozens of birth defects (thalidomide-like affecting the cardiovascular, nervous, chromosomal, digestive, and kidney systems), and accelerated aging of human cells and organisms. All of this accelerates exponentially at the higher doses, which inevitably accompany cannabis legalisation. Our findings have been confirmed in Colorado, Canada,

Australia, Hawaii, the U.S., and most recently in Europe and can be found via Google Scholar. (Published with Dr. Reece's permission.)

What is already known about the harm caused by the uncontrolled use of marijuana is enough to keep it listed as a dangerous drug. Only FDA-approved medicine produced from marijuana should be permitted.

But by now, marijuana has become the cigarette of the twenty-first century. Smoking cigarettes never fogged the mind or served as a conduit to abuse more dangerous drugs.

Suppose compassion was the reason for Soros's crusade to legalize marijuana. In that case, he should pay for a huge, multi-year campaign to stop the use of marijuana, similar to what was done to limit cigarette smoking.

However, Soros's drug legalization campaign was not motivated by compassion for the sick. He has been funding the legalization of marijuana throughout the U.S. under the guise of "equality" and "justice." And as more people get high, he and his neo-Marxist, progressive-Left cabal are free to undermine the country's legal system, moral values, and sovereignty.

It seems that in Soros's neo-Marxist, divided, crime-ridden, racist America, the marijuana-addicted, doped citizenry will be as easy to subdue and control as in Aldous Huxley's *Brave New World*. While Elon Musk spends his billions to enrich society by opening new horizons, Soros has been investing his wealth in policies that have already and will increasingly harm millions of people while robbing them of their rights to individual freedom and free enterprise.

What a legacy!

3

JUSTICE, SOROS-STYLE

"I have been involved in efforts to reform the criminal-justice system for more than 30 years I have been a philanthropist."[1]

—GEORGE SOROS, JULY 31, 2022

"Few men have done more harm to public safety and justice in America than George Soros. Even now, as he surveys the carnage wreaked by the prosecutors he bankrolled, he has no regrets."[2]

—SENATOR TOM COTTON (R-ARK.), AUG 3, 2022

SOROS'S SUCCESSFUL USE OF "COMPASSION" to make "medical marijuana" legal in California in 1996 validated the manipulative megalomaniac's assumption that he could change what Americans once held illegal and improper to legal and normal. Encouraged, Soros used "compassion" to advance his "criminal justice reform" plan for all Americans.

Later, the plan was adjusted to focus on criminal justice for Blacks, and soon after, the OSF added health justice, racial justice, social justice, climate and environmental justice, and transitional justice, including programs for diversity, equity, and inclusion (DEI), and more.

The need to reform the US criminal justice system has long been acknowledged and debated by Democrats and Republicans alike. The ideas of how to and what to improve are varied, and changing the system customarily requires legislative changes, which take a long time and are expensive and uncertain.

Traditional political negotiations do not encumber Soros. He sets his rules and changes them when they don't suit him anymore.

He has often argued that the US criminal justice system is flawed and has laid out his arguments for reform in articles, essays, and public speeches. Through his various nonprofit foundations and private organizations, he funded research validating his views and proposed policies.[3]

As with the legalization of marijuana, Soros chose to support directly and indirectly groups claiming the U.S. criminal justice system is racist. The 2012 incident involving Hispanic neighborhood watch coordinator George Zimmerman shooting his attacker, the black teenager Trayvon Martin, in Florida, allowed Soros to funnel money into organizations that support the Dream Defenders, whose website calls it "a project of Tides Center."[4] Dream Defenders claimed the shooting was racially motivated.

Local protests against the shooting soon developed into a national campaign for "racial justice," which led to the firing of the local police chief and the charging of Zimmerman with second-degree murder twice. When he was not found guilty in both trials, new, extensively publicized, and well-organized demonstrations advanced the perception that the U.S. justice system discriminates against Blacks. Soros's investment in the organizations that led the protests paid off; they heightened the perception of racial division in American society.

In 2014, for example, Soros gave $50 million to ACLU's Campaign to End Mass Incarceration, which was "strongly endorsed" by Obama's attorney general, Eric Holder.[5]

Again using his overwhelming financial resources through special PACs, such as Democracy II, the Justice & Public Safety PAC,[6] and his foundations, Soros has been backing the election of handpicked district attorneys who share his extreme views. Once in office, these DAs (known as "Soros DAs") apply the power of selective enforcement of the law, redefining the criminal code and deciding what constitutes criminal behavior and who gets charged. His strategy worked. The Soros DAs and Democratic mayors and governors have released tens of thousands of criminals from prisons across the country,[7] most allegedly due to the COVID pandemic. How many of these have caused an unprecedented spike in crime throughout the nation is unknown.

Soros, through his foundations, also targeted the federal criminal justice system for its alleged unfair "mass incarceration."

The latest available statistics from "Recidivism of Prisoners Released in 24 States in 2008: A 10-Year Follow-Up Period (2008–2018)" showed that "during the 10-year follow-up period, an estimated 2.2 million arrests occurred among the approximately 409,300 prisoners released in 2008."[8] Among persons released from prison in 2008 in the 18 states that provided data on persons returned to prison, about half (49%) had parole or probation violation or an arrest that led to a new sentence within three years. This rate increased to about 6 in 10 (61%) within 10 years. "By the end of Year 10 following release, a greater percentage of prisoners age 24 or younger (90%) had been arrested than prisoners ages 25 to 39 (85%) or prisoners age 40 or older (75%)."[9]

The study also found that "forty-four percent of male prisoners were arrested at least once in Year 1, and 22% in Year 10 . . . By comparison, 34% of female prisoners were arrested in Year 1," and 98% of all the recidivists were not charged for "probation or parole violation," but for more serious offenses."[10] However, the more Soros-funded DAs are elected, and the more directives listing what crimes should or should not be charged are written, the fewer offenders will be jailed. As the number of incarcerated offenders plummets, the danger to the public's safety will increase. This would surely satisfy the pro-criminal radical Left.

Former New York City police commissioner Ray Kelly told WABC Radio, "George Soros is a major cause for the systematic decline of American law enforcement. The mindset of his DAs—that criminals are victims—has done immeasurable harm, especially to poor minorities in our inner cities. Meanwhile, the complex network of nonprofits Soros uses to disperse his funds makes it nearly impossible to track what he's doing to undermine our justice system. It's ironic," said Kelly, "that his foundation is called The Open Society Institute, yet his anti-law-enforcement programs are deliberately designed to avoid public scrutiny."[11]

Soros's numerous foundations' excessive support of candidates for the 2020 elections in the US—including state legislators and district attorneys plus unqualified candidates—got many elected in major American cities. His PACs and the OSF's various "justice" and "equality" program recipients have functioned and continue to serve as "echo chambers" for past and future candidates whose primary qualification is adherence to Soros's seemingly progressive ideas, which aim to increase racial and social division and chaos in the streets of America.

The "progressive" ideology for Soros DAs includes anti-law enforcement; no bail; anti-incarceration; open borders; illegal immigration; sanctuary cities; and gender, race, environmental, and climate justice "equities" as promoted by Soros-funded organizations.

In October 2016, when Soros's OSF endorsed the abolition of the police, the OSF's *Voices* posted this, written by a "2015 Soros Justice Fellow":

> The United States is facing a policing crisis. Far from being a new issue, as the media might have us believe, this crisis extends back to the country's earliest days, when plantation owners and their legislative counterparts felt it necessary to suppress the activities of the African peoples they conscripted into slavery.

Policing has *always* been a sensitive issue for the Black community in the United States, especially in inner cities with high crime rates. In August 1979, *Ebony*'s publisher John H. Johnson issued a special edition of "Black on Black Crime: the Cause, the Consequences, the Cures."[12] Johnson wrote, "It is our belief, and it is the basic premise of this issue, that Black on Black crime has reached a critical level that threatens our existence as a people. It is a threat to our youths, to our women, to our senior citizens, to our institutions, to our values." He explained, "However, we are not responsible for the external factors that systematically create breeding grounds for social disorder; we cannot avoid the internal responsibility of doing everything we can to solve a problem that is rending the fabric of our lives." Johnson continued, "Homicide is a major cause of death among young Black males, and most of these murder victims are killed, not by racists or members of the Ku Klux Klan, but by other young Black males."[13]

Radical Left groups, such as Black Lives Matter, used the condemnable killing of George Floyd, a black man, by Minneapolis cops on May 25, 2020, to organize more than "8,700 protests, 574 of them violent riots in 69 of the largest cities in the U.S.," causing billions of dollars in damages, according to a report by the Major Cities Chiefs Association. While the report "can't be found" anymore, its findings have been reported elsewhere.[14]

The violent protestors used the opportunity to attack police stations and vehicles and injured and killed law enforcement officers. According to the FBI, "Nationally, 60,105 law enforcement officers were assaulted while performing their duties in 2020. These assaults were reported to the FBI by 9,895 law enforcement agencies. Based on these reports, there were 4,071 more officers assaulted in 2020 than the 56,034 assaults reported in 2019."[15]

According to the National Law Enforcement Memorial Fund's report for 2020, by the end of the year, "264 federal, State, military, tribal, and local law enforcement officers died in the line-of-duty in 2020, an increase of 96% over the 135 officers killed in the line of duty the year before."[16]

While police reform is certainly needed in the U.S., the protestors have been calling to defund and abolish the police, ideas that Soros's OSF has been advocating for years. As a 2016 post suggested, "Maybe instead of thinking about how to improve policing, however, we would do better to reduce the role law enforcement plays in our day-to-day lives."[17]

Soros, the Connoisseur of Chaos, aptly dubbed so by the late Stefan Kanfer,[18] liked the idea so much that his OSF granted $3 million to the Community Resource Hub for Safety and Accountability (CRH) in 2020.[19] Notwithstanding its lofty name, the CHR serves to train agitators "to address the harms of policing in the U.S." and "reviews alternatives to policing in the context of police abolitionist frameworks, offering insights and sharing successful strategies for advocates in the field. . . . The hub 'houses and staffs' the website defundpolice.org in partnership with several national movement organizations." Fox News investigations into Soros's funding of anti-law enforcement groups revealed that according to Soros's "group's tax forms, CRH is a fiscally sponsored project of the New Venture Fund, a nonprofit incubator managed by the Washington, D.C.-based consulting firm Arabella Advisors."[20]

The New Venture Fund, one of the four managed by Arabella, "raked in $965 million in anonymous donations in 2020." While other investors did not disclose their donors, "Soros' nonprofit outright states the cash is going to the New Venture Fund to be passed off to the CRH."[21]

Soros's daughter, Andrea Soros Colombel, joined his fundraising committee. Their Lead the Way 2022 includes the Way to Lead PAC, Missouri representative Cori Bush's campaign committee, and the campaigns of the twelve other progressive politicians attempting to enter Congress.[22] Fox News reported that the hundreds of thousands of dollars "from Andrea and George Soros put them among Lead the Way 2022's and Way to Lead's top, respective backers for the 2022 elections."[23]

Using different venues to finance groups advocating the abolishment of the police and training agitators around the country are good ways to spread chaos in the streets of America. To assure further destruction of law and order, Soros has been supporting downgrading the criminal code, eliminating bail, and pretrial diversion programs, ending incarceration as punishment, and electing administrative officeholders, including DAs, who refuse to enforce the laws. The Soros-selected progressive-radical activist DAs ignore drug-related offenses, oppose detention, support the early release of convicts from prison, expunge their records, give them voting rights, facilitate homelessness and neglect, and even assist addicts' use of all drugs openly. Oregon, which in 2020 seemingly followed Soros's Drug Policy Alliance's advice to decriminalize drug use, became the first State to legalize all drugs. In 2021, 1,069 drug users died from an overdose, a 41 percent increase from the previous year.[24]

Funding, mostly from Soros's foundations, also went to organizations supporting illegal immigration, funding illegal immigrants' lodging, and more. All in the name of "compassion" and "justice."

In May 2020, when the COVID-19 epidemic was in full swing in the U.S., George Floyd, a Black man, was killed by police officer Derek Chauvin in Minnesota. (In 2021, Chauvin was "sentenced to 22-and-a-half years in prison for second-degree unintentional murder, third-degree murder and second-degree manslaughter in Floyd's death. And in July 2022, he was sentenced to 22.5 for violating Floyd's civil rights, which he'll serve concurrently in federal prison.[25] The trial of two other former police officers was scheduled for October 2022.[26]) Another former police officer who pleaded guilty was sentenced to three years for manslaughter.[27]

With the 2020 presidential election around the corner, the Democrats, who never let a crisis go to waste, used Floyd's killing to endorse, organize, and often participated in nationwide demonstrations of Black Lives Matter, Antifa, and "defund the police" groups that erupted all over the country. The protests often turned violent. Large and small businesses were raided and set on fire, as were police stations and cars. Police officers and bystanders from Portland to Austin, New York, Philadelphia, and elsewhere have been shot at or beaten. The rioters caused billions of dollars in damages, disrupted the lives and livelihood of millions of people, and created fear, increased anxiety, uncertainty, and insecurity. According to the National Police Association, more than two thousand police officers were injured in 574 incidents of rioting and looting in 2020.[28] By May 2021, influenced by organizations and activists, some directly, most circuitously supported by Soros, more than fifty major cities had reduced their police budgets.[29]

By mid-2022, in New York City, attacks on the police resulted in the departure of 1,596 police officers, "a 38% surge over the same period in 2021, when 1,159 officers left, and an astonishing 46% leap over 2020's numbers, when 1,092 left the force." Joseph Giacalone, a John Jay College of Criminal Justice professor and a former NYPD officer, stated, "It will take 20 years to fix this mess. The city is bleeding blue, and only the cop haters will be celebrating . . . There's no way to stop it. Activists, abolitionists, and their pandering politicians have done so much damage to the profession that it will take a generation to fix, if at all."[30]

In early June 2022, more than 75 percent of New Yorkers polled "said they were concerned about becoming victims of violent crime."[31] In mid-2022, rising crime and high taxation drove hundreds of thousands of people out of New York.[32]

In July 2020, in reaction to the violent demonstrations and rioting following Floyd's killing, Patrick Gaspard, then OSF's president, announced a new investment of $220 million in Black-led racial justice groups.[33] Gaspar declared, "Now is the moment we've been investing in for the last 25 years."[34] A strange statement.

Perhaps he had in mind the millions of dollars in investments Soros has made over the years (as noted on the OSF's varying websites[35]) promoting radical black organizations (as mentioned elsewhere, including at Influence Watch[36]) and academic institutions promoting anti-police, anti-incarceration notions as viewed through the lenses of critical race theory. CRT, as conservative propagandist Christopher Rufo explains, is "an academic discipline, formulated in the 1990s, built on the intellectual framework of identity-based Marxism," using euphemisms such as "equity," "social justice," "diversity and inclusion," and "culturally responsive teaching." CRT "prescribes a revolutionary program that would overturn the principles of the Declaration and destroy the remaining structure of the Constitution," writes Rufo. He goes on to detail how activists of CRT are promoting racist theories in the federal government. The Treasury Department's training session, for example, told "staff members that 'virtually all white people contribute to racism.'"

A chilling example of the teaching of this pernicious movement is the three-day "reeducation camp" of white male executives from Sandia National Laboratories, "which designs America's nuclear arsenal." Rufo reports that "they were told that 'white male culture was analogous to the 'KKK,' 'white supremacists,' and 'mass killings.'" As if this were not enough, "the executives were then forced to renounce their 'white male privilege' and write letters of apology to fictitious women and people of color."[37] Similar reeducation programs have been taking place in all government departments, as well as in academic institutions and large and small businesses.

CRT plays a significant role in Soros's programs to "reform" the criminal justice system and support initiatives to provide "reparations" to the allegedly oppressed.[38]

Another example is the OSF's $500,000 in 2007 to CUNY's John Jay College of Criminal Justice in Manhattan.[39] Its Institute for Innovation in Prosecution, "with the help of controversial figures such as Chicago prosecutor Kim Foxx, Los Angeles DA George Gascón, and San Francisco's [recalled DA,] Chesa Boudin—has been instrumental in reshaping how prosecutors [and law enforcement officials] across the country view crime and punishment."[40]

"There is this call for justice in Black and brown communities, an explosion of not just sympathy but solidarity across the board," Gaspard declared as he announced the OSFs $220 million in support of Black Justice. "It's time to double down . . . If we're going to say, 'Black lives matter,' we need to say, 'Black organizations and structures matter."[41]

This significant investment has put Soros and his foundations "near the forefront of the police protest movement."[42] Some $150 million went to "emerging organizations like the Black Voters Matter Fund and Repairers of the Breach, founded by the Rev. Dr. William J. Barber II of the Poor People's Campaign. The money will also support more established organizations like the Equal Justice Initiative." The rest, $70 million, went to "local grants supporting policing and criminal justice changes. Some funds will pay for civic engagement opportunities and to organize internships and political training for young people."[43]

Alexander Soros, deputy chair of the OSF, remarked, "These investments will empower proven leaders in the Black community to reimagine policing, end mass incarceration and eliminate the barriers to opportunity that have been the source of inequity for too long."[44]

Gaspard was right. Twenty-five years of millions of dollars pumped into advancing Soros's radical progressive theories on criminal justice have been paying off.

The Democrats and their presidential candidates fully supported demolishing America's rule of law structure. On July 8, 2020, presidential candidate Joe Biden affirmed that "some funding should 'absolutely' be redirected from the police,"[45] even though police budgets are decided locally, not by the federal government. Biden denied it but did not retract his statement as crime skyrocketed around the country.

In June 2020, Kamala Harris, then Biden's running mate as vice president, tweeted and posted on Facebook an appeal on behalf of George Howard, a Minneapolis domestic abuser with previous convictions. "If you're able to, chip in now to the @MNFreedomFund to help post bail for those protesting on the ground in Minnesota [for Howard's release]." The bail was quickly raised, and less than a year later, when Howard was charged with two counts of second-degree murder, Twitter and Facebook removed Harris's post.[46]

The bail paid on February 16, 2022, to release Black Lives Matter (BLM) activist Quintez Brown, who two days earlier was charged with the attempted murder of the Jewish Democratic mayoral candidate, Craig Greenberg, in Louisville, Kentucky, exemplifies but one indirect method of Soros's funding.

The $100,000 bail was paid by the Louisville Community Bail Fund,[47] a BLM project which is part of the Alliance for Global Justice (AFGJ). The Louisville group received more than $737,000 from the San-Francisco-based Tides Center,[48] which includes Tides Network, Tides Center, Tides Foundation, Tides Two Rivers Fund, and Tides Inc., serving as a clearinghouse for Soros's and other Left-supporting individuals and foundations. In 2020, Tides received more than $3.5 million from Soros's Foundation to Promote Open Society (FPOS).[49]

According to the most recent available 990 tax form, the FPOS also gave $250,000 to the AFGJ, which is dedicated to "catalyz[ing] Black communities into the global movement for climate justice,"[50] including allegedly funding Palestinian terrorism and the anti-Israel Boycott, Divestment, and Sanctions (BDS) movement.[51] In reaction to Brown's release on bail, Greenberg stated, "Our criminal justice system is broken. It is nearly impossible to believe that someone can attempt murder on Monday and walk out of jail on Wednesday."[52]

According to Capital Research Center, the Tides Nexus is a collection of Bay Area nonprofits that collectively brought in over $1.6 billion in 2020 alone—and more than $6 billion since 2007. "If one can call a 'dark money' network famous," wrote the center's Hayden Ludwig, "this is it."[53]

The unprecedented surge in violent crime since Biden took office was exacerbated by applying Soros's soft-on-crime policies, utilized by crime-friendly DAs, and the reduction and suppression of police forces. It caused a loud public outcry. Several Democratic mayors put aside their radical progressivism and requested millions to refund the police. Even congressional representatives called for more, not less, policing.

On March 1, 2022, during his second State of the Union Address, Biden, who had to address the crime surge, said: "The answer is not to Defund the police. The answer is to FUND the police with the resources and training they need to protect our communities."[54]

BLM received billions of dollars in contributions from mega-corporations such as Amazon, Microsoft, Tinder, major banks and businesses, Wall Street and Hollywood, and Left-leaning NGOs. Soros's OSF has been a significant advocate and supporter. By the end of 2020, the *Economist* reported at least $10.6 billion in pledges to BLM and affiliated groups claiming to help black communities.[55] The *Economist* noted that "Exact sums received will be known when the central body overseeing BLM spending publishes its finances."

According to BLM's Impact Report in February 2021, after Floyd's killing, in 2020 alone, BLM raked in $90 million.[56] However, it kept its finances secret until February 2022, when it shared its "financial snapshot" with the Associated Press. Since 2020, a few leaders of the organization network have been charged with embezzlement, fraud, and money laundering but have yet to be convicted.[57]

Moreover, Black American organizations claimed that BLM did nothing to help impoverished inner cities.[58] BLM activist co-founder and until May 2021 executive director, Patrisse Cullors (who, as mentioned elsewhere, supports the BDS and has links with the PFLP),[59] opened a consulting firm, Janaya and Patrisse Consulting, and paid herself "over $20,000 a month," a "total of $191,000 over the course of 2019 via payments from Reform LA Jails, while she served as the chairwoman of a Los Angeles jail reform initiative."[60]

Other BLM activists and affiliates, quite a few who received training and financial support from the OSF—which for decades, under different programs, has been funding and training hundreds of activists[61]—jumped on the bandwagon. They offered reeducation programs on race and gender fluidity and equity and criminal justice, conducted workshops, and provided relevant literature on critical race theory to US government agencies, including the Defense Department, big and small corporations, academic institutions, medical and elementary schools, and businesses.

In its 2021 IRS filing, BLM reported it spent "$8.4 million on operating expenses while disbursing $21.7 million in grants [of $500,000 each] to Black Lives Matter groups in Boston, Philadelphia, Detroit, and 11 Black Lives Matter chapters around the country," and additional grants to some 30 groups affiliated with BLM.[62]

On May 17, 2022, the Black Lives Matter Global Network Foundation (BLMGNF) disclosed its IRS filing. The group, which according to a previous filing, raised $90 million in 2020,[63] was left with $42 million in assets by mid-2021. The *New York Times* says, "More than half of the money [was] spent on consultants and real estate." The

Times cited Jacob Harold, a nonprofit expert, saying: "This 990 tells a story of weak nonprofit governance."[64]

When Soros decided to change the US legal system, he targeted the penal code and used the argument of "compassion" to divert attention. He initiated and funded "criminal justice reform" and racial and gender "equity" programs. He has been awarding fellowships to individuals and grants to think tanks, organizations, and universities; and paying for policy papers, such as "Changing Public Attitudes Toward the Criminal Justice System."[65] All advocate pro-criminal, anti-victim policies and function as echo chambers to bolster the public's support for the progressive-Left candidates' promises of "justice" and "policing" reforms (defund the police) in every national and local election.

Since 47 of the 50 states elect district attorneys, Soros's open checkbook goes a long way, especially in cities run by Democratic mayors. The primary qualification of the candidates for the DA's office is adherence to Soros's progressive-socialist, anti-law enforcement, anti-incarceration, gender, social, economic, and racial justice "reforms," enthusiasm for climate, as well as the support of illegal migration, and other radical ideas that Soros and his foundations' functionaries could conceive.

Christopher F. Rufo wrote that the "new trend in criminal-justice activism of rationalized stealing" is the concept of "survival crime," promoted by Soros and his cohorts.[66]

"The theory holds that the homeless, the poor, and people of color commit property crimes and low-level infractions in order to secure their basic survival," Rufo continued. "Any enforcement of these laws is thus a violation of their basic human rights and should be relaxed—that is, local governments should stop enforcing any laws that 'criminalize homelessness' and 'criminalize poverty.'

"Survival crime theory is the flipside of Broken Windows theory. They deal with the same class of offenses—mainly property crime, drug possession, and public nuisances—in precisely the opposite way. Broken Windows theory argues that everyone is responsible for their own behavior. If we permit low-level crimes, it will lead to a general breakdown in law and order. Survival-crime theory, by contrast, argues that local governments should decriminalize these offenses because vulnerable individuals have been compelled by social conditions to commit them," Rufo explained.[67]

To enforce and hasten the acceptance of survival crimes, which ties into Soros's criminal justice reform, he picks and funds the election of local progressive-radical candidates for local sheriffs, district attorneys, and judges.

The public initially votes for "Soros DAs" because their platform always promises "justice reform" to increase the community's safety. However, once in office, their policies lead to more, not less, crime and violence, devastating the community and causing more, not less, poverty.

In May 2018, the *Los Angeles Times* reported that Soros had funded at least 21 local prosecutorial campaigns. According to the *LA Times*, from 2014 to 2018, Soros "spent more than $16 million in 17 county races in other states. His favored candidates won in 13 counties."[68] Soros didn't rest on his laurels; he increased his direct and indirect funding of potential DA candidates throughout the country.

How much Soros has spent on changing America since he established his OSF in New York in1993 is unknown. However, according to the June 2022 report by the Law Enforcement Legal Defense Fund (LELDF), available campaign spending reports between 2014 and 2021 show that Soros spent $40 million to elect "social justice" prosecutors throughout the U.S.[69]

But it was only in December 2019, in the run-up to the 2020 presidential election, Soros's unrestricted funding of progressive-Left candidates for district attorneys finally caught the attention of President Trump's attorney general, William Barr. Speaking on Martha MacCallum's *The Story*, Barr remarked: "There's this recent development [where] George Soros has been coming in, in largely Democratic primaries where there has not been much voter turnout and putting in a lot of money to elect people who are not very supportive of law enforcement and don't view the office as bringing to trial and prosecuting criminals but pursuing other social agendas." Barr accurately predicted a dramatic rise in crime in cities where Soros's handpicked, paid-for DAs were elected.[70]

The Biden administration's support of soft-on-crime policies and aversion to enforcing the laws has led to rising crime and chaos in the streets of America. From 2021 through early 2022, crime has been skyrocketing everywhere, especially in cities and states run by progressive-Left mayors and governors, who eliminated bail significantly and defunded and often vilified the police. The violent demonstrations, riots, and mass looting that erupted in May 2020 after a policeman killed George Floyd in Minneapolis also ushered in a new era of ambushing and killing police officers. According to CNN, 2021 "saw the highest number of law enforcement officers who were intentionally killed in the line of duty since the terrorist attacks of Sept. 11, 2001."[71]

Soros has been financing the marketing of crime-friendly district attorneys and prosecutors who, while swearing to enforce the State's laws, refuse to do so. For example, when the state legislature classifies an armed robbery as a "B" felony punishable by incarceration, that is not a suggestion subject to the whim of a local prosecutor, such as NYC's DA Bragg. That is the law. Indeed, Soros's DAs' refusal to enforce the laws has significantly contributed to the unprecedented upsurge in crime everywhere they are in office. From organized "grab and run" looting of stores, robberies, carjacking, selling and using drugs in public, to shooting sprees, rapes, and murders, all are undermining the security and safety of the people and the economic infrastructure of cities and towns by causing businesses to shut their doors and residents to move to safer cities and states.

Soros's backing of "alternative justice and policing," such as no-bail policies, no-incarceration efforts, and Black Lives Matter and similar radical black activist groups, aided the movement to defund the police in Democrat-run states and cities. The FBI reported 2021 as the "deadliest for law enforcement officers in recent years: 73 officers killed on duty, compared with 46 the year before."[72]

In October 2018, the *New York Times* credited Soros with pioneering "the push to overhaul prosecutors' offices."[73] The Washington-based Capital Research Center has kept an eye on Soros's efforts to systemically change criminal justice laws by placing soft-on-crime, anti-incarceration, pro-illegal migrants, pro-drugs prosecutors and judges throughout the country. While he began decades ago, he got more serious about it during Obama's term in office. In addition to direct contributions, he invested millions of dollars in a vast network of national, state, and local political action committees (PACs), dedicated to Soros's and the woke's version of "justice" (racial justice, public safety justice, economic justice, gender justice, environmental justice, etc.).

Whitney Tymas, aka Soros PAC consigliere,[74] who runs Soros's "prosecutor initiative," explained that Soros's "single overarching goal" is "to end mass incarceration. That's our North Star," she declared. "We've won twice as many races as we've lost. We're not going to win them all. But we're really trying to because that's the difference between people unjustly sitting in jail or not," she said.[75]

Soros has expressed his desire to end American supremacy since 2003.[76] His successes in changing the U.S. from within increased the aging megalomaniac's resolve to achieve what he set out to do in 1993. So the financial speculator boosted his war chest and expanded his funding to undermine law and order in America further.

Candidates whose war chests were crammed with Soros's money have repeatedly overwhelmed their opponents by dominating the airwaves with TV and radio ads, billboards, and orchestrated events. Everywhere voters have looked, Soros's lackeys were front and center, promising racial equality–based changes to criminal justice that would guarantee the citizens' safety and security. Their high-sounding rhetoric is always dominated by squishy, throwaway jargon such as "social and restorative" racial and gender justice, as well as "environmental" and "climate justice"—standard and ever-changing catchphrases of "woke" elites.

In early June 2022, in the run-up to the 2022 midterm election, to silence conservative radio, Lakestar Finance LLC, a Soros Fund Management–based communication and technology company, invested

$60 million to purchase eighteen Spanish-speaking, mostly conservative radio stations for the Latino Media Network, a media group headed by longtime supporters of the Marxist founder of Black Lives Matter, Alicia Garza.[77]

Once they win and take the Oath of Office, swearing to "support the Constitution of the United States and the state's Constitution, Soros financed soft on crime," district attorneys and prosecutors inevitably refuse to enforce the law. Instead, they often issue directives heeding the Soros Justice Reform doctrine.

In early June 2022, the Law Enforcement Legal Defense Fund's (LELDF) report "Justice for Sale" documented that Soros has funded the elections of "at least 75 . . . social justice prosecutors" who are supposed to protect more than 72 million U.S. citizens, "including half of America's 50 most populous cities and counties."[78] According to the thorough report, "In 2021, more than 40% (9,000+) of the approximately 22,500 homicides in the US occurred in areas overseen by these DAs. Similarly, these jurisdictions reported more than a third of all violent and property crime last year."[79]

Their policies have contributed to a substantial increase—not a decrease—in all crimes, especially violent crimes, homicides, and overdosing on fentanyl-laced drugs. Thus far, the public's outcry has done little to reverse such policies, except for the successful recall of San Francisco's soft-on-criminals DA, Chesa Boudin, on June 7, 2022. More than 60 percent of the city's voters have had enough of the increasing violence caused by his policies.[80]

In early June 2022, Angelinos, who had had enough of Soros-backed DA George Gascón's disregard for the public's safety, collected more than 500,000 signatures for the petition to recall the DA on July 6, 2022. This second attempt to recall Gascón seemed to generate more support than the September 2021 failed effort. By July 12, 2022, over 715,000 signatures supporting the petition to oust him were submitted.[81]

On June 8, 2022, Fox News released the audio of Willie Wilkerson, a California gang member accused of murder and two attempted murders during a home invasion robbery. He told his mother he should "cut a plea deal quickly before District Attorney George Gascón is potentially recalled."[82] This illustrates how Gascón's policies embolden criminals and explains why Angelinos want to recall Gascón.

While many Americans fed up with the increasing chaos and violence hoped the upcoming midterm elections would help oust Soros-backed DAs and reverse the radical-progressive pro-criminal policies, Soros has already increased his funding of super PACs funding the elections of prosecutors and state secretaries everywhere. "It takes real money to meet this moment," said Whitney Tymas, who runs the major Soros-funded Justice and Public Safety PAC. She declared a $300,000 contribution to their favorite candidate in Maine's DA's primary in June 2022.[83] Until then, the combined war chest of both candidates was $70,000. Tymas reportedly explained that vast amounts of money are "necessary to bring change to an office that is overwhelmingly white and male, and where most incumbents run unopposed for reelection."[84]

Parker Thayer at the Capital Research Center has carefully detailed DAs that Soros helped elect with at least $29 million. Here are a few of them, some with my additional comments (the list below is published with permission from the authors and the organization):[85]

Diana Becton—Contra Costa County, CA. "Backed by $275,000 from Soros in 2018, Becton became the first woman and first African American elected to serve as DA for Contra Costa County. She is also one of the first in the position to have zero prior experience as a prosecutor. During Becton's first years in office, four Contra Costa cities made the list of the top 100 most dangerous cities in California in 2018. Both violent crime and property crime increased by several percentage points during 2019."[86]

George Gascón—Los Angeles County, CA. Elected in 2020. Gascón served as San Francisco's DA from 2011 to 2019, overseeing a huge rise in crime. "Under his tenure as the San Francisco DA, crime exploded," according to the Heritage Foundation's January 2021 report. "He was, on the merits, a complete failure. Ask virtually any resident of

San Francisco, and they will tell you how dangerous the city became under Gascón's tenure."[87]

Charles Stimson and Zack Smith, the authors of the report, documented how "*one minute* after he was sworn into office on December 7 [2020], . . . Gascón issued nine sweeping 'Special Directives' to all deputy district attorneys to supersede entire chapters of the office's existing legal policy manual. . . . Effective the next day, the diktats from the front office apply to virtually all potential cases, incoming cases, ongoing cases—and to those cases that have already been completed in which a defendant was convicted and is serving a sentence."[88]

"Soros has spent a combined $6 million on California DA races, much of it wasted on failed candidates, but almost half was spent on the successful campaign of George Gascón for Los Angeles DA. Soros was the largest spender in the race, and Gascón won easily."[89]

Gascón's transition team included 13 different advisors teams, "many with direct ties to Soros, are anti-law-and-order activists and zealots."[90]

Under Gascón's directives of December 8, 2020, one can commit at least 13 crimes with impunity in Los Angeles. Not surprisingly, homicide rates soared, organized shoplifting sprees ravaged the city, and trains were stopped and ransacked by mobs of looters.[91]

The city of Los Angeles has rapidly become a national disgrace. Like other Soros rogue DAs, Gascón has been using the Orwellian techniques of doublethink and newspeak to dupe the public into believing their policies are reforming the criminal justice system while undermining the safety of the people.

The new directives include limitations on police officers' and prosecutors' efforts to arrest and charge criminals, even on violations that Gascón's directives have not redefined. For example, prosecutors are not allowed to ask for pretrial bail.[92] Special Directive 20–12, entitled Victim Services, should be, as Stimson and Smith suggest, called "We Don't Care About Victims."[93] In short, Gascón ignores the laws that existed when he entered the office, which he swore to enforce. His policies ensure criminals are free to commit as many crimes as they like, endangering the public's safety.

An attempt to recall Gascón in 2021 failed. But by the end of January 2022, Angelinos, including wealthy Hollywood liberals, seemed fed up with the spiking murder rate, robberies, car hijacking, and crime. A new recall initiative was set in motion. However, the renewed effort to recall Gascón was launched only after a murder of a Beverly Hills resident and several grab-and-run robberies in tony, wealthy areas of LA. Suddenly, crime had come to the elites' doorsteps, thanks to Gascón's boneheaded policies.

On February 8, 2022, the Association for Los Angeles Deputy Sheriffs, representing eight thousand LA County sworn sheriff's deputies, joined the effort to recall Gascón in the midterm election.[94] The Association of Deputy District Attorneys (ADDA), representing over eight hundred deputy district attorneys of Los Angeles County, also joined the recall effort. Their statement noted that Gascón's pro-criminals policies caused "more than 30 cities within Los Angeles County" to issue "votes of no confidence in the District Attorney. In addition, multiple cities are exploring options to avoid Gascón's no prosecution policy on quality-of-life crimes."[95]

On June 3, 2022, Justice John L. Segal of California's Second District Court of Appeals rejected DA George "Gascón's position that he has absolute discretion to decide what to charge or not charge, not subject to being countermanded by the courts; Segal said: 'The district attorney overstates his authority. He is an elected official who must comply with the law, not a sovereign with absolute, unreviewable discretion.'"[96]

Eric Siddall, vice president of the ADDA, brought the case against Gascón (*The Association of Deputy District Attorneys for Los Angeles County v. Gascón*), commented: "Today, the judiciary affirmed the rule of law. Mr. Gascón's authority is not absolute. He must follow the rules. While we are heartened by the Court's ruling, we continue to be disappointed that Los Angeles's chief prosecutor forced his own employees to take him to court to stop him from breaking the law."[97]

By July 20, 2022, the recall efforts gathered 715,833 signed petitions (the requirement was for 650,000 signatures) to recall Gascón. The groups organizing the recall collected additional signatures in an effort to ensure his recall. However, since Boudin was recalled, Soros, who is adamant about getting progressive-Left DAs elected everywhere, and a few other progressive billionaires injected millions of dollars into countering Gascon's recall. On August 15, 2022, the effort to recall Gascon failed when "California county's registrar-recorder, Dean Logan, announced that 195,783 of the 715,833 signatures on the recall petition "were found to be invalid," with nearly 90,000 of them not registered to vote and nearly 45,000 signatures being duplicates."[98]

Monique Worrell—Ninth Judicial Circuit (Orange and Osceola Counties), FL. "Monique Worrell is the second Soros candidate to become state attorney for Orange and Osceola Counties. Her predecessor, Aramis Ayala, was a 'long-shot candidate' elected in 2016 with the help of more than $1.3 million in spending by the Florida Safety and Justice PAC. Ayala immediately earned a reputation for her activist approach, which led to her removal from multiple high-profile murder cases by two different Republican governors. During Ayala's tenure, violent crime increased dramatically, with murders rising by 26 percent during 2020.

"After Ayala left office to run for Congress, Worrell filled her shoes with $1 million from Soros's Democracy PAC surging into the race at the last minute to help her claim victory against her moderate opponent in 2020."[99]

Darius Pattillo—Henry County, GA. "Receiving just under $150,000 from Soros through the Georgia Safety and Justice P.A.C., Patello [sic] was elected in 2016 and has remained the most unremarkable Soros-backed DA elected . . . Soros's funding of Patello [sic] nearly went unreported, possibly because Patello [sic] does not seem to share the radical views of his fellow Soros DAs."[100]

Kim Foxx—Cook County (Chicago), IL. "Probably the most famous Soros-backed DA, Foxx was boosted into office with the help of $2 million in Soros cash. Foxx has recently been in the news for potential ethics violations in her 2019 decision to drop charges against Jussie Smollet for his infamous hate crime hoax. (On December 9, 2021, Smollett was "found guilty on 5 out of 6 charges at his hate crime hoax trail."[101]) Foxx has also made headlines for presiding over Chicago's most significant spike in homicides in more than 30 years while her office dropped charges against 30 percent of felony defendants during 2020."[102]

James Stewart—Caddo Parish, LA. "Probably the least well-known and least radical Soros-funded DA, James Stewart was elected as the DA of Caddo Parish, Louisiana, in 2015 with the help of more than $930,000 in funding from Soros. Stewart has enacted few radical reforms since his election, potentially a disappointing result for Soros. His opponents at the time worried that his progressive views on criminal justice would be 'detrimental to the safety of Caddo Parish.'"[103]

Scott Colom—Circuit Court District 16, MS. Another lesser-known Soros-funded DA, "Colom quietly received over $9,000 in funding from Soros to help unseat a long-time incumbent in 2015. Colom oversees District 16 in Mississippi, including Lowndes, Oktibbeha, Clay, and Noxubee Counties. Colom was recently recommended by Rep. Bernie Thompson (D-MS) for a position as a judge for the U.S. District Court of the Northern District of Mississippi. Meanwhile, violent crime, specifically gun violence, remains a serious and growing problem for cities and counties in the 16th Circuit, a problem Colom has been accused of doing little to combat."[104]

Jody Owens—Hinds County, MS. "Aided by a $500,000 contribution from Soros's Mississippi Justice and Public Safety PAC, Owens was elected in 2019 after running on a platform that promised reform and 'alternatives to incarceration.' Owens brought controversy with him to the DA's office. In 2019, Owens was accused of harassing his female colleagues while working at the Southern Poverty Law Center, an organization with a well-documented propensity for enabling and ignoring sexual harassment in the workplace.[105] Moreover, on September 3, 2022, he was accused by Mississippi State Capitol Police of pointing a gun at another man who was visiting a woman who "is an employee in Owens' office." Ownes denied all allegations.[106]

"Owens has also recently brought highly questionable murder charges against two police officers. The charges were dismissed with prejudice for lack of evidence that officers 'caused any injury to the alleged victim. Under Owens, Jackson has become one of the deadliest cities in the nation, and in 2021 the city saw over 150 homicides (98 murders per 100,000 residents), an all-time high."

Kim Gardner—St. Louis, MO. "One of the most famous and polarizing Soros-backed DAs, Kim Gardner, has served as the circuit attorney of crime-ridden St. Louis since 2017 and has repeatedly used her office to prosecute conservatives while allowing criminals to walk free. According to Missouri's Ethics Commission, on January 2, 2019, Gardner violated campaign finance laws, dating back to her time as a state representative, [107] for which she signed "a Consent Order" and paid a fine of $6,314. [108, 109]

"In 2018, Gardner launched a bogus criminal investigation against Missouri's Republican governor. "Greitens claimed he had been the victim of a political witch hunt."[110] On August 30, 2022, "the Missouri Supreme Court reprimanded Gardner, for professional misconduct rules during the investigation of former Missouri Gov. Eric Greitens, and fined her $750."[111]

Gardner was also the lead attorney in the deliberate prosecution of Mark McCloskey; [112, 113] however, she and her office were removed from the case by Circuit Judge Thomas Clark II,[114] who wrote, "The Circuit Attorney's conduct raises the appearance that she initiated a criminal prosecution for political purposes." Indeed, Gardner's time as St. Louis Circuit Attorney "has often been tumultuous."[115]

After one year in office, Gardner's mishandling murder cases turned St. Louis into the murder capital of the nation, but this did not stop Soros from contributing $116,000 to aid her reelection in 2020. In early 2021, "St. Louis became one of the deadliest cities in the world."[116]

Raul Torrez—Bernalillo County (Albuquerque), NM. "Although his ties to Soros are less well known, and his ideas are slightly less radical, Albuquerque's DA also got his start from $107,000 in Soros cash, boosting his unopposed campaign in 2016. As of mid-November, Albuquerque had experienced 102 homicides in 2021, the highest number ever recorded, compared to the 67 reported at the same time last year. Meanwhile, Torrez is busy campaigning for New Mexico attorney general. Soros's money is likely to make an appearance in that upcoming race as well."[117]

Alvin Bragg—Manhattan, NY. "One of Soros's newest DAs, Bragg was elected in 2021 as the DA of Manhattan, largely thanks to approximately $1.1 million given by Soros that year to groups supporting Bragg. Even though Bragg has barely been in office, his tenure is already shaping up as a disaster. After Bragg released a memo stating that his office would not seek prison sentences for crimes such as armed robbery, drug dealing, and burglary, more than nine prosecutors in Manhattan quit. Interestingly, one area where Bragg is *not* expected to be overly lenient is an investigation into President Donald Trump's business practices, which Bragg conveniently took over after assuming office."[118] On March 24, 2022, Bragg announced his decision to suspend Trump's investigation "indefinitely." However, according to former assistant U.S. attorney for the Southern District of New York, Andy McCarthy, there are "many cases in prosecutors' offices that have not been closed. What matters is whether there is activity in the investigation," he told Fox News.[119]

David Clegg—Ulster County, NY. Soros cash to the tune of at least $184,000 was used to push Ulster County DA David Clegg across the finish line in his 2019 election, but it was also the source of a major controversy at the time. In an embarrassing snafu (guffaw), the New York Justice and Public Safety PAC paid for mailers that featured Clegg shaking hands with a prominent criminal and Left-wing activist. Under Clegg, gun crimes and shootings have surged dramatically, and high-profile cases have been badly mishandled, including a murder case in which the suspect was released because Clegg's office failed to file an indictment on time."[120]

Larry Krasner—Philadelphia, PA. Among the most famous

Soros-backed DAs is Krasner, whose election and reelection campaigns received more than $2 million from Soros. Krasner had no experience as a prosecutor when he was first elected in 2017 in Philadelphia, but Soros's $1.7 million got him the job. In 2021, Soros contributed $259,000 toward Krasner's reelection. Soros funneled most of his contributions through the Pennsylvania Justice and Public Safety PAC and the Philadelphia Justice and Public Safety PAC. "Under Krasner's watch, crime rates have soared, and in 2021, Philadelphia became the murder capital of the United States with the highest per capita homicide rate of the country's ten largest cities."[121]

Jack Stollsteimer—Delaware County, PA. "Lesser known but also well financed by Soros, Stollsteimer was the first Democratic DA ever elected in Delaware County, boosted by roughly $100,000 in ads paid for by Soros during 2019. While still undoubtedly a progressive, Stollsteimer is much less radical than Krasner and has not been openly hostile to police. He did, however, recently feud with police over the graphic details of a report on rape in broad daylight on a train with many witnesses, none of whom tried to intervene. During Stollsteimer's first year in office, homicides in Delaware County increased 127 percent, though many attribute this to the county's proximity to Philadelphia."[122]

Joe Gonzalez—Bexar County (San Antonio), TX. "George Soros has even dared to mess with Texas. Joe Gonzalez is one of Soros's favorite DAs, receiving nearly $1 million in backing from the billionaire during his 2018 campaign, upsetting incumbent Democrat Nico LaHood in the primary. Like in Dallas, violent crime reportedly increased by 15 percent in San Antonio under Gonzalez, while convictions dropped by 17 percent."[123]

John Creuzot—Dallas County, TX. Backed by an estimated $236,000 from Soros, Creuzot became the DA of Dallas County in 2018 and immediately moved forward with a plethora of radical reform policies. He stated, "Criminalizing poverty is counter-productive for our community's health and safety. For that reason, this office will not prosecute theft of personal items less than $750 unless the evidence shows that the alleged theft was for economic gain." But he told his prosecutors "to dismiss" all misdemeanor criminal trespass,[124] and drug possession. During his first year in office, crime reportedly increased by 15 percent, while total convictions dropped by 30 percent. Most recently, Creuzot failed to get a conviction in [the] straightforward case against Billy Chemirmir, a Kenyan immigrant charged with murdering and robbing 18 older women in assisted living facilities. He was found with his alleged victims' personal papers and jewelry in his possession."[125]

Brian Middleton—Fort Bend County, TX. "Although it went unnoticed and unreported by the media, Soros played a major role in the 2019 Fort Bend County DA Brian Middleton campaign, spending nearly $200,000 on advertising in support of his campaign. Middleton has been extremely moderate as far as Soros-backed candidates go, so Fort Bend County has not seen a dramatic spike in crime."[126]

Kim Ogg—Harris County (Houston), TX. "In 2016, Kim Ogg became the State's first Soros-backed DA after Soros spent more than $600,000 on the race. As one of the first reform DAs backed by Soros, Ogg is also one of the most moderate. She has stopped prosecuting marijuana offenses but often seeks high cash bail, causing her to be ostracized by many progressives and apparently Soros."[127]

José Garza—Travis County (Austin), TX. "In 2020, Garza was elected as Austin's DA with more than $400,000 in ads paid for by the Texas Justice and Public Safety PAC, one of Soros's private PACs that has received roughly $3.6 million from the billionaire since its creation in 2018. Since assuming office, Garza has developed a reputation for letting violent offenders go free on little to no bail.

"In 2020, Garza released hundreds of inmates from jail over COVID-19 protocols, even though only six people in Austin at the time were known to have COVID-19. On May 27, 2021, Garza released his guideline on "bail and sentencing policies."[128] However, earlier in January 2021, his office released David Olmos, who had eight prior felony convictions, after he was caught toting a gun in a meth-fueled car chase with police. After his release with an ankle monitor, the man allegedly went on a crime spree committing 10 armed robberies. On June 10, 2022, Olmos was sentenced to 18 years in prison.[129] Since Garza was elected, police budgets have been slashed, and Austin has experienced skyrocketing crime rates and a record number of homicides.[130]

Parisa Dehghani-Tafti—Arlington County and City of Falls Church, VA. "Backed by over $600,000 from the Justice and Public Safety PAC, one of George Soros's many personal PACs, Dehghani-Tafti won her 2019 election by toppling a moderate Democratic incumbent and has been a center of controversy ever since. Dehghani-Tafti, along with several other Soros-backed DAs in Virginia, is facing a recall petition after crimes like felony aggravated assault rose 40 percent during her first year in office."[131]

Steve Descano—Fairfax County, VA. Steve Descano is also facing a recall petition.[132] He was elected in 2019 and has endorsed the progressive-Left platform. Reportedly, he told his staff, "Don't listen to victims" of sex crimes because "they're overly dramatic."[133]

Descano has made it his office's official policy not to prosecute more than 20 different crimes, including shoplifting for goods under $1,000, prostitution, and indecent exposure. Descanso's initial campaign benefitted from approximately $600,000 from Soros."[134]

Buta Biberaj—Loudoun County, VA. "As Loudoun County District Attorney, Buta Biberaj has championed an anti-incarceration approach to the job but made headlines for personally seeking jail time for Scott Smith, a father who was arrested for misdemeanor disorderly conduct at a Loudoun County School Board meeting for protesting the School Board's failure to protect his 14-year-old daughter, who was raped by a transgender boy in a school bathroom. Smith's defense attorneys reported that it was "completely unheard of" for a DA to personally handle a misdemeanor, much less to pursue jail time, court-ordered anger management, and a hefty fine.[135] In September 2022, the efforts to recall her were boosted by a VA judge's decision to remove her from the case. However, Biberaj's campaign in 2019 was boosted by over $650,000 in Soros cash,"[136] and she probably relies on his funding to defeat her recall.

Ramin Fatehi—Norfolk County, VA. "One of the latest additions to Soros's collection of rogue prosecutors, Ramin Fatehi was one of very few Democrats to win a Virginia election in 2021, largely thanks to about $220,000 in funding from Soros. Fatehi has yet to make a name for himself as DA, but he ran on the typical progressive platform of promising to abolish cash bail and decriminalize marijuana possession."[137]

In December 2021, Senator Tom Cotton wrote:

Last year, our nation experienced the largest increase in murder in American history and the largest number of drug overdose deaths ever recorded. This carnage continues today and is not distributed equally. Instead, it is concentrated in cities and localities where radical, Left-wing, George Soros progressives have captured state and district attorney offices. These legal arsonists condemn our rule of law as "systemically racist" and have not simply abused prosecutorial discretion; they have embraced prosecutorial nullification. As a result, a contagion of crime has infected virtually every neighborhood under their charge.

He explained that the DAs funded by Soros refuse to "enforce laws against shoplifting, drug trafficking, and entire categories of felonies and misdemeanors."[138]

"In 2020, the murder rate in Baltimore was higher than El Salvador's or Guatemala's," he said.[139]

Intriguingly, several Soros-financed DAs—Kim Foxx, Kimberly M. Gardner, Buta Biberaj, and Marilyn Mosby, to name a few—have been running afoul of the law.[140] Thus, their striking lack of moral integrity as they dismiss the criminal code is not surprising.

Soros's PACs also funded the election of San Francisco's radical Left DA, Chesa Boudin, who, like Soros, proclaims "compassion" as his motive to defy the criminal laws he is supposed to enforce. Boudin's goal was "to restore a sense of compassion" to the justice system, including for "the people who, themselves, have caused harm."[141]

In his excellent book: *San Fransicko: Why Progressives Ruin Cities*

(New York: Harper 2021), Michael Shellenberger documents how the Left's misguided policies have exacerbated homelessness, drug addiction, and crime in progressive Democrat-run cities in America. As crime continued to escalate in San Francisco, Shellenberger wrote in the *Wall Street Journal*:

> When Chesa Boudin ran for San Francisco district attorney in 2019, he said crime was caused by poverty, wealth inequality, and inadequate government spending on social programs. He called prostitution, open drug use, and drug dealing "victimless crimes" and promised not to prosecute them. The increase in crime has been so sharp that San Francisco's liberal residents are now paying for private security guards, taking self-defense classes, and supported Mr. Boudin's recall in June 2022. Retailers like Walgreens and Target are closing stores in the city, citing rampant shoplifting. A shockingly organized mob of looters ransacked downtown Louis Vuitton and other designer stores.[142]

Under Boudin's soft-on-crime policies, including "elimination of cash bail, restriction of pretrial detention and letting out as much as 40% of the city's jail population," burglaries increased by "40% from pre-pandemic levels and homicides up almost 37%."[143]

The Tenderloin is a district "so riddled with crime and drugs that the city's Board of Supervisors declared it an emergency zone in December [2021]." By mid-2022, assaults had risen by 11% to 1,035 cases, there was an increase of 10% in rape cases, and drug overdose had risen to likely surpass the 474 people who died of fentanyl in 2021 alone." Boudin's shocking response? "This is not a new problem."[144]

San Francisco residents, most of whom are Democrats, thought differently. They have had enough of the radical-progressive DA's pro-defendants' policies, which only encouraged criminals to commit more violent crimes. On June 7, 2022, 60 percent of them booted him out of office.

Did Boudin get the message? According to the *New York Post*, he did not. Instead, he "blamed 'right-wing billionaires'" for his defeat,[145] which is amusing since he and other Left-wing prosecutors in New York, Philadelphia, and elsewhere were elected with the help of George Soros.[146]

So, don't count him out yet. Boudin's credentials as the son of Weather Underground terrorists and his status as a radical progressive could help him be elected to some office in 2023 or a prominent position in the Soros-backed Justice Reform movement.

Before the recall, a Democratic strategist was cited by *Forbes*, saying: "Chesa is the unfortunate victim, the unfortunate recipient of all of the anger from the investor class and the billionaire class."[147] Indeed, Boudin's radical-Left supporters have done what they always do; they accused Republican billionaires of funding the campaign to oust him while disregarding the billionaires that got him elected in the first place.

The ousting of Boudin did little to lessen the radical Left's vehemence to reconsider their crime-inducing policies that endanger the public's safety and create chaos in large and small cities alike. They may tone down their public message but expect them to double their efforts to take over as many elected offices as possible—especially the offices of state secretaries, whose role is to certify elections.

In New York City, new Soros-funded DA Alvin Bragg's campaign rhetoric got him elected, but his contrasting initial actions directly contributed to a dramatic increase in crime.

Before the election, Bragg spoke of his commitment "to reshape and repurpose the DA's office to end racial disparities."[148] That translated to *not* prosecuting what he decided were "minor offenses." Bragg reclassified robberies, commercial and some residential burglaries as "petty larceny." Marijuana possession and "low-level" drug dealing were reclassified as misdemeanors, Turnstile-jumping, trespassing, driving with a suspended license, prostitution, resisting arrest for non-criminal offenses, weapons possession (of non-firearms), and obstructing the work of the New York City Police Department are not to be prosecuted under Bragg.[149]

Bragg issued "Day 1 Memo" as his first official action, underscoring and broadening previously stated objectives, instructing the career prosecutors in his office to ignore the law, to not charge, or reduce charges for activities that the city, the State, and the country have defined as crimes. There would be a presumption of no jail time for almost any crime, and life sentences without parole would be banned, even for cop killers, barring "exceptional circumstances."[150] And "prosecutors can only request incarceration in 'extraordinary circumstances' and must first receive approval from a supervisor."[151]

Soros-financed progressive DAs across the nation have also instructed their staff on their pro-criminals policies.[152] Their brash instructions to ignore laws endanger citizens' lives in dozens of Democrat-governed cities and states that either eliminated or limited the use of bail.

The combination of pro-offenders' directives at both the state and local levels has raised threat levels substantially. A particularly egregious example is the synergy of DA Bragg's radical instructions and New York State's elimination of bail and barring judges from detaining criminals because they're deemed a danger to public safety. Together, such measures expose Manhattan residents to rampant crime and personal harm.

According to Barry Latzer, a former professor of criminal justice at John Jay College of Criminal Justice in New York City, "DA Bragg is content with New York's reforms and seems bent on making things even worse. He opposes giving New York judges (and prosecutors) the discretion to determine a defendant's dangerousness when deciding whether to release him. Why? He thinks dangerousness determinations are racist. 'I have no confidence,' he says, that 'there is any race-neutral way to predict who is dangerous at such an early stage in the case.'

"This is preposterous," Latzer concluded. "Suppose there is compelling evidence that a defendant has committed a violent crime and that he has, in addition, a prior conviction for a crime of violence. Assume as well that he has a history of failing to appear in court. Under such circumstances, most people would conclude that the judge should have the authority to send the defendant to jail or impose bail. It would create a real danger to the public to release such a person willy-nilly."[153]

Bragg reduced felony robbery charges to several misdemeanor petty larceny counts. William Rolon was one of the first beneficiaries of Bragg's redefinition of crimes. "Cops charged Rolon with first-degree robbery," but when he got to court, that count was reduced to petit larceny under the "Day One" memo that Bragg issued on January 3, his first full day in office, the *New York Post* reported.[154] According to the court complaint, the 43-year-old Rolon had lifted $2,000 worth of products from a Duane Reade/Walgreens pharmacy and threatened a female manager with a pocketknife. Police officers said a bag of heroin fell from Rolon's sock during his arrest. Rolon has sixteen previous arrests dating back to 1991, which included charges of "rape, robbery, assault, and drug dealing." The police reported that Rolon is a habitual criminal with first-degree robbery and criminal possession of a weapon. But the prosecutor dropped his robbery charge, reduced his blatant theft to petty larceny, and reduced Rolon's threatening the manager with a knife to "second-degree menacing."[155] Manhattan Criminal Court judge Jay Weiner told Rolon, "Based on your record, you would have faced a long period of time in jail if convicted." Yet Rolon was granted "supervised release."[156]

Bragg's memo stated his office would not prosecute certain robberies if there were no "genuine risk of physical harm." At the time of his arrest, Rolon was also wanted in Brooklyn for failing to show up in court, where he faced charges that included felony assault with a weapon. But according to Bragg's new policy, Rolon is "a prime example of a person in need of treatment and resources, not incarceration."[157]

Bragg's pro-criminals approach caused a dramatic increase in crime in the Big Apple. On July 18, 2022, the *New York Post* reported that the city's major crime rate has increased by 37% since January. "Grand larceny has shot up 49% this year over last year—from 18,058 to 26,908. Auto theft has spiked by 46.2%, from 4,855 to 7,100. Robbery is up 39.2%, from 6,530 to 9,091, and burglaries increased by 32.9%, from 6,251 to 8,305, the numbers show. Felonious assault rose by 18.6%, and rapes saw an 11%."[158]

As NYC's reported crime cases have been skyrocketing, Bragg insisted on not enforcing the laws protecting the city's residents and properties from criminals. He deliberately decided to ignore them. His "Day One" memo directed his staff not to prosecute serious crimes, such as armed robbery.[159]

Bragg, like others who support "racial justice" pro-criminal policies, seems to believe that the "criminal justice system must [be based on] equality, equity…focused on reducing the number of people incarcerated [and] focused on redemption," as stated in President Biden's "Plan for Strengthening America's Commitment to Justice,"[160] which resembles the criminal justice reform policies proposed by Soros's OSF.[161]

Bragg seems to believe criminal offenders are less likely to become recidivists if sent into drug treatment or mental-health programs instead of jail time or heavy sentencing. His vision of public safety emphasizes sympathetic and trusting treatment of criminals and downplays the risk for future victims of the criminals he coddles.

Bragg's approach is consistent with the George Soros playbook for undermining America's rule of law, thus encouraging chaos. His memo prompted the resignation of nine seasoned prosecutors from his office. And NYPD commissioner Keechant Sewell emailed every officer in the force an email, saying she was "very concerned" Bragg's agenda would impact their "safety as police officers, the safety of the public and justice for the victims."[162]

In the first two weeks of January 2022, NYC's transit system had a 65.5 percent rise in crime over the previous year. Community and business leaders called on the city's newly elected mayor, Eric Adams, to fire Bragg. But Adams insisted "the city had 'a safe subway system.'" He said, "What our battle is in the subway system is fighting the perception of fear." In response, former NYPD commissioner Howard Safir (1996–2000) commented, "The fact is, crime is up in the subways . . . Perception often is reality, and if you happen to be one of the victims, it's certainly a reality."[163] In May 2022, a New Yorker who must take the subway to get to work was heard saying: "Taking the subway is a leap of faith. I pray each time."

The heavily criticized Bragg hired a crisis-communication expert.[164]

On January 20, 2022, instead of walking back to his pro-crime policy, the progressive DA issued a doublespeak declaration that would have made Orwell proud. "I understand why those who read my memo of January 3 have been left with the wrong impression about how I will enforce New York's laws," he said. Still, he defended the memo: "The purpose of the memo is to provide prosecutors with a framework for how to approach cases in the best interest of safety and justice. Each case is fact-specific," he said.[165] But his statement was greeted with skepticism.

Judging by the NYPD's CompStat report for the month of January 2022, Bragg's pro-criminals policies were working. There was a "38.5% increase in overall index crime compared with January 2021 (9,566 v. 6,905)."[166]

"Actions speak louder than words," reacted the NYPD's Detectives' Endowment Association president, Paul DiGiacomo. "There is a penal law, and those laws are there for a reason and should be prosecuted. You can't just disregard the law. If you don't like a law, you act to get it changed. You don't ignore it," he said.[167]

But Bragg did just that. So, February in NYC was even worse. "According to NYPD statistics, major felonies in New York City rose by 58.7%, rising from 5,759 reported crimes in February 2021 to 9,138 reported crimes in February 2022. Every crime category saw an increase except for citywide shooting incidents decreasing 1.3%."[168] By mid-March 2022, homicide, including shootings, was rising again everywhere in the city, including Fifth Avenue, the Museum of Modern Art, Columbus Circle, Soho, the Upper West Side, And the Upper East Side.

NYS progressive-Left Governor Kathy Hochul's early release of hundreds of convicts from prison into the general population, coupled with former NYC's progressive very-Left Bill DeBlasio's disbanding of NYPD's special plainclothes anti-crime unit in 2020, exacerbated the situation, as violence and crime rates ballooned. New York City's law-abiding residents have lost their freedom, and many lost their lives.

The public outcry caused mayor Eric Adams and his police commissioner to declare they would tackle the city's surging crime rates by focusing on getting gun-toting criminals off the streets.[169] But NYC's 8.85 million residents are plagued by crimes that continue to rise despite assurances from the mayor, who declares new plans to stop the violence. However, most violent crimes in this and other cities across the country include grand larceny, auto thefts (in June 2022, increased by 51.1% in NYC[170]), armed robberies, and spontaneous physical attacks and stabbing, which, while less noisy, are equally deadly.

In mid-March 2022, the new Neighborhood Safety Team of recognizable police officers, wearing clothing with "NYPD" written on the back and front and patches bearing the officers' names, shields, ranks, and commands," began patrolling neighborhoods prone to gun violence. "I don't know if this new team will be a good thing, but something has to be done," Joseph Burachio, owner of Clearview Cleaners in Queens, told the *New York Post*. "Crime rates are elevated. Crazy is elevated. Something needs to change. Juveniles are getting away with murder, and people don't feel safe. Go on the subway, and you're taking your life in your own hands."[171]

While hopeful, the effectiveness of 168 additional police officers on a rotating basis in preventing such attacks did nothing to reduce New York's soaring crime. NYPD's crime statistics for March 2022 showed a sharp increase of 36.5 percent for shootings, rape, robberies, and car thefts compared to March 2021.[172]

As NYC's reported crime cases have been skyrocketing, Bragg insisted on not enforcing the laws protecting the city's residents and properties from criminals. He deliberately decided to ignore them. His "day one" memo directed his staff not to prosecute serious crimes, such as armed robbery.

On August 3, 2022, three days after Soros's pontification[173] in the *Wall Street Journal*, the *New York Post* exposé highlighted how the combination of the State's "bail-reform" and DA Bragg's pro-criminals policies are leading to spiking crime in the city. The paper reported as an example of how a small group of just 10 career criminals was allowed to run amok across the Big Apple and rack up nearly 500 arrests after

New York enacted its controversial bail reform law—and most of them are still out on the streets," *The Post* cited New York City's Mayor Eric Adams, saying: "Our criminal justice system is insane. It is dangerous, it is harmful and it's destroying the fabric of our city," he complained. Adams added: "Time and time again, our police officers make an arrest, and then the person who is arrested for assault, felonious assaults, robberies and gun possessions, they're finding themselves back on the street within days—if not hours—after the arrest."

Adams repeated his call to Gov. Kathy Hochul to revoke the State's 2020 "bail reform," which resulted in skyrocketing crime rates and recidivism. "And those who say that the predicted wave of recidivism wouldn't happen, and the studies that claim to show that the rate of arrest for violent felonies has not changed since the reforms were passed, I have one word for you: Wrong. You are wrong," said the angry mayor.

However, Adams said nothing about Manhattan DA Bragg's policies contributing to the city's "insane" criminal justice system, "It is dangerous, it is harmful and it's destroying the fabric of our city," he fumed.

As long as Bragg is the DA, and bail reform laws allow violent offenders to return to the streets quickly,[174] and there are not enough police officers to patrol the streets, the steady rise in crime will increase the pace of the great migration out of New York City.

Another example of a Soros DA and judge promoting their (and Soros's) political agenda instead of the law is their successful efforts to undermine Texas's immigration law. Texas Democrats have been forum shopping for progressive-Left prosecutors and judges to successfully repeal Gov. Greg Abbott's efforts to enforce the laws punishing illegal crossing from Mexico to stem the flood of illegal migrants to the state. They found what they were looking for in Austin, Texas's, liberal Travis County DA, José Garza. The progressive-Left Democrat's election was funded by Texas's Justice and Public Safety PAC, which received $652,000 from George Soros.[175] Garza did not disappoint his funder.

The case involved Jesus Guzman Curipoma, an Ecuadoran man who illegally crossed the border from Mexico to Texas, "who hoped to submit a request for asylum, was arrested in September 2021 at a railroad switching yard in Kinney County on a criminal trespassing charge."[176]

DA Garza, who represented the state's prosecution, openly sided with Guzman's defense attorneys. "Mr. Guzman Curipoma's prosecution for criminal trespass as part of Operation Lone Star violates the supremacy clause of the United States Constitution and represents an impermissible attempt to intrude on federal immigration policy," Garza declared.[177]

The case was brought before Judge Jan Soifer, who is a former chair of the Democratic Party of Travis County; raised millions of dollars; served as a volunteer lobbyist for many progressive groups, including Planned Parenthood; and was a member of the National Advisory Council of Soros's funded J Street,[178] which is not "a pro-Israel, pro-peace group," as she and the organization claim. Careful research has documented J Street's sponsorship of groups supporting the BDS that "call for the elimination of Israel."[179] Soros has been highly critical of Israel's policies towards the Palestinians, as well as towards the main Israeli lobby in Washington, the American Israel Public Affairs Committee (AIPAC).[180] In an effort to counter the pro-Israel lobby in Washington[181] and reduce U.S. public support of Israel, Soros secretly funded J Street. "In 2010, *The Washington Times* revealed that J Street executive director Jeremy Ben-Ami lied about George Soros's three-year, $750,000 contribution.[182, 183, 184, 185] According to Prof. Alan Dershowitz, "J Street is one of the most virulent anti-Israel organizations in the history of Zionism and Judaism."[186]

So, while J Street and its supporters claim to support Israel, its activities and statements prove otherwise.

As expected, Soifer ruled that the arrest of Jesus Guzman Curipoma, who sought asylum in America, on a state criminal trespass charge amounted to illegal enforcement of federal immigration laws. Her ruling opened the door to similar court challenges of migrants arrested and detained on state trespassing charges under a border initiative led by Gov. Greg Abbott. Indeed, lawyers filed similar appeals for 11 men arrested in Operation Lone Star. The applications were routed to Soifer's court and set for a hearing, and many more are expected to follow.

Texas Attorney General Ken Paxton reacted, saying, "Ridiculous. Biden has FAILED to secure the border. Texas stepped in. We have the right to defend our border if the feds refuse. I'll fight this nonsense on appeal."[187] The state's appeal was dismissed "for want of jurisdiction."[188]

The sharp increase in crime in Colorado has been directly linked to the state's progressively criminal-friendly public policy that "has focused on being offender-friendly vs. victim-friendly."[189]

In December 2021, the Common Sense Institute published "The Colorado Crime Wave." The report, authored by two former DAs, showed that Colorado was leading "the nation in its rates of increased property crimes and, separately, auto thefts in 2020," according to the *Denver Gazette.* "The average monthly crime rate was 28% higher than a decade ago, and the violent crime rate spiked 35% over 2011."[190]

This spike is also attributed to Soros's funded successful multi-year campaign for marijuana legalization in the state.

The economic cost of this crime surge "has a high price tag; the research shows $27 billion in total, equal to 77% of the state budget, which works out to an average cost of $4,762 a year for every Coloradan."[191]

Several other studies showed similar results, though the growingly woke political atmosphere in Democrat-led states, and lack of funding for such politically incorrect research, have dampened the incentive to conduct such studies.

Nevertheless, the Council on Criminal Justice's study on 2021 homicide trends displayed the effect of implementing Soros's soft-on-crime justice reform policies. It found "an additional 5 percent rise in homicides (on the heels of a 30 percent increase in 2020) in 22 major American cities. Los Angeles, Louisville, and Washington, DC, saw homicides increase by more than 10 percent."[192]

Despite a virtually perfect record of failure, Democrat-run cities and states continue their soft-on-crime policies, telling the voters the outcomes will be different. These politicians blindly double down on Soros-touted policies, ignoring "red" States and cities' successful measures, such as:

- Funding the police;

- Enforcing the criminal codes;

- Attacking homelessness by developing programs that focus on the treatment of mental illness and jobs;

- Setting up law enforcement joint task forces focused on arresting all illegal drug dealers and users of drugs in public;

- Backing these up by enforcing the laws, effective prevention programs, and addressing addiction for the incarcerated;

- Acknowledging properly licensed citizens' right to carry concealed firearms (although anathema to "progressives," concealed-carry laws have invariably deterred and reduced crime, particularly robberies and assaults).

Notwithstanding the progressive Left's claim that "guns kill people," the 1996 University of Chicago Law School paper "Crime, Deterrence, and Right-to-Carry Concealed Handguns" proved the opposite.

The abstract of John R. Lott. Jr. and David B. Mustard's paper says:

Using cross-sectional time-series data for U.S. counties from 1977 to 1992, we find that allowing citizens to carry concealed weapons deters violent crimes, and it appears to produce no increase in accidental deaths. If those states which did not have right-to-carry concealed gun provisions had adopted them in 1992, approximately 1,570 murders; 4,177 rapes, and over 60,000 aggravated assaults would have been avoided yearly. On the other hand, consistent with the notion of criminals responding to incentives, we find criminals substituting into property crimes involving stealth and where the probabilities of contact between the criminal and the victim are minimal. The largest population counties where the deterrence effect on violent crimes is greatest are where the substitution effect into property crimes is highest. Concealed handguns also have their greatest deterrent effect in the highest crime counties. Higher arrest and conviction rates consistently and dramatically reduce the crime rate. Consistent with other recent work (Lott, 1992b), the results imply that increasing the arrest rate, independent of the probability of eventual conviction, imposes a significant penalty on criminals. The estimated annual gain from allowing concealed handguns is at least $6.214 billion.[193] (With permission from the authors.)

In his follow-up book, *More Guns Less Crime*, in 2010, Lott "found that increasing arrest rates in the most crime-prone areas led to the greatest reductions in crime." He also pointed out that "of all the methods studied so far by economists, the carrying of concealed handguns appears to be the most cost-effective method for reducing crime." Lott noted "no crime-reduction benefits from state-mandated waiting periods and background checks before allowing people to purchase guns" and concluded that "guns also appear to be the great equalizer among the sexes."[194]

But progressive-Left Democrat mayors, such as New York City's Eric Adams and Chicago's Lori Lightfoot, continue blaming guns for the spiking homicide rates. Instead of demanding that soft-on-crime DAs enforce the laws, punish violent criminals with jail time that would prevent them from having access to guns, and fire DAs refusing to follow the laws, they have created special police units to confiscate illegal guns. So the shootings continue, killing children, young and older men, and women, while these mayors double down on their irrational and empty promises to reduce crime.

Soros's DAs pro-defendant, anti-victim policies emboldened repeat offenders to commit more brazen crimes. Soros's arrogant response to the growing public outcry was to dismiss them. "The most rigorous academic study [probably funded by him], analyzing data across 35 jurisdictions, shows no connection between the election of reform-minded prosecutors and local crime rates."[195] This, however, contradicts the reality of the enormous rise in crime in American cities and towns where Soros's "reform-minded" prosecutors refuse to enforce the laws. Soros does not deny his funding elections of soft-on crime DAs, "I have done it transparently," he says. Moreover, Soros, the dystopian "Connoisseur of Chaos,"[196] declared he has "no intention of stopping" because, as the progressive-Left billionaire claims, "the funds I provide enable sensible reform-minded candidates to receive a hearing from the public." He rationalizes, "Judging by the results, the public likes what it's hearing." He forgot to mention he also funded groups that successfully and stupidly defunded the police, allowing criminals to terrorize cities and towns freely. Electing "soft-on-crime" DAs serves Soros's purpose of increasing chaos and social polarization in America, turning it from a melting pot into a boiling pot.

Soros rightly points out that the public elected the DAs he funded in Democrat majority-led cities. But that was before the public was exposed to their pro-criminal policies. When Soros's piece appeared in the *Journal*, most cities with his "reform-minded" DAs were fed up with the constantly rising crime. Since the beginning of 2021, the media has been reporting how *"the nation's largest cities are leading the call to crack down on lawlessness"* and *"how Democrats went from defunding to refunding the police."* [197] Hundreds of thousands of residents who could afford it and police officers[198] got so fed up that they moved to "red" States and cities that uphold the laws. The pro-criminal policies forced businesses, such as Starbucks, CVS, Walgreens, Target, and many others, to close many stores due to safety concerns and declining profits caused by the "growing impact of organized retail crime on retail employees and communities."[199]

On August 4, 2022, Florida's Governor, Ron DeSantis, had had enough. He suspended the Soros-backed State Attorney, Andrew Warren, for refusing to enforce the State laws. DeSantis's office stated: "We are suspending Soros-backed 13th circuit state attorney Andrew Warren for neglecting his duties as he pledges not to uphold the laws of the state." DeSantis declared, "The constitution of Florida has vested the veto power in the governor, not in state attorneys. We are not going to allow this pathogen of ignoring the law to get a foothold in the state of Florida."[200] Would other Republican governors or mayors follow DeSantis's move and fight back the Soros agenda?

The megalomaniac nonagenarian billionaire who has "no intention of stopping," is adamant about continuing.[201] He is adamant about continuing financing the elections of DAs, judges, mayors, state secretaries, state governors, and others, touting "reformative justice." The more he can get elected while he is still around, the more anarchy will prevail in American cities and towns, turning the once "law and order" society into a deeply divided, drug-infused, and lawless society.

4

SOROS'S OPEN BORDERS: UNDERMINING NATIONAL SOVEREIGNTY

Sovereignty is an anachronistic concept...the principle
of sovereignty stands in the way of outside intervention
in the internal affairs of nation-states.
—GEORGE SOROS, "THE PEOPLE'S SOVEREIGNTY,"
FOREIGN POLICY, OCTOBER 28, 2009[1]

"I live in one place, but I consider myself a citizen of the world...
and, I believe certain universal principles apply everywhere,"
—GEORGE SOROS, 1998[2]

SOROS BEGAN CHALLENGING the United States national sovereignty in 1996. As Soros tells it, he became enraged by new federal laws signed by President Bill Clinton.

The Personal Responsibility and Work Opportunity Reconciliation Act "required state professional and occupational licenses to be withheld from undocumented immigrants,"[3] thus, restricting food stamps and Supplemental Security Income Benefits to non-citizens. Soros declared this was "a clear-cut case of injustice."[4]

This was followed by the Illegal Immigration Reform and Immigrant Responsibility Act (IIRIRA), which aimed to reduce the surge of illegal immigration to the U.S. The IIRIRA "increased penalties on immigrants who had violated US law in some way (whether they were unauthorized immigrants who'd violated immigration law or legal immigrants who'd committed other crimes)" and required their detention and fast-tracking deportation.[5] The Lazarus Fund, created through Soros's Open Society Institute, believed that this kind of "open hostility" (against lawbreakers, mind you) was "antithetical to the values of an open society.»[6]

The first U.S. naturalizing law of 1790 required that the applicant be a "free white person" with a "good moral character" who resided in the country for two years. In 1870, the law was amended to include applicants of African origin. According to the Pew Research Center, "Starting in 1875, a series of restrictions on immigration were enacted. They included bans on criminals, people with contagious diseases, polygamists, anarchists, beggars, and importers of prostitutes." In 1965, "the landmark Immigration and Nationality Act created a new system favoring family reunification and skilled immigrants."[7] By 1986, lax controls of the Mexican and Canadian borders allowed six million unauthorized immigrants, mostly from Latin America, to cross the border. To better control the flow of immigrants to the country, the Reagan administration enacted the Immigration Reform and Control Act, which offered—with some stipulations—legalization to the illegals who applied, strictly penalizing employers who hired illegals and tightening security on the borders. Only 3 million of the 6 million illegals applied and received legal status. Also, "the strict sanctions on employers were stripped out of the bill,"[8] and the borders remained porous, incentivizing millions more to cross into the country illegally.

So, when the Clinton administration decided to tighten the immigration laws, activist/philosopher/billionaire Soros allocated $50 million to the aforementioned new fund, the Emma Lazarus Fund, whose mission was to provide legal defense to immigrants, helping them to stay in the country . . . and stay on welfare too.

Soros's naming of his pro-migration organization after Emma Lazarus—whose poem "The New Colossus," welcoming immigrants, was etched in bronze and mounted on the Statue of Liberty's pedestal in 1903—[9] is typical of Soros's use of Orwellian doublespeak.

The organization was said to have folded into his OSF. Still, the 2016 publication of OSF correspondence by DCLeaks revealed an Emma II, which has been funding, directly and indirectly, many other groups supporting illegal immigration into the U.S. and Europe.

A 1997 report published by Capital Research Center listed the first Emma Lazarus grants to twenty-three organizations. The list included the following[10]:

ACLU Immigrants' Rights Project, San Francisco, $200,000

Asian American Legal Defense and Education Fund, NYC, $150,000

Asian Law Caucus, San Francisco, $150,000

Asian Pacific American Legal Center of Southern California, Los Angeles, $200,000

Catholic Legal Immigration Network, Washington DC, $3 million

Coalition for Humane Immigrant Rights of Los Angeles, Los Angeles, $80,000

Fund for New Citizens, NYC, $2.5 million

Illinois Coalition for Immigrant/Refugee Protection, Chicago, $100,000

Immigrant Legal Resource Center, San Francisco, $500,000

Massachusetts Immigrant and Refugee Advocacy Coalition, Boston, $80,000

National Asian Pacific American Legal Consortium, Washington, DC, $500,000

National Association of Latino Elected & Appointed Officials Educational Fund, Los Angeles, $750,000

National Citizenship and Welfare Collaborative of the Immigration Coalitions. Boston, Los Angeles, San Francisco, Chicago, New York, and Dallas, $750,000

National Council of La Raza, Washington D.C., $1 million

National Immigration Forum, Washington DC, $200,000

National Immigration Law Center, Los Angeles, $1 million

New York Association for New Americans, New York, $150,000

New York Immigration Coalition, NYC, $100,000

Northern California Coalition for Immigrant Rights, San Francisco, $100,000

Texas Immigration and Refugee Coalition, Dallas, $100,000

Travelers' Aid of New York, NY, $210,000

Urban Institute, Washington DC, $50,000

In its cover story, "Saint George (Soros) and His Unlikely Crusade," on September 1, 1997, *Time Magazine* remarked that less than a year after the fund was established, it awarded "forty-five additional grants."

Since then, Soros has poured untold funds into groups promoting and arranging for illegal migration to the U.S. and organizations, mayors, and DAs who advocate and support sanctuary cities and benefits to illegals.[11] He reportedly works with the UN to help the caravans of illegal migrants to the U.S.[12] On September 20, 2016, his letter to the *Wall Street Journal* announced a $500 million investment to help the unlawful (forced) migration to Europe.[13] "This commitment of investment equity will complement the philanthropic contributions my foundations have made to address forced migration," he stated.[14]

In 2012, Soros welcomed President Obama's decision to bypass the lengthy legislative process of reforming immigration laws. Obama's executive order, the Deferred Action for Childhood Arrivals (DACA), was much to Soros's liking. It stopped the deportation of "people who were brought into the United States as children and did not have citizenship or legal residency status."[15] The protection was to last for two years at a time and was renewable. The program was not supposed to provide "a pathway to citizenship." Nevertheless, it legalized the status of at least 10 million illegals.

On May 28, 2015, when the U.S. Court of Appeals for the Fifth Circuit declined to lift the injunction on specific provisions of President Obama's "hallmark immigration executive actions,"[16] the Open Society Foundations announced "an initial investment of $8 million to support efforts to maximize successful applications for Deferred Action for Childhood Arrivals (DACA) and Deferred Action for Parents of Americans and Lawful Permanent Residents (DAPA)."[17]

Soros continued pouring undisclosed sums of money into programs benefiting illegal migration to the U.S. and Europe.[18]

The 2016 WikiLeaks of Soros and the OSF emails revealed that Soros has been funding Left-leaning or secular and religious organizations supporting illegal immigration to the U.S.[19] For example, between 2000 and 2014, the OSF gave more than $4.5 million to sixteen Catholic organizations.[20] The lion's share of these grants went to fund the activities of organizations supporting illegal migration to the U.S. According to an Urban Institute study in 2013, "At least 684 nonprofits nationwide provide some form of legal aid to immigrants."[21] How much of the OSF's money trickles down to fund them is unknown.

On March 21, 2021, the OSF website offered its executive

summary for the Lazarus Campaign's International Migration Initiative: Open Society–U.S. program. The site described the "Emma Lazarus Campaign as "an unprecedented collaboration between the Open Society Foundations and partners across the United States to provide direct relief to hundreds of thousands of undocumented immigrants and vulnerable workers in response to the COVID-19 pandemic."[22] The program's summary reviews several essential insights from experience that will help policymakers, civil society groups, and the philanthropic sector advance similar policy responses at the municipal, state, and federal levels.

An example of the OSF's utilization of the Emma Lazarus Campaign to undermine illegal migration laws in states and cities across the U.S. is the Emma Lazarus Resilience Fund partnership with Communities Foundation of Texas in August 2021. The Emma Lazarus Resilience Fund was set up to "distribute $500,000 to nonprofits that provide direct financial assistance to immigrant/refugee individuals and families who are otherwise ineligible for federal COVID-19 relief programs."[23]

The Soros grants went to the following entities:

Catholic Charities of Dallas, Inc.

Center for Survivors of Torture

Children's Food Ministry

Community Action Organizers

The Concilio

Family Independence Initiative

Heard That Foundation

ImmSchools

International Rescue Committee

Mi Familia Vota Education Fund

Open Arms, Inc. dba Bryan's House

Rosa Es Rojo, Inc.

The Stewpot of First Presbyterian Church

UNT Dallas Foundation

Wilkinson Center

Workers Defense Project

On February 24, 2022, as Russian forces invaded Ukraine, the Lutheran Immigration and Refugee Service (LIRS) encouraged the United States to "lead by example and live up to its highest ideals in welcoming more refugees" fleeing the violence in Ukraine. The Council on National Security and Immigration and the Catholic Legal Immigration Network (CLINIC) pleaded with the Biden administration "to extend an immediate 18-month designation of Temporary Protected Status (TPS)" for Ukrainians "to ensure they cannot be deported."[24] The same request was made for more than 100,000 unvetted Afghans—including the Taliban and al-Qaeda members.

Not all refugees are the same, and it could prove dangerous to treat them similarly.

What is the annual cost of refugee resettlement to American taxpayers? The latest available report from 2018, before the Biden administration opened the southern border to millions of illegal migrants, all in need of food, clothing, cash, shelter, welfare, social services, and job training programs, is the 2018 study of the Federation for American Immigration Reform (FAIR). According to this study, "the annual cost to U.S. taxpayers is $1.8 billion, and over five years, that financial burden skyrockets to $8.8 billion." This was the guesstimated cost for 3.5 million refugees sheltered in the U.S. between 1980 and 2018.[25]

Since then, especially as the Biden administration embraced Soros's and the globalization clan's open border policy, the cost of subsidizing millions of illegal migrants, minted as "refugees," has reached new heights, adding billions of dollars to the U.S. deficit.[26]

In 2021, the first year of the Biden administration's "open border" policy, U.S. Customs and Border Protection (CBP) reported that "more than 2 million unauthorized migrants [who] came across the Mexican border . . . were apprehended or turned themselves in."[27] By July 2022, the *New York Post* editorial reported: "By the administration's own estimates, 4 million have come in under President Joe Biden, plus another 800,000 who made it without getting intercepted."[28] However, the accurate number of illegals who entered the U.S. is unknown.

How many and what kind of crimes do these illegals commit? Hard to tell, especially since many Democratic governors, mayors, and Soros-elected DAs refuse to cooperate with federal authorities, such as the U.S. Immigration and Customs Enforcement (ICE), and even ban their presence in the cities and states they control.

Contributing to the chaos is the Biden administration's secret policy of distributing illegal migrants throughout the country, under cover of darkness, using special charter flights and other means of transportation. The administration does not notify or seek approval of the governors (especially Republicans) or mayors of towns and cities where they drop hundreds of illegals in the middle of the night, leaving state and local government with the responsibility and cost of providing housing, food, health, welfare, education, jobs, and so on. The spike causes additional costs in life and treasury, resulting from crimes committed by many unscreened illegals, including members of violent M18 and MS13 gangs.

According to the CBP's report for 2021, "heroin seizures were up 113 percent, cocaine seizures increased 28 percent; methamphetamines and fentanyl seizures were down 59 and 51 percent, respectively."[29] The CDC announced that 2021 saw an increase of 15 percent in overdose deaths.[30] Many of the 107,622 Americans who overdosed consumed dangerous drugs, such as heroin and other opioids, methamphetamines, and cocaine, often laced with fentanyl. Fentanyl[31] is a synthetic opioid, about 100 times more potent than morphine and 50 times more potent than heroin. It is highly addictive and frequently deadly; 2 milligrams are enough to kill a person.

As mentioned earlier, China is the major exporter of huge volumes of precursors of many synthetic drugs, including fentanyl, most of which finds its way to the Mexican drug cartels that produce millions of counterfeit pills, either laced with fentanyl or, more frequently, containing only fentanyl. The millions of pills smuggled through the open southern border have already killed hundreds of thousands of Americans in what should be considered chemical warfare. So, why does the Biden administration keep the border open? Moreover, it has been providing "Safe injection" sites for edicts and drug paraphernalia, justifying it as a "harm reduction" effort, just as Soros has been recommending and funding since 1997. But "Safe injection sites have not delivered on their promises and have caused a significant increase in trash, crime, and disorder,"[32] but the Biden administration follows Soros's plan.

The enormous quantities of illegal drugs (millions of fentanyl and methamphetamine pills, hundreds of kilos of cocaine and heroin, and tons of cannabis) apprehended by the Border Patrol since the Biden administration opened the southern border is merely an indication of the immense quantities that are pouring into the U.S. together with millions of illegal migrants.

"The January 2022 apprehension numbers of illegal migrants nearly doubled the totals for the same month one year before (75,316), which in turn was 158 percent higher than the number of Border Patrol apprehensions at the Southwest border in January 2020 (29,205)—before the Covid-19 pandemic shutdowns that brought most immigration (legal and illegal) to a halt," the CBP reported.[33]

Are all these illegal supposedly "asylum seekers" from Central and South America? Almost half of those caught by the Border Patrol in January 2022 were not refugees, but "Long-Distance" economic migrants, migrants"[34] from some 160 countries.[35]

As the number of illegal migrants apprehended crossing the southern border in January 2022 doubled, by July 2022, the guesstimated number of "gotaways" was over 500,000.[36] Different guesstimates put the number of illegal migrants who crossed the border from Mexico by September 2022 between 4 and 5 million.[37] At the same time, law enforcement seized record quantities of fentanyl, cocaine, and other dangerous drugs. But how much more was smuggled in? How many more thousands of Americans will overdose on these drugs? What does the Biden administration do to stop the flow of dangerous drugs to the U.S.? Nothing.

Mass illegal migration to the United States is of concern because many of the illegal migrants, relabeled as "refugees," crossing the borders to the U.S. come from countries where democracy, freedom of speech and religion, and individual rights, including the rights of women and the LGBT, are rejected and even forbidden. These illegal migrants do not know English, are semiliterate or illiterate and have no money and no skills for jobs other than manual work. Many are afflicted with contagious diseases that have long been eradicated in the U.S., and many are unfamiliar with basic hygiene practices. Settling such people in the U.S. imposes a huge financial burden on the economy and endangers the public's health and safety.

None of these considerations seems to deter Soros and his affiliates from bringing additional illegal migrants to the U.S. Moreover, the growing revenues of organizations engaged in illegal migration, especially to the U.S., suggests they are not charities or NGOs, as they claim, but profitable businesses. Instead of being given tax exemptions, they and their funders/supporters should be held accountable. And more important, they should be brought to justice for violating federal and state laws and held responsible for human trafficking.

* * *

Soros extended his activities to Europe in 2010 as waves of refugees fled from the horrors of the Arab Spring. Soros supported German chancellor Angela Merkel's open-border policy, encouraging refugees from Syria and the region to come to Europe. He expediently dismissed criticism that Merkel's policy opened the floodgate to millions of paperless "refugees" from Africa and the Middle East into Europe and chided countries that closed their borders and refused to accommodate tens of thousands of illegal immigrants on their way to Merkel's welfare state.[38]

Soros was especially pleased with Merkel's announcement that it was Germany's "national duty" to open its borders" to refugees from Syria and the Middle East"[39] but criticized her for a "lack of adequate controls" and appropriate plans to absorb the large number of newcomers."[40]

To reach Germany, the refugees—most turned out to be illegal, undocumented economic migrants from other Middle Eastern countries, Africa and Asia—had to cross other European countries. Not all European nations shared in Merkel's and Soros's enthusiasm.

Soros's nemesis, Hungarian premier Victor Orban, denounced Merkel's "open-door" policies. "(A Hungarian) does not want to see throngs of people pouring into his country from other cultures who are incapable of adapting and are a threat to public safety, to his job and his livelihood." He said, "The Hungarian man is, by nature, politically incorrect. That is, he has not lost his common sense." And he vowed to fight the wave of migration that threatened "to turn his country into a 'refugee camp.'"[41]

Over decades of meddling in government affairs worldwide, Soros rarely encountered outright opposition. And there is nothing like a scorned Soros. So he has launched multiple personal attacks on Orban in articles and speeches,[42] parroted by Left-leaning, Soros-adoring, and sometimes Soros-sponsored media outlets everywhere. Moreover, Soros personally lobbied the EU leadership to punish Hungary. He succeeded in tarnishing Hungary's image and Orban's reputation but, thus far, has failed at removing Orban from office.

How many illegal migrants have made their way to Europe? Hard to tell. Reporting by national and international agencies varies. According to the European Union's migration data from 2015, when the so-called refugees and migrant crisis erupted, through 2018, "Europe . . . has dealt with 2.4 million refugees and people in refugee-like situations and 860 thousand asylum-seekers."[43] The migration spike intensified several European countries' economic, financial, and social problems. The arrival of additional 1.2 million illegal migrants between 2019 and 2020 did not help ease the burden.

The cost of welfare, housing, health care, education, and training of millions of illegal migrants continues to burden the economies and threaten the security of the countries that accept them. Violent crimes, including murder, rape, and stabbing, have soared, as have terrorist and anti-Semitic attacks in Europe and the U.S.

In the report titled "What Terrorist Migration over European Borders Can Teach About American Border Security," Todd Bensman, a senior national security fellow at the Center for Immigration Studies, detailed how "terrorists disguised as migrants have entered the European Union to commit terrorist attacks." According to Bensman, "Between 2014 and 2017, 13 of the 26 member states lining the so-called Schengen Area's external land borders recorded more than 2.5 million detections of illegal border-crossings along several lands and sea routes, a historic, mostly unfettered surge that came to be known as the 'migrant crisis.'"[44]

Bensman reported that "most migrant terrorists involved in thwarted or completed attacks were purposefully deployed to the migration flows by an organized terrorist group to conduct or support attacks in destination countries." His report validated Hungary's, Poland's, Slovakia's, and the Czech Republic's security concerns as their main objection to allowing illegal migrants into their countries.[45]

Despite constant criticism and pressure campaigns initiated by OSF-linked international media and organized demonstrations to shame and bully the leaders of countries that refuse to open their borders, labeling them racists and xenophobic, these countries' leadership remains firm regarding illegal migrants from Africa and the Middle East. However, since Russia attacked Ukraine in February 2022, the Visegrád states—Czech Republic, Hungary, Poland, and Slovakia—have accepted a limited number of Ukrainian refugees.

Soros has lobbied the Council of Europe[46] and marshaled his well-paid army of European Human and Justice Rights organizations to badger the European Commission (EC) to threaten penalties and other restrictions against the objecting member-states. Unsurprisingly, the EC[47] took legal proceedings against Poland, Hungary, and the Czech Republic. However, the leaders of the defiant countries asserted that the goal of their governments' policies is "ensuring security for our citizens."[48]

Unsurprisingly, the European Court of Justice (ECJ) ruled against Hungary. The premier insisted, however, that it would continue its migration policies and that "it doesn't matter what the European court ruled. Hungary must continue to defend its borders."

"We decided that we will not do anything to change the way the border is protected," Orban said. "We won't change it and we aren't going to let anyone in."[49]

But as millions of refugees fled Ukraine after Russia's attack in February 2022, Orban announced, "We're letting everyone in." Hungary has opened its border to all Ukrainian citizens and legal residents, even providing them with travel documents and "allowing in those who have arrived from third countries after the proper screening," he stated.[50]

By April 2022, Hungary had taken in more than 540,000 Ukrainian refugees—"between five and six refugees for every 100 Hungarian inhabitants." Other neighboring countries—Poland, Slovakia, Romania, and Moldova—also provided Ukrainian refugees shelter, food, and legal papers. Yet, Hungary's support has been mostly ignored by the Leftist media. When noted, it regularly repeats the Soros-affiliated Hungarian Helsinki Committee's claims that these statistics are "misleading,"[51] and routinely denouncing Orban, among other things, as "Putin's puppet."[52]

Hungary has maintained close economic relations with Russia, which supplies Hungary's gas, and offered better conditions for funding, building, and expanding the Paks nuclear power plant. Hungary's ties to the West could have probably been closer had Soros, the influential financial guru, refrained from interfering in the country's domestic affairs. Constantly vilifying it didn't help.

Soros's constant interference in the country's politics, attacking Hungary's patriotism and immigration policies, and efforts to oust Orban were amplified by his many well-placed and well-paid supporters in the media and academia. Soros's fiefdom in Budapest, the Central European University (CEU), also functioned as an extension of the OSF. That did not sit well with Orban and the ruling national-conservative party, Fidesz, which he established in 1990 and has led since then.

Russia's attack on Ukraine on February 24, 2022, exacerbated Europe's migration problems. By August 23, the Russian bombardment of Ukrainian cities and towns resulted in more than 11.5[53] million refugees who fled to neighboring countries, including Poland and Hungary, where they were received with open arms.

In the run-up to the April 3, 2022, parliamentarian election and a national referendum, "the Soros empire—with all its money—the international mainstream media," and "Brussels bureaucrats" have been in full gear to defeat Orban, his party, and the referendum on his policies, which include prioritizing national sovereignty, tax cuts for families, traditional Christian values, and immigration. Soros and his affiliates, the EU, and the Leftist media failed. Orban won the election. "The entire world can see that our brand of Christian democratic, conservative, patriotic politics has won," he declared.[54] Soros lost again.

Russia's war on Ukraine's sovereignty, the energy crisis, and worsening supply chains caused produce shortages just as the COVID pandemic seemed to ebb increased nationalist sentiments among other European countries, who now question the trend of globalization. No doubt Soros and the globalization cabal are busy planning how best to stop such developments.

Soros and the globalizers will rejoice as long as Joe Biden is in office. Biden's woke administration and the progressive-Left Democrats will continue opening the border with Mexico, incentivizing millions more to smuggle their way into the U.S. Even rumors of lifting Title 42 enforcement law,[55] which Trump's administration imposed to stop the COVID virus spread—have already increased the number of illegal migrants, not refugees, who have crossed or are on their way to the southern border. How many more million illegal migrants are expected to join the millions that the Biden administration dispersed under cover of darkness in chartered flights and buses across the country is anybody's guess. The administration is moving fast to turn Soros's dream into reality, resulting in a borderless, poor, crime-ridden, racist, drugged, and chaotic America. And then what?

5

THE STATELESS STATESMAN: SOROS'S REVOLUTIONS

Soros sometimes refers to himself as "a stateless statesman."[1]

—CONNIE BRUCK, THE *NEW YORKER*, 1995

SOROS'S MEDDLING in the affairs of countries all over the world began in the mid-1980s. He supported resistance movements and politicians and acknowledged on several occasions that his cash earned him respect and influence in unstable countries than would typically be the case. Indeed, Soros not only made his fortune exploiting unstable markets but also used and created political instability to his or his supporters' advantage.

Soros gained recognition as a pro-democracy activist through the financial support his foundations distributed in the former Soviet Union and the Eastern Bloc. It didn't cost Soros much to fund libraries, scholarships, fax machines, printers, milk for schoolchildren, and stipends for young, promising students to study abroad. But the serious money to instigate resistance, revolution, and regime change, often originated from the United States Agency for International Development (USAID) and other U.S. government agencies. Using the local Soros foundations when needed afforded them plausible deniability.

The breadth and consequences of Soros's brazen meddling in U.S. and international politics directly and through his vast network of NGOs have yet to be fully explored. When exposed, all criticism of such intervention is regularly labeled by Soros and his aficionados as anti-Semitic, for Soros his alleged victimhood as a shield decades ago to deflect attention and elude scrutiny.

In June 2019, Soros and isolationist libertarian billionaire Charles Koch declared the creation of their Quincy Institute (QI) for Responsible Statecraft as a "once-in-a-generation opportunity" to diminish America's "interventionist foreign policy" and military power. Their initial contribution to QI was $500,000 each.[2] Serving as executive vice president for the new think tank is Iranian Trita Parsi. "The institute's titular director and president is Andrew Bacevich, a historian, former U.S. Army colonel." However, the Institute's 2019 "tax exemption application lists Parsi's estimated compensation at $275,000 a year, compared with $50,000 for Bacevich—a fair indication of who is actually running" it.[3]

Parsi's lobbying Washington on behalf of Iran was launched in 1997 from Sweden, where he resided. There, he founded and was president of "a small lobby organization, Iranians for International Cooperation" (IIC).[4] From Sweden, Parsi used IIC's members in Washington to "send petitions and letters to Congress." The ICC stated, "Our agenda is topped by the removal of US economic and political sanctions against Iran. . . . IIC is capable of organizing the grassroots and pressure US lawmakers to pose a more Iran friendly position."[5]

In 2001, Parsi's activities from Sweden led to his next job as director of development of the American Iranian Council (AIC), founded in 1997 by anti-sanction and pro-Iran advocate Hooshang Amirahmadi.[6] Backed by Iran, AIC received funding from U.S. oil companies eager to do business in Iran as the Clinton administration deferred the 1996 Iran-Libya Sanctions Act (ILSA).[7]

In interviews with Iranian government press agencies, Amirahmadi stated that AIC is Iran's "prominent lobby in the U.S. that strives to defend the interests of Iran and oppose the pro-Israeli lobby AIPAC."[8] The AIC website also boasts that its influence led to "Vice President Joe Biden's and Senator John Kerry's proposals for dialogue between the US Congress and the Iranian Parliament."[9]

In 2002, after a few months at AIC, Parsi left and, for 16 years, presided over the nonprofit organization National Iranian American Council (NIAC) and its lobbying arm, the NIAC Action, which is dedicated to "building political power" favoring the Iranian regime's agenda, "with supporters in all 50 states."[10]

In addition to launching the new Iran lobby, the NIAC, Parsi also began working for the Tehran-based Iranian advisory firm Atieh Bahar. The Iranian American Forum, which opposes the mullahs' regime, posted on its website copies of Parsi's 2002 and 2003 reports from Washington to the Bahar agency in Tehran, as well as the fees he received for this work.[11] Some of these documents were made public because of Parsi's and the NIAC's failed lawfare and intimidation tactics against Hassan Daioleslam (aka Dai), an activist of the pro-democracy opposition to Iran in the U.S., who, on August 23, 2007, published a detailed account titled "Iran's Oil Mafia, Penetrating US Political System." His investigation included examining public documents and explaining how and why NIAC and Trita Parsi lobby in favor of the Iranian regime.[12] Daioleslam's report produced a wave of criticism against Parsi and the NIAC. So Parsi sued him for defamation in 2008. However, during the discovery process in court, Daioleslam provided documents proving that between 2002 and 2003, Parsi sent his reports to Bahar and was paid for them.[13] Parsi and the NIAC lost the case. D.C. District Court Judge John D. Bates ordered: "a $183,480.09 fine because of the abuses which NIAC and Parsi perpetrated for over two years during discovery." In his ruling, Judge Bates said, "There is no question that plaintiffs have repeatedly tried to evade their discovery obligations" (p. 23). "In awarding sanctions, the Court is mindful not just of the need to compensate defendant, but also of the need to deter plaintiffs from future discovery abuses." (pp. 22–23)[14]

Another thorough exposé, "How Trita Parsi and NIAC Used the White House to Advance Iran's Agenda," was published by *Tablet* magazine in June 2017.[15]

On January 13, 2020, a group of U.S. senators led by Sen. Tom Cotton, petitioned the attorney general, William Barr, to investigate the NIAC "for potential violations of the Foreign Agents Registration Act (FARA)."[16] While NIAC registered as a nonprofit organization, from the beginning, it has been spreading the Iranian regime's propaganda and employing pressure to manipulate U.S. foreign policy.[17]

According to the petition, the NIAC, which claims to be a "nonpartisan, nonprofit organization advancing interests of [the] Iranian-American community,"[18] is a pro-Tehran advocacy group with deep ties to the Iranian regime. It played a key role in the Obama administration's pro-Iran "echo chamber," which misled Congress and the American people about the terms of the landmark 2015 nuclear deal.[19]

Missing from the petition was the OSF's support to the NIAC, which the organization does not disclose, although, according to the *Washington Free Beacon*, NIAC admitted that Soros "is a major donor."[20] However, it has been reported that between 2006 and 2009, Soros's OSI and his Foundation to Promote Open Society gave $200,000 to NIAC.[21] And according to the *Guardian*, NIAC received $281,000 to lobby for the Iran Deal from the Soros-funded Ploughshares Fund.[22]

Once again, the *Stateless Stateman* has been funding the globalist, anti-American, anti-Israel agenda. On whose behalf?

On January 3, 2020, a day after a US drone strike killed the leader of the infamous Iranian al-Quds force, Qassem Soleimani, QI issued a press release written by Trita Parsi, denouncing the alleged "assassination of Qassem Soleimani," calling it an "act of war," and attacking President Trump.[23] Roxane Farmanfarmaian, an outspoken advocate of the mullahs regime in Iran, who was hired by QI as a nonresident fellow in September 2022, has also attacked Trump for Soleimani's assassination, calling it "a colossal strategic blunder." She also favors Iran's building a nuclear bomb, claiming, "It's inconceivable that Iran would bomb Israel because it would isolate it." [24]

Soros followed suit. Speaking in Davos on January 23, 2020, he condemned President Trump for ordering the killing of arch-terrorist Soleimani—who had the blood of thousands, including many Americans, on his hands.

Siding with the mullahs in Tehran is nothing new for Soros. His foundations have been operating in Iran in complete disregard of its U.S. designation as a State Sponsor of Terrorism in 1984. The Open Society Institute's 2002 annual report described its Iranian activities as holding "meetings and seminars on open society issues"—an oxymoron in the Shite theocracy—and promoting "a deeper understanding between the United States and Iran."[25] Was Soros promoting his foreign policy agenda?

Perhaps not.

Soros's promotion of Iran's interest in the U.S. was not limited to funding the NIAC. He has also been funding the pro-mullah regime, the American Iranian Council (AIC).[26]

In 2002, then-Senator Joe Biden, chairman of the Foreign Relations Committee, "applauded" the AIC and praised George Soros's Open Society Institute" for its "important" and critical role" in forging U.S.-Iran relations. "I believe that an improved relationship with Iran is in the naked self-interest of the United States, and I would presume to suggest Iran's interest as well," Biden declared.[27]

Over the years, despite constant Iranian aggressions and terrorist activities everywhere, including the U.S., neither Biden and his previous boss, Obama, nor Soros seemed to recant their fictitious claims that the mullahs' "naked self-interest" is to advance peace and prosperity in the region or develop nuclear power stations to supply electricity. They willfully ignore the regime's mantras "Death to America" and "Death to Israel," ignoring Iran's attacks on U.S. forces and Iranian surrogates'

attacks on Saudi Arabia or Israel, and on and on. Instead, in his eagerness to salvage Obama's 2015 nuclear agreement with Tehran, Biden
agreed to Iran's contemptuous condition to allow Russia to lead the
negotiation, with China as a reserve!

Biden's submission to Iran's demands stuck another knife in
America's fading image of a superpower, advancing Soros's intention.

In January 2005, the AIC and the Open Society Institute "hosted a
talk with Iran's Ambassador to the United Nations, Javad Zarif." The OSF
website said, "This event is one of many OSI has hosted over the years
on contemporary Iran covering a wide spectrum of issues and views."[28]

The OSF's May 2007 statement, discussing its activities in Iran, said
it "focused on humanitarian relief, public health, and arts and culture.
These activities were undertaken with the knowledge of the Iranian government and in full compliance with the specific licenses granted by the
Office of Foreign Assets Control, United States Treasury Department."
It further declared, "None of OSI's Iran activities have been funded or
initiated by the U.S. government" and noted that the "OSI has relied
on the expertise of consultants on the ground."[29]

Who were these expert consultants? Since Iran is a totalitarian
country, it is common knowledge that little happens there, especially
concerning foreign entities, without the regime's control. So, were these
"consultants" agents of Iran's KGB-trained Ministry of Intelligence and
Security (MOIS), known as VEVAK (Vezarat-e Ettela'at va Amniat-e
Keshvar)? The Basij Force? The Islamic Revolutionary Guard Corps
(IRGC) intelligence (Ettalaat-e-Pasdaran)?[30]

In September 2007, the AIC, with the OSF, helped arrange a
meeting between President Mahmoud Ahmadinejad of Iran and
U.S. academics, business leaders, and media members at Columbia
University. The primary topic of the discussion was "the difficulties
and problems in the ongoing relationship between the two countries."[31]

On September 5, 2018, as Iran's foreign minister Javad Zarif
addressed the Iranian parliament, he praised the "long and successful
working relationship with the Open Society Foundations." According

to the translation provided by Iran Gateway, "Zarif claimed that the Open Society Foundation was legally operational inside Iran . . . with significant collaborations with city councils and other organizations."[32]

In May 2020, then Democratic Party presidential candidate Biden belittled China's threat to the U.S. "China is going to eat our lunch? Come on, man," the former vice president said, reported NBC News. "I mean, you know, they're not bad folks, folks. But guess what? They're not competition for us," he added.[33]

Biden has held such opinions for a long time. In 2011, in an op-ed in the *New York Times*, he said similar things about America's relationship with the Chinese Communist Party, asserting, "I remain convinced that a successful China can make our country more prosperous, not less," and concluded, "Some may warn of America's demise, but I'm not among them. And let me reassure you: based on my time in China, neither are the Chinese."[34] This and similar statements he made since he took office seem, first and foremost, to reflect his family members' financial arrangements with the CCP. A detailed account of this and many similar deals the CCP has with other prominent American individuals and corporations is available in Peter Schweizer's excellent book *Red-Handed*.[35]

One of Biden's priorities as president was reviving Obama's corrupt deal with Iran, which Soros endorsed and supported by funding "echo chambers"[36] to promote the deal despite the regime's continuing calls for death to both America and Israel, deployment of terrorist groups across the globe, vows to kill all "infidels" (non-Muslims), conducting cyberattacks against the U.S., and collaboration with China, Russia, North Korea, Venezuela, and Cuba, which are hostile to the U.S.

Does Soros delude himself into thinking he could subvert the fanatical, radical terrorist Shiite regime from within? The mullahs would be glad to part him from his money—until the moment they suspect his operatives are attempting to influence the locals. The radical regime is known for its paranoia of anything Western.

Of course, Soros has been known to meddle in the domestic affairs of countries with rich natural resources. And Iran has large natural gas reserves, coal, chromium, copper, iron ore, lead, manganese, zinc, sulfur, . . . and pistachios. Could this be the reason for his interest in Iran?

Soon after he settled in the White House, Biden appointed Robert Malley as his special envoy to Iran.[37] Malley is the former president and CEO of the Soros-funded, Brussels-based International Crisis Group,[38] which, like Soros, has been criticizing Israel and praising Hamas.[39] Since he served as President Bill Clinton's special assistant for Arab-Israeli Affairs, he demonstrated his pro-Syria, pro-Iran, pro-Palestinian, and always anti-Israel attitudes.[40] As Obama's lead negotiator in the 2015 very-bad Iran deal,[41] Malley was instrumental in secretly delivering at least $1.7 billion in cash to Iran, of which $400 million was paid as ransom to release American prisoners held by Tehran.[42] The cash was delivered in unmarked European currencies and transferred by unmarked plane under cover of darkness.[43] He was also instrumental in arranging the transfer of $150 billion[44] to the mullahs in Tehran, which then secretary of state John Kerry boasted about in Davos in January 2016. Kerry claimed Iran would get only $55 billion[45], as he acknowledged, "Some of [the money] will end up in the hands of the IRGC or other entities, some of which are labeled terrorists . . . I'm not going to sit here and tell you that every component of that can be prevented."[46]

Reacting to Biden's appointment of Robert Malley, international columnist and author Amir Tahari tweeted, "Robert Malley, a protege of George Soros, as #JoeBiden's 'Iran man' may please 'New York Boys' faction."[47]

To disguise his support of the mullahs, Soros declared he would favor "moderates" to win power in Tehran. After meeting with Islamic president Khatami in Davos in 2004, Soros tried to help Khomeinist "'moderates' come on top," Tahari wrote on January 24, 2021.[48]

To help generate the public's support for Obama's appeasement efforts, Soros's OSF awarded $750,000 to Ploughshares Fund to increase the influence of "echo chambers" in support of the proposal titled "Defending Iran Nuclear Diplomacy." Special efforts were made to deceive the public by broadening and better coordinating the "circle of experts and validators who support diplomacy," including Left-leaning, prominent US and European "military and diplomatic personalities" often known for their "America Last" and anti-Israel views, "as well as Iranian human rights and civil society leaders."[49]

The *Israel Times* reported that soon after Obama's very bad nuclear deal was signed, "Iran has . . . increased its financial support for two of the largest terror groups in the region . . . Hamas and Hezbollah."[50]

A few months later, Hassan Nasrallah, the leader of Hezbollah, the Lebanon-based Shia terrorist group, publicly praised Iran for its generous financial support.[51]

On September 5, 2018, as Iran's foreign minister Javad Zarif addressed the Iranian parliament, he praised the "long and successful working relationship with the Open Society Foundations." The OSF hosted Zarif in 2005 when he served as Iran's ambassador to the UN.[52]

Soros has successfully changed the political landscape of the U.S., several of the former Soviet Republics, and the EU's and other international bureaucracies, successfully facilitated the legalization of marijuana in most Western countries and bullied them into opening their borders to millions of illegal, predominantly Muslim migrants, claiming they are "refugees." However, his foundations were forced to exit China and Russia. He left Hungary to avoid complying with local laws. That, however, is not surprising since he repeatedly said he learned not to follow the rules at a young age.[53] In reaction to Hungary's demand to comply with the law, he, again, used his favorite attack weapon, accusing the prime minister of anti-Semitism.[54]

COLLABORATING WITH COMMUNIST REGIMES

In 1984 Hungary, a Soviet satellite was ruled under "the basic principles made up in Moscow." Soros could not have opened his Budapest office without Moscow's approval.

Miles Yu, a professor of East Asian and military history at the United States Naval Academy, described the circumstances that led to Soros's foundation in Hungary. "To reverse a vicious cycle of stagnation in the Soviet Union [in the early 1980s], the Brezhnev government conducted a bold but risky experiment with a limited market economy through a special economic zone. The experiment was conducted in Mr. Soros' native Hungary, which had become a vibrant and semi-open society within the Soviet system," Yu wrote.[55]

In *Soros on Soros*, in 1995, the financier admitted to becoming cozy with elements in the Communist regimes where his foundation was active: "Of course, we collaborated: The communists wanted to use me, and I wanted to use them," he said. "That was the basis of our collaboration."[56]

It is hard to imagine that the Communist regimes allowed the OSI to choose who to aid. The recipients were chosen or allowed to receive aid provided by Soros's foundations.

On June 28, 2016, in London, at Mikhail Khodorkovsky's Open Russia Club, which Soros supports, he told the gathering that he had decided to return to the Soviet Union upon hearing that Gorbachev asked Nobel Laureate Andrei Sakharov "to return to Moscow . . . When I heard about it, I understood that something had really changed."[57]

When Soros told Sakharov about his plan to form an Open Society Institute in the Soviet Union, the Russian scientist warned Soros, "Young man, you are going to fill the coffers of the KGB." That, however, did not seem to deter Soros.[58]

On the contrary, he opened the OSI Moscow office in 1987 with help from the KGB. "Actually, the KGB played an important role in the setting up of the foundation," he said. "It was a reformist cell, and they took me in their confidence," he added with a straight face.[59]

How could he tell this was a "reformist" KGB cell? Why has no one challenged this and many similar asinine statements by Soros?

Was this KGB's "reformist cell" that instructed the Hungarian Ministry of Internal Affairs III (in Hungarian Belügyminisztérium III) to facilitate the opening of Soros's OSI Budapest office in 1984? Soros also collaborated with similar "reformist cells" in Bulgaria's notorious "State Security" that approved the establishment of his Sofia office.[60]

The DS (Durzhavna Sigurnost), like other security services in the Eastern Bloc was a subsidiary of the KGB.[61] The Soviet KGB "founded, dominated and managed the intelligence services of the communist bloc states," said the Declaration of the International Conference on the NKVD/KGB Activities and its Cooperation with Other Secret Services in Central and Eastern Europe 1945–1989, which was held in Bratislava, Slovakia in November 2007.[62]

By the early 1990s, he had foundations throughout eastern Europe, Russia, and the former Soviet republics. It is difficult to overestimate the impact of Soros's decisively applied millions of dollars, providing libraries, traveling scholarships, milk for schoolchildren, and vitally needed equipment, like fax machines, PCs, and photocopiers. *Newsweek* characterized Soros at that time as a "one-man Marshall Plan."[63] In real dollar terms, Soros was said to have spent $2 billion more than the $11 billion spent by the Marshall Plan. But how much of this was his own money?

Soros Management Fund, funded by USAID, provided training to foreign officials.[64] It also used $9 million in USAID money to change governments in Albania and Macedonia[65] and at least $18 million from USAID[66] to operate in the West Bank and Gaza. The Soros-USAID alliance extended to other former Communist courtiers, including Romania and Macedonia, and Latin American countries, such as Colombia.[67] The OSI/OSF website occasionally listed other governments and American and foreign organizations that funnel through the OSI/OSF, especially in eastern Europe, the former Soviet republics, the Balkans, the Middle East, and elsewhere. The updating of the OSF website at the beginning of 2022 made such a listing difficult to find.

In response to my inquiries at the State Department and USAID as to why they used Soros's foundations to distribute grants at his will, with no acknowledgment it was U.S. government money, most officials claimed they had no idea this was done. One senior official at USAID volunteered when I persisted, "Soros's foundations' presence and reach in every country is wider. So, it seemed more efficient to distribute grants through them."

Perhaps. But why was Soros allowed to claim it was his money? Who did he afford with plausible deniability?

Exhaustive research would expose a few of those who used Soros's distribution channels, but not all of them. Soros's foundations, as his business operations are notoriously opaque.

Even before the fall of the Soviet Union in 1991, the West, including the U.S., decided to pretend "revisionism" had disappeared from international politics. Soros's OSI, which was already active in the former Soviet republics and eastern Europe, spent millions of dollars creating NGOs, "ostensibly to assist them in transforming their country into a more "open" and "democratic" society. This was how he transferred the "Soviet Empire" to the "Soros Empire," he bragged at a meeting at the Asia Society in 2015.[68]

Soros used his contacts with officials and public figures in the former Communist regimes—many of whom later served in the transitional governments, academia, and media, as well as scientists who received stipends from the OSI (and the U.S. government)—to sway the political, economic, and social agendas of the newly established governments. And to advance his businesses.

Soros's OSI, with U.S. backing, supported the nonviolent transition of power, known as the Velvet Revolution,[69] in what was then Czechoslovakia (November–December 1989).[70]

Next came Georgia's Rose Revolution. It culminated when demonstrators led by Soros's protégé Mikheil Saakashvili stormed the Parliament session with red roses in hand. Soros, through his foundations, spent $42 million orchestrating the demonstrations to oust the last remnant of the Soviet leadership President Eduard Shevardnadze. Saakashvili became Georgia's president for two consecutive terms (January 2004 to November 2013). Soros paid the salaries of Saakashvili and many of his ministers who had been working at the OSI.[71] The USAID and the Organization for Security and Co-operation in Europe (OSCE), which have supported many Soros initiatives, supplemented the salaries of all government officials.

Visiting Tbilisi in June 2005, Soros stated, "I'm very pleased and proud of the work of the foundation in preparing Georgian society for what became a Rose Revolution."[72]

UKRAINE

In 1995, Soros boasted to the *New Yorker* about his and his foundations' activities in Ukraine after the fall of Communism. "It was a vacuum" with "a great willingness to accept this kind of support, which would in normal times be rather intrusive," Soros said. "I mean, I can't try and do that in America. They would tell me where to get off!" Soros further exclaimed, "If this isn't meddling in the affairs of a foreign nation, then I don't know what is!"[73] However, by the time Soros made this statement, he was already meddling in U.S. domestic and foreign politics and policies. Yet, no one told him "where to get off." Why not?

Soros established the Kyiv branch of his Open Society's growing empire, branding it the International Renaissance Foundation (IRF) in April 1990. At that time, Ukraine was still part of the Soviet Union. According to the OSF's website, "By 1994, it was the biggest international donor in the country, with an annual budget of roughly $12 million."[74] It didn't stop there.

According to the OSF's webpage, "In the early 2000s, the foundation (IRF) oriented itself around European integration,"[75] pushing for Ukraine's acceptance into the European Union. But Soros didn't use his extensive influence in the EU to push very hard. Ukraine ratified the Association Agreement on September 16, 2019.[76]

The OSF's webpage also talks about "mobilizing resources to help those affected by conflict after Russia's invasion and illegal annexation of Crimea in 2014."[77] But it says nothing about Soros's role in fomenting and funding the Orange Revolution (2004–5), which was also assisted by OSCE, the State Department, and other international bodies.

On the flight from London to Kyiv, two days before Ukraine's 2004 presidential election, Soros's delegates—all wearing some orange-colored clothing items, some holding little orange flags—were brazenly debating the potential efficacy of their plans to disrupt the election. Sure enough, early evening of November 22, 2004, before the election was over, thousands of people wearing orange color items gathered in Kyiv's central square in freezing weather. Many carried professionally made signs protesting the election results, even before the counting ended, and called for a new election. The icy square was filled early the following day with small tents and thousands of additional demonstrators who were bused there overnight. An international election monitor group that questioned many of the mostly young demonstrators found out that each was offered $100 per day—at a time when the average income was $50 per month—to join the demonstration. This windfall brought in thousands of people from all over Ukraine. They were provided with individual tents, food, and warm beverages. Soros's Orange Revolution was underway. It took more than two months and two more elections before Soros's and the State Department's choice, Viktor Yushchenko, was declared the winner on January 23, 2005.

In 2013–2014, Soros funded the demonstrations of the Maidan Revolution, which ousted President Viktor Yanukovych—who was no longer useful—and supported the election of Petro Poroshenko as president. Soros also publicly lobbied the EU to invest more than €50 billion in Ukraine.

Soros-funded organizations have influenced every aspect of Ukraine's politics and public institutions. Soros's International Renaissance Foundation has invested in groups such as Transparency International Ukraine, StateWatch, and the Anti-Corruption Action Center (AntAC), to mention a few.[78] He also funded StopFake, an "anti-disinformation" organization established after the 2014 Maidan Revolution. The *Nation* reported that the group was "lauded as a model of how to combat Kremlin lies."[79] But within four years, "StopFake began aggressively whitewashing two Ukrainian neo-Nazi groups with a long track record of violence, including war crimes."[80] Allegedly, Soros was also behind StopFake's successful blocking of the Belarusian pro-Moscow government efforts to publicize the EU's and Soros's $6 billion to fund a wave of protests against the government that erupted in 2020. StopFake dismissed the allegations. However, it failed to disclose Soros's large donations to the group.[81]

Nina Jankowicz, the Biden administration's Disinformation czarina, "hosted *StopFake Episode 117*,[82] whose lead story dealt with a perennial obsession of Russian propaganda: Ukraine's volunteer battalions." The *Nation* commented, "Painting neo-Nazi paramilitaries with an extensive record of war crimes as patriots helping refugees, all while working with a "disinformation" group that turned out to run interference for violent neo-Nazi formations—that's the experience Biden's new disinformation czar brings to the table."[83] Jankowicz, who served as a consultant to the Ukrainian government, supported the "Russia collusion" lie that involved officials in Ukraine and denied the existence of Hunter Biden's laptop, which also included information on payments to the president's son.

In May 2015, Soros told the Austrian daily *Der Standard* he was willing to invest $1 billion in Ukraine because "Ukraine is defending Europe's borders . . . But above all, the country is fighting for European values such as the rule of law and freedom . . . There are concrete invest-ment ideas, for example, in agriculture and infrastructure projects. I would put in $1 billion," he declared. But this investment, according to Soros, was purely altruistic. "This must generate a profit. My foundation would benefit from this, not me personally."[84]

Soros's declaration made the headlines on CNN. However, and not for the first or the last time, Soros's spokesperson announced that the "investment would depend on the West doing 'whatever it takes' to rescue Ukraine." [85]

Soros has often been lauded for announcing large international financial contributions. However, the conditionality of many of these contributions (which Soros long ago declared were investments) or their realization was rarely, if ever, reported.

In November 2015, Soros was awarded Ukraine's Order of Freedom by the Ukrainian president he helped elect, Petro Poroshenko.[86] In 2019, Soros supported Poroshenko's reelection campaign, but Poroshenko lost to Volodymyr Zelenskyy.

By then, Soros has been deeply involved in Ukraine. His foundation also gave nearly $290,000 to the Anti-Corruption Action Center, which received $4.4 million from the U.S government.[87]

John Solomon's thorough reporting in the *Hill* revealed how Obama's Justice and State Departments and the FBI "outsourced some of its work in Ukraine" to AntAC.[88] Soros's role in that affair has yet to be explored. But don't hold your breath for any revelations. Once the war in Ukraine is settled, any evidence of possible Soros involvement will surely disappear.

Investigations showed that AntAC targeted opponents of Soros's involvement in Ukraine and, at least in one case, in 2015, "petitioned the United States Justice Department on behalf of Ukrainian civil society to dedicate the nearly $3 million in forfeited and seized assets."[89]

AntAC and the Democracy Integrity Project, also funded by Soros, played an important role in creating the infamous "Steele dossier" alleging Trump-Russia collusion.[90]

It is possible that Russian President Vladimir Putin's mention of AntAC in his public address about Ukraine—on the eve of the Russian invasion of Donbas—was an implicit threat to the Biden administration to report that he knows how Ukraine has been used by the Clinton, Obama, and Biden administrations? While he did not mention Soros by name, Putin said, "The United States directly controls the National Agency on Corruption Prevention, the National Anti-Corruption Bureau, the Specialized Anti-Corruption Prosecutor's Office, and the High Anti-Corruption Court. All this is done under the noble pretext of invigorating efforts against corruption. All right, but where are the results? Corruption is flourishing like never before."[91] He was right.

On January 19, 2022, Biden predicted "Russia will invade Ukraine" and suggested that the West's response could be more muted for a "minor" incursion." Did he imply this might be acceptable?[92]

Was Biden influenced by Kyiv's corrupt regime that for decades prospered with fraud and bribes? Or was he influenced by the sordid financial dealings of his son Hunter in Ukraine? On September 18, 2022, when President Biden was asked on *60 Minutes*[93] about "conflicts for you or for the United States" in places such as China, Russia, and Ukraine," Biden responded, "There's not a single thing that I've observed at all that would affect me or the United States relative to my son Hunter," he said, though the question was not about Hunter.

Does he fear the possibility of the reelection of President Trump would entice the Ukrainians who paid his son to spill the beans? How does Soros's influence on the Biden administration's Ukraine policy of sending billions of dollars and weapons to assist Kyiv's war against Russia instead of looking for ways to resolve the conflict peacefully? On February 26, 2022, Soros tweeted, "I have witnessed Ukraine transform from a collapsing part of the Soviet Union to liberal democracy and an open society. It has faced countless acts of Russian aggression but has persisted."[94]

While Ukraine changed its political system in 1991, it has been mired in corruption from the beginning. Soros and his Open Society Foundations have been very active in Ukraine, spending more than $180 million between 1989 and 2021 on various projects.

Matt Palumbo, who wrote *The Man Behind the Curtain*, noted that Soros also "financed Mikheil Saakashvili, the president of Georgia (2004–2013), who became governor of Ukraine's Odesa region (2015–2016), and Svitlana Zalishchuk, a former member of the Ukrainian parliament. He's also given money to Mustafa Nayyem; an MP appointed VP of Ukroboronprom, a state association of the nation's major defense conglomerates."[95]

In Davos on May 24, 2022, Soros used the opportunity to speak about open society and his role in advancing it as he declared, "The invasion of Ukraine didn't come out of the blue. The world has been increasingly struggling between two systems of governance that are diametrically opposed to each other: open society and closed society."[96]

Many share his observation that "the invasion may have been the beginning of the Third World War and our civilization may not survive it." The only way for civilization, which for Soros represents his versions of "open society," "is to defeat Putin as soon as possible."[97]

RUSSIA

In the early 1990s, Soros pumped so much cash into shaping the former Soviet republics' sociopolitical and economic structure to his liking that he bragged that the former Soviet Empire had turned into the "Soros Empire." That "Empire" did not last for very long.

In 1997 Soros's Fund Management reportedly lost some $2 billion during Russia's financial crisis.[98] This, however, did not reduce Soros's funding of OSI's activities in Russia. But in November 2015, Soros and his foundations outlived their usefulness to the former Soviets. The Putin government "branded foundations run by the financier George Soros a threat to the country's constitutional order and banned them from disbursing grants to Russian partners."[99] Putin took away his empire and forced Soros to close his OSF Moscow office. But Soros's efforts to influence Russian politics did not stop.

HUNGARY

In her article "The Gravedigger of the Left," Dr. Mária Schmidt, director-general of the House of Terror Museum and the XXI Century Institute in Budapest, noted that "when George Soros appeared in Hungary in 1984 the Soviet rule still seemed solid and indestructible."[100]

Curiously, a few days before launching his Hungarian operation, Soros criticized the Reagan administration's hardline stance against Communism. "Anti-Communism, as it is professed and practiced by the Reagan administration, runs a great risk. If we interfere in the internal politics of countries within our orbit in order to prevent them from falling into the Communist orbit, we must deny them the privilege of choosing their own form of government," Soros opined in the *Financial Times*.[101]

Per his agreement with the Hungarian Academy of Science, Soros has arranged fax machines and Western textbook deliveries to Hungarian universities and libraries. These were much prized by the Hungarians. He also provided generous grants to promising young students to study in the U.S., England, and other Western European countries. They were grateful to Soros for the exposure to democratic capitalistic systems. As the Communist regime ended in Hungary, many of his grantees became the new elite in the new democratic state, just as Soros had hoped.

However, it did not take long before several of his beneficiaries began loosening the Soros strings, distancing themselves from Soros because of his increasingly anti-capitalist, pro-Socialist rant. This started soon after the demise of the USSR, which led to the collapse of Communism in central and eastern European countries. Soros no longer preached capitalism. Instead, he ranted against it and pushed for socialism instead.

Schmidt details how in 1990, when the Communists were toppled, "Soros had already recruited a broad circle of supporters and proposed to take over Hungary's complete sovereign debt and, in exchange, asked for Hungary's industry, that is, the bulk of the country's national wealth."[102] His offer was turned down.

But Soros wanted to control Hungary's economy. He twice failed to buy Hungary's then-troubled largest retail bank, Posta Bank (OTP), for a song ($50 million). Faced with negative publicity for his attempts to exploit Hungary's troubled economy, Soros preposterously claimed he wanted to buy the bank "on behalf of his foundation and university" in Budapest.

Schmidt, who, like Hungary's Prime Minister Viktor Orban, was an early Soros grantee who soon became disillusioned, has identified his modus operandi:

> He buys influence in the world of the intelligentsia, among opinion makers in academia and the financial world, as well as in the media. He builds and takes over political parties and NGOs. He organizes them into a network and uses them as covers. He creates chaos and apprehension. He weakens incumbent powers by all available means. He cries electoral fraud, if necessary, economic hardships whenever possible, or finds some other pretext. He gets large demonstrations organized, or if they are organized by others, his people join them immediately and take over the lead.[103]

Soros's vociferous attempts to overthrow Viktor Orban, Hungary's prime minister, and defeat his Fidesz (Hungarian Civic Alliance) party, failed.

CHINA

Soros's successful collaboration with Communist regimes was not limited to the Soviets and their satellites. According to Professor Miles Yu, Deng Xiaoping, the paramount leader of the People's Republic of China (1978–1992), was "partly inspired by the Hungarian model" and began to set up China's own "special economic zones" along its southern coast." Soros used his contacts to approach Premier Zhao Ziyang, "a reformer," who "was in charge of China's economic policies" proposing to set up a Chinese branch of his OSI. Soros "received the approval in 1986" and "set up his "China Fund,"[104] initially with an annual budget of at least $1 million to support China's Open-Door policy. Not a word about "open society."

Soros told Connie Bruck about a newspaper that had called him an anti-Communist in the late 1980s. Embarrassed, Soros, who then collaborated with the KGB and their sister security services in the Eastern Bloc, vehemently protested that he was *not* an anti-Communist. Though he did use the phrase "Open Door Policy" in that interview, he was careful not to use his motto "open society." Not in China.[105]

Soros reflected on his China foundation with Michael Kaufman, portraying himself as a babe in Communist China. He told Kaufman that he hoped, and was promised, the Foundation's Beijing office would run "by Chinese for Chinese," independent of the government. It was only in early 1989 that Soros learned that the foundation was run by "state security operatives."[106]

It is hard to believe that the worldly Soros, who already operated in other Communist-run countries, was that naïve. Or was he foolish enough to think he could outsmart the Chinese and use one of his programmatic interventions to influence or undermine the Communist regime?

Soros was forced to shut down the Foundation's Beijing office just before the Tiananmen Square demonstrations in May 1989.

According to Yu, the "security forces used the Soros operation in China as a potent weapon to purge the Zhao wing of economic reformers, who were purged in the aftermath of the Tiananmen Square massacre."[107]

We have yet to find out why and on whose behalf Soros was allowed to operate in the Communist bloc freely and how Soros and his foundations' operatives served the KGB and its subsidiaries and aided their supporters in the West.

Soros's organizations have been meddling for years in the domestic affairs of independent nations to sway political alliances and remove leaders who won't toe the Sorosian line. Under the guise of anti-corruption and justice reform programs, often backed by the U.S., the UN, the EU, the World Bank, and other national and international organizations, the OSF's consultants influence local laws, economic developments, and politics by "developing potential strategic litigation options" through their Open Society Justice Initiative.[108]

Despite the OSF's claim to operate independently, their regional and country-based activists get their marching orders from the organization's headquarters. The OSF's representatives always enjoy access to the political leadership, including presidents and prime ministers, government officials, opposition leaders, and, of course, the local media. In many countries, they are treated as representatives of an empire, the Soros Empire.

Or is it Sorostan?

6

SOROS'S ANTI-ISRAEL CRUSADE

George Soros has done more to vilify the state of Israel and to fund anti-Israel propaganda machines than almost any individual on the face of the earth. The idea that by criticizing George Soros, I am anti-Semitic, or I'm indicating anti-Semitic tendencies, when George Soros is himself one of the great enemies of the Jewish people and the state of Israel, turns the world on its head. Just because he's nominally of the Jewish faith does not mean he gets a free pass on being criticized.

–DAVID FRIEDMAN, FORMER U.S. AMBASSADOR TO ISRAEL, 2016[1]

IN HIS 1995 BOOK *Soros on Soros*, George Soros declared that Zionism "doesn't appeal" to him because it is "the founding of a nation [Israel] where the Jews are in the majority." For Soros, "being a Jew [is] being in a minority." He also argued that sometimes, in response to persecution, Jews choose to "identify with their oppressors" and even "try to become like them."[2]

Soros told the *New Yorker* in 1995, "I don't deny the Jews their right to a national existence—but I don't want to be part of it."[3] Since then, he has done a lot to undermine the Jewish State of Israel.

Soros's distorted version of Middle Eastern history serves to better

140

jibe with his idea of the "poignant and difficult case" of Israel, another nation, like the U.S., of "victims turning perpetrators." Soros echoes the virulently anti-Semitic, anti-Israel propaganda in the Arab newspapers that retroactively erase and reverse historical facts daily, to Israel's self-defense against the PLO, Hamas, and Islamist/ Arab terrorists' repeated attempts and commitment to annihilate the Jewish State, to Nazi atrocities: "Jews were the victims of the Holocaust, which can itself be ascribed, in part, to a process of victims turning perpetrators: Hitler rose to power by capitalizing on a wave of resentment caused by an onerous peace treaty and runaway inflation," Soros wrote.[4]

Sure, the Germans hated the Treaty of Versailles, but that was not the reason for Hitler's anti-Semitism and his decision to exterminate the Jews.

In *The Bubble of American Supremacy,* Soros wrote that "Jews resorted to terrorism against the British in Palestine in order to secure a homeland in Israel. Subsequently, after being attacked by Arab nations, Israel occupied additional territory and expelled many of the inhabitants. Eventually, the Arab victims also turned perpetrators, and Israel started suffering terrorist attacks."[5]

Soros's interpretation seriously downplays and denies the number of Arab invasions and the brutal tactics that led Israel to occupy the territories these attacks were launched from in the first place. And as for being "expelled," many of those Arab people left of their own accord because the surrounding Arab nations ordered them to go and because Muslim edicts forbid[6] interaction with the Jews. But Soros wasn't through.

He went on to accuse Israel of making "the habit of retaliating vigorously" against Arab attacks and "enlarging the circle of Arab victims . . . The situation deteriorated," he claimed, until the victimized Palestinians resorted to "suicide bombings" which "became commonplace."[7]

Soros's warped account of the Palestinian attacks on Israel could have been written by Noam Chomsky or originated with Yasser Arafat, who, like Soros, excelled in playing the victim card. For whatever reasons, Soros conveniently ignores the bald truth that the Arab plan has always been to kill all the Jews as soon as possible and take over the Jewish State's territory. That plan has never changed.

Israel's successful defense against terrorism, especially preemptive actions, is never appropriate in Soros's book. Instead, Soros's foundations have increased support for the Palestinians and doggedly continued attacking Israel.[8]

In November 2003, as Operation Iraqi Freedom was underway and anti-American and anti-Israeli/anti-Semitic demonstrations spread throughout Europe, Soros spoke at a meeting of the Jewish Funders Network in New York. The Jewish Telegraphic Agency reported that Soros claimed, "The policies of the Bush administration and the Sharon administration contribute" to the rise of anti-Semitism. He assured his audience that the world would return to not hating Jews once Bush and Sharon were removed from office. "If we change that direction, then anti-Semitism also will diminish. I can't see how one could confront it directly," he said.[9] Ira Stoll reported in the *New York Sun* that Soros declared, "Israel 'likely' was a big but secret reason for America's war in Iraq."[10]

Unlike Soros, and uncharacteristically, when the Palestinian leader of the Islamic Jihad, Sheikh As'ad Bayyud al-Tamimi, spoke about the Gulf War, he said nothing about Israel. Was the Sheikh ill-informed?

"Bush and Thatcher have revived in the Muslims the spirit of *Jihad* and martyrdom," al-Tamimi said and promised that all Muslims "will fight a comprehensive war and ruthlessly transfer the battle to the heart of America and Europe. . . Islamic *Jihad* has the forces to carry out strikes in Europe and America."[11] Nothing about Israel or the Jews.

Soros's comments did not sit well with quite a few public figures:

"Let's understand things clearly: Anti-Semitism is not caused by Jews; it's caused by anti-Semites," said Elan Steinberg, senior advisor at the World Jewish Congress. "One can certainly be critical of Bush policy or Sharon policy, but any deviation from the understanding of the real cause of anti-Semitism is not merely a disservice, but a historic lie."

Abraham Foxman, [then] national director of the Anti-Defamation League, called Soros' comments "absolutely obscene." Fuming, Foxman added, "It's a simplistic, counterproductive, biased, and bigoted perception of what's out there. It's blaming the victim for all of Israel's and the Jewish people's ills."

"Furthermore, Foxman said, "If he sees that his position of being who he is may contribute to the perception of anti-Semitism, what's his solution to himself—that he give up his money? That he close his mouth?" Foxman asked.[12]

The *New York Daily News* ran an editorial describing Soros as a "man who lacks even a remotely balanced view of history and the nature of evil. He has demeaned the Holocaust and placed moral responsibility for anti-Semitism on its victims rather than its perpetrators." Former Democratic representative Eliot Engle called Soros's statements "morally reprehensible" and advised his "hear no evil/see no evil" Democratic brethren that "people shouldn't kiss up to" Soros simply because "he wants to give money."[13] Such a comment today would "cancel" Engle from all progressive Democrat public forums forever.

Yet, when Soros claimed that the U.S. had invaded Iraq to some degree on behalf of Israel, the Democratic leadership kept silent. Maybe they didn't hear him say it. Maybe they were in line at the bank, waiting to deposit another one of Soros's massive donations as he went public with that gem.

Soros has been funding groups rejecting the existence of Israel as the Jewish State, such as al-Haq[14] and others, as detailed in this chapter. These include Israeli-Jewish and Israeli-Arab Leftist groups, as well as media. His largesse extends to Palestinian-led groups everywhere, promoting boycotts, divestments, and sanctions against Israel (BDS), anti-Israel, pro-Palestinian Jewish, Christian, and even Muslim organizations in the U.S. Several have links with the U.S.-designated Palestinian terrorist groups and support the elections and appointments of anti-Israel proponents in the U.S. government and international organizations.

In *Bad Investment*, which thoroughly examined the role of Soros's funding in increasing tensions between Israel and the Palestinians, Alexander H. Joffe and Gerald M. Steinberg documented the opacity and secrecy of Soros's funding of anti-Israel, pro-Palestinian groups. Indeed, lack of transparency and secrecy has been the staple of Soros's organizations.[15]

In August 2016, after Barack Obama became president, Soros's OSF's and OSI's documents were released by DCLeaks.com. A 2009 Soros's Open Society Institute paper clarified that Soros "began an ambitious project to persuade Europe and the U.S. to hold Israel accountable for violations of international law." However, Soros "did not want to be open about its advocacy," as is clearly evident from another leaked document, a 2013 summary of the OSF's "Palestine/ Israel International Advocacy Portfolio." It says, "For a variety of reasons, we wanted to construct a diversified portfolio of grants dealing with Israel and Palestine . . . building a portfolio of Palestinian grants and in all cases to maintain a low profile and relative distance—particularly on the advocacy front."[16]

Eli Lake, a former senior national security correspondent for the *Daily Beast* and *Newsweek*, fittingly remarked, "Let's take a minute here to savor the irony. An outfit that promotes the 'open society' is shielding its efforts to influence public policy. It's true that plenty of foundations take a similar sub rosa approach to funding advocacy work in Washington. But those foundations are not named for Karl Popper's famous defense of liberal democracies. It's enough to make you wish there was a new Open Society Foundations to expose the old one."[17]

The OSF's "Palestine/Israel International Advocacy Portfolio" goes on to say, "Our theory of change was based on strengthening the advocacy efforts of civil society organizations and platforms in order to maintain sustained and targeted international advocacy that would oblige the international community (mostly Europe and America) to act and to hold Israel accountable to its obligations under the international law." And again, it emphasized the need for secrecy to avoid "politically motivated investigations."[18] By whom?

Soros's foundation decided the Israeli response to Hamas's 2008–2009 rocket barrage of Israeli cities and towns was an excellent opportunity to "hold Israel accountable." In 2010, Soros's Washington, DC office arranged a meeting with Richard Goldstone, who led the UN "fact-finding mission." They provided him with "evidence" that Israel had deliberately bombarded civilians in Gaza. Much of the so-called evidence was submitted by Soros-funded pro-Palestinian groups and publicized by, among many others, the Palestinian media center I'lam, which between 2003 and 2016, according to the OSF's leaked documents, received $1,083,000 million from Soros, is demonizing Israel, "promotes boycott campaigns, and engages in political advocacy against Israel," accusing it of ethnic cleansing.[19] As expected, Israel was condemned. But a year later, on April 1, 2011, Goldstone, in an op-ed titled "Reconsidering the Goldstone Report on Israel and War Crimes" in the *Washington Post*, recanted, saying, "If I had known then what I know now, the Goldstone Report would have been a different document."[20]

When did Soros begin funding Palestinian NGOs and anti-Israel groups? Hard to tell since Soros has insisted on secrecy, and his foundations notoriously lack transparency.[21] However, his funding of anti-Israel, and anti-Zionist organizations is not a new development.[22]

In 2007, the *New York Review of Books* published Soros's "On Israel, America, and AIPAC," in which he protested that "attitudes toward the Jewish community are influenced by the pro-Israel lobby's success in suppressing divergent views."

Soon after J Street, which advocates "alternative" views of Israel, was established, the Soros family, through their foundations, gifted some $750,000 over three years (2007–2010) to the new anti-Israel lobby.[23] They have continued their support ever since.

From 2001 to 2015, OSF and other Soros-related foundations funneled nearly $10 million to various liberal Jewish and Palestinian groups to intensify anti-Israel propaganda.[24] In 2010, for example, the OSF pledged $100 million over ten years to Human Rights Watch (HRW), whose funds were dwindling despite its 2009 efforts to raise funds in, of all places, Saudi Arabia.[25] The $470,000 grant from a Saudi billionaire in 2012 was given to HRW after its Executive Director Kenneth Roth "signed a memorandum of understanding with al-Jaber containing language that said the gift could not be used for LGBT rights work in the region." [26] Writing in the *New York Post* on September 13, 2020, Gerald Steinberg, president of the Jerusalem-based NGO Monitor, maintained that Soros's Open Society Institute "exclusively supports advocacy groups . . . such as Adalah, Peace Now, Breaking the Silence, Gisha and Yesh Din," who oppose the existence of the State of the Jewish people and "campaign internationally to undermine the elected governments of Israel."[27]

Steinberg added, "George Soros, whose own biases are well-established," has extended his "control over HRW." Indeed, Soros funded the expansion of the HRW staff "to reposition it as a major international player and restore its influence as an arbiter on universal human rights."[28]

Soros turned the HRW—which for decades has been promoting the Palestinian cause, including support of the BDS and demonizing Israel—into a powerful organization with a reported annual budget of more than $129 million.[29]

The HRW and Amnesty International—another beneficiary of Soros's largess—work closely with the United Nations Human Rights Council (UNHRC). OSF's president since January 2021 is George Soros's decades-long friend, Mark Malloch-Brown,[30] whose involvement with the OSF began in 2009 and who held executive positions at the UN. Malloch-Brown is well-known for his anti-Israel, pro-Palestinian, anti-American, and pro-globalization views.

Soros's support extends to Christian evangelists to amplify anti-Israeli voices in the U.S. He has chosen to fund fringe American Christian evangelists. In *Hijacked: How George Soros and Friends Exploit Your Church*, John Aman, director of communications at D. James Kennedy Ministries (DJKM), unveils that "Soros has been giving six-figure grants to the Telos Group, which takes evangelical influencers on expense-paid tours to Israel and brings 'Israeli and Palestinian leaders and activists' to speak in the U.S., as 'part of a propaganda or cognitive war against Israel.'"[31]

As Aman points out, "Soros has been an 'angel investor' for Telos."[32]

Additional reports identified the Foundation to Promote Open Society, which awarded Telos $713,500, half of the start-up funding it needed for its first three years (2008–2011). Soros followed up with $1.6 million to Telos "from 2012 to 2019."[33] "Telos, which leverages evangelical celebrities to reach the evangelical community, may be eroding support for Israel among younger evangelicals," Aman reported. "A recent survey registered a 42% drop since 2018 in support for Israel among evangelicals aged 18–29. Some say the drop is not that steep, but it's still a cause for alarm."

"George Soros might consider it a return on investment. Dubbed 'one of Israel's most dangerous and powerful enemies in the Western world,' Soros is at least getting his money's worth," Aman concluded.[34]

While Soros's financial speculations do not always succeed, he must be pleased with his investments promoting anti-Israel, pro-Palestinian radical groups. These anti-Israel activists are also the disciples of radical progressive, neo-Marxist, and other Leftist anti-American agendas that Soros promotes.

Soros has been funding progressive-Left, anti-Israel, pro-Palestinian individuals' training and "continuing education" programs for decades. The "graduates" go on to occupy positions in academia, nonprofits, and media and win local and national elections with further support from Soros. Though not always disclosing the identity of their funder.

Take Rep. Rashida Tlaib, the Michigan progressive Democrat, a member of the Squad. In December 2018, investigative reporter Joe Schoffstall documented that "Tlaib did not report any income in the amount of $85,307 on financial disclosure forms submitted as she was running for office, . . . as required by the House Ethics Committee. . . . Candidates are required to disclose the name of groups and organizations that provide their sources of income."[35] However, she was listed as a 2016 "Leadership in Government" fellow of the OSF.[36] (Another recipient that year was Gigi B. Sohn, who was nominated twice by President Biden to head the FCC in October 2021, but as of August 2022, she was still waiting to be confirmed.[37]) Page 97 of the OSF's

321-page 2017 Form 990-PF reported she was paid an $85,307 expenditure.[38] In her 2018 financial disclosure, she listed an income of $68,307 stipend for the aforementioned Leadership in Government Fellowship but did identify the OSF as the source.[39] "Tlaib was paid $139,873 by Soros's group in 2016, tax forms show. Between 2016 and 2017, Tlaib received a total of $225,180," the *Washington Free Beacon* reported. [40]

Soros's "Leadership in Government Fellowship" is a finishing indoctrination program. According to OSF's 2021 statement, which has since changed,[41] the program aim is "to increase involvement of disenfranchised urban communities of color with their local governance process by creating a community benefits strategy for equitable development and creating a leadership training for impacted residents focused on negotiation skills and identifying leverage at the local level."[42]

Tlaib, a virulent anti-Israel, pro-Hamas activist who supports boycotting Israel, comparing it "to boycotting the Nazi regime,"[43] and claims Israel is an apartheid state and has a "map in her office where Israel is covered with a sticky note that says 'Palestine.'"[44] She was widely criticized for her ugly antisemitic dog-whistling, even by the Left-leaning Anti-Defamation League's head, Jonathan Greenblatt.[45] However, like other progressive-Left Democrats who share Tlaib's repugnant views, such as Rep. Ilhan Omar, she can count on Soros to fund her reelection campaign in 2024.

Another example of a vitriolic anti-Israel, pro-Palestinian former Soros grantee is Michelle Alexander, who was among the first grant recipients from the Soros Justice program in 2005. As "a Soros Justice Fellow," she received a stipend of $35,000 to $97,000—"to complete a book called *The New Jim Crow* [46] about the so-called war on drugs and mass incarceration as the defining racial justice issues of our time."

Since then, Alexander has been affiliated with numerous Soros-funded organizations, such as the Ella Baker Center for Human Rights, which promote "color Justice" and "nationally organize and coordinate demonstrations for illegal-alien amnesty and manage voter-registration campaigns for Democratic candidates."[47] She also supports the BLM movements,[48] including Dream Defenders. This NGO and Interfaith Peacebuilders openly "support and promote the mission of the Popular Front for the Liberation of Palestine (PFLP)," a designated terrorist organization by the U.S.,[49] EU,[50] Australia,[51] Canada,[52] Japan,[53] and Israel.[54]

In 2018, shortly after Soros increased its investment in the *New York Times* by more than $3 million, the paper hired his disciple, Alexander.

Using the pretext of commemorating Martin Luther King Jr. Day, the *New York Times* "Sunday Review" published Alexander's op-ed, "Time to Break the Silence on Palestine," an unhinged anti-Israel, anti-Semitic, pro-Palestinian rant.[55] Constitutional/criminal lawyer Alan Dershowitz fittingly described the article as "one of the most biased, one-sided, historically inaccurate, ignorant and bigoted articles ever published by that venerable newspaper."[56] Both the *Times* and the Alexander article were widely criticized.

Vitriolic smears against Israel are nothing new to the *NYT*. What was new about this slanted article was that it displayed how George Soros's propaganda machine works.

While the "paper of record" brags about its transparency, the 10,000-word fawning profile of the billionaire in the *New York Times Magazine* in July 2018,[57] shortly after he made his additional investment in the paper, did not bother to disclose Soros's holdings in the paper. Similarly, it failed to disclose Michelle Alexander's affiliation with Soros.

According to the US Securities and Exchange Commission (SEC), in May 2018, Soros Fund Management LLC purchased 126,400 shares worth $3,046,000 in the New York Times Company. This investment increased Soros's holdings in the newspaper from the 470,000 worth of shares he bought in 2007.[58] Though this was not a big investment, it is nonetheless significant when the investor is Soros.

In 2011, Dan Gainor, then vice president of business and culture at the Media Research Center, exposed Soros's funding/investment strategy "in media both in the United States and abroad."[59] By then, Soros had invested more than $48 million "in media properties, including the infrastructure of news—journalism schools, investigative journalism, and even industry organizations."[60]

Gainor further revealed "that Soros' influence doesn't just include connections to top mainstream news organizations such as NBC, ABC, The *New York Times*, and *Washington Post*. It's bought him connections to the underpinnings of the news business. The *Columbia Journalism Review*, which bills itself as 'a watchdog and a friend of the press in all its forms,' lists several investigative reporting projects funded by one of Soros foundations."[61]

Since then, Soros has directly and indirectly (often through other family members) greatly expanded his political investments, aka "charitable" funding, to influence major media outlets in print and online, including book publishing, films, documentaries, TV, radio, and social media. But not American-based social media—an industry he has come to criticize of late loudly.

It is important to remember that Soros is not a philanthropist. Take his word for it: "Philanthropy goes against the grain because our civilization is built upon the pursuit of self-interest, not on any preoccupation with the interests of others," he said, according to his website in 1994.[62]

Dershowitz pointed out that "the most outrageous aspect of the [Alexander] column is the claim by Alexander that Martin Luther King Jr. inspired her to write it. But he was a staunch Zionist who said, "When people criticize Zionists, they mean Jews. You are talking anti-Semitism."[63] This, however, is to be expected from anyone funded by Soros, especially since he has expressed his loathing of the Zionist Jews who live in Israel (i.e., most Israelis) because they are "nationalist."

The Soroses often use other organizations to pass through funding to groups they support. The San-Francisco–based Tides Foundation is a public charity that, through donor-advised funds, acts as a fiscal sponsor to smaller charities. It is regularly used as a pass-through distribution center for many Left-leaning foundations, including the OSF and other Soros-related not-for-profit groups.

Soros is free to spend his money as he pleases. Under the pretext of "open society," he has been using his nonprofit business—which he calls "political philanthropy"[64]—to invest in promotions of political indoctrination, social engineering, and revolutionary policies that, while not always successful, cause social, economic, and political upheaval.

Between 1998 and 2018, for example, Tides received $22,389,530 million from the "George Soros Foundation to Promote Open Society and his OSF. In 2019 Soros's OSF gave Tides $4.4 million.[65]

Tides, which serves as an intermediary to many Left-leaning charities[66], regularly passes funds from Soros's various foundations to organizations promoting progressive/socialist causes in the U.S., including a few pro-BDS, anti-Israeli groups, such as CODEPINK,[67] a leader of U.S.-based anti-Israel BDS campaigns, and Grassroots International,[68] which funds NGOs active in the Arab-Israeli conflict with ties to the PFLP, which we discussed earlier.[69]

The Jerusalem-based NGO Monitor is probably one of the most reliable sources on "non-governmental organizations (NGOs), their funders, and other stakeholders, primarily in the context of the Arab-Israeli conflict."[70] Their website lists Palestinian NGOs that thrive on anti-Israeli, anti-Zionist, and anti-Semitic activities. Many are linked with the radical-Left, Marxist, woke organizations in the U.S. that are also beneficiaries of Soros's largess. Keep in mind that Palestinian NGOs lack transparency. Information about their funders is mostly available from their foreign donors, such as European, U.S., and major international organizations, sometimes directly from some Soros foundation or indirectly through other organizations he funds that transfer money to Palestinian groups with close links to the PFLP and that were identified and some designated as terrorist organizations by the Israeli government's report in February 2019 titled "Terrorists in Suits: The Ties Between NGOs Promoting BDS and Terrorist Organizations."[71] In October 2021, the Israeli government added six more NGOs with links to terrorist organizations, a few with both direct and indirect funding from a Soros foundation.[72]

Here are a few examples of such NGOs:

DREAM DEFENDERS[73]

Dream Defenders initially formed in 2012 to "protest . . . Florida's 'Stand Your Ground Laws' in the wake of the Trayvon Martin shooting."[74] It soon morphed into one of the key groups in the Black Lives Matter movement and also exists "to serve the anti-Israel BDS movement."[75]

"Dream Defenders' Education Fund " is a "partner" of Tides, which carries the organization's mission and Dream Defenders' logo on its website. Tides regularly pass funds from Soros's various foundations, not only to organizations promoting progressive/socialist causes in the U.S. but also to groups such as Dream Defenders, which Tides lists on its website as a "Social Venture."[76]

Remember that Dream Defenders backs the PFLP, whose tactics include the murder of Israeli civilians, bombing, shooting, and even plane hijackings.[77] Dream Defenders also demanded the release of Ahed Tamimi, who was "charged with assaulting a soldier, incitement to terrorism, among at least nine other charges." Tamimi has commented, "Whether it is stabbings or martyrdom operations or throwing stones, everyone must do his part and we must unite in order for our message to be heard that we want to liberate Palestine." This is the kind of person Dream Defender celebrates.[78]

In January 2015, *Ebony* magazine posted an article titled "Dream Defenders, Black Lives Matter & Ferguson Reps Take Historic Trip to Palestine," which featured Black Lives Matter co-founder Patrisse Cullors. According to Ahmad Abuznaid, a fervent anti-Israel, anti-Semitic Palestinian-American, the trip highlighted in the article "represented a chance to bring the power of Black organizing to Palestine." At the time of this article, Abuznaid was Dream Defenders' legal and policy director. It was he who organized the ten-day trip, as well as another trip in 2016. Participants included Dream Defender and BLM activists, and the trip was guided by a former PFLP terrorist who was released in 1985 by the Israelis after serving seventeen years in prison in a prisoner swap of "1,150 Arab prisoners in exchange for three IDF soldiers held by the Popular Front for the Liberation of Palestine-General Command."[79]

In August 2016, various organizations involved in Black Lives Matter released a platform called the Movement for Black Lives (M4BL) statement. In particular, the document contained a section called "Invest/Divest," which accused Israel of "genocide" and of being an "apartheid state."[80]

Dream Defenders likens the PFLP's activities against Israel to their struggle against America. "They [the PFLP] want to be free from global imperialism. They want liberation. They want equal rights. Just like the Dream Defenders."[81] Not surprisingly, Dream Defenders' 2016 alternative school curriculum featured the PFLP as one of nine "heroes" that should be used to teach "rebellion" strategies and tactics.[82]

"In 2014, Dream Defenders created an 'educational' campaign called 'Blacked Out History,' which was a tribute to 'overlooked heroes' in history," says a writer at legalinsurrection.com. "One of the heroes is the PFLP. The heroes are celebrated by creating artwork in their commemoration and teaching about them in schools."[83] At some point, Dream Defenders offered the "BLACK OUT: History, Rebellion Curriculum Toolkit" for "grades 6–11 (common core compatible)," saying, "The curriculum toolkit was created by traditional and radical educators in Dream Defenders membership body. Rebellion features nine organizations, including Left Roots, FRELIMO, Brown Berets, Sandinistas, Young Lords, Zapatistas, South African Student Movement, Black Panther Party, and the Popular Front for the Liberation of Palestine."[84]

In 2020, Dream Defenders SunDDay School hosted radical Marxist Angela Davis,[85] a member of both the Communist Party USA and the Black Panther Party, who in 1979 was awarded the Lenin Peace Prize in Moscow.[86]

ADALAH

Adalah is a supposedly "independent" Israeli/Arab NGO that uses "legal warfare (Lawfare) campaigns against Israel in international courts and other legal forums. It aims to convince foreign governments to sever diplomatic relations with the only democracy in the Middle East, slandering Israel as a racist and undemocratic state, and partners with anti-Israel BDS (boycotts, divestment, and sanctions) groups."[87] Adalah, like Dream Defenders, maintains working relations with the PFLP.[88, 89]

Adalah's branch in the U.S., the Boston-based Adalah Justice Project (AJP),[90] is supported by the OSF with mostly undisclosed funds. The OSF's 2016 hacked emails included a document from the Open Society's Arab Regional Office dated August 6, 2015, detailing some of Soros's funding of "civil society groups in Israel" between 2001 and 2015. Adalah's share was $2,688,561.[91]

Another major U.S. charity that supports many Palestinian groups, including BDS activists with ties to the PFLP, is the Rockefeller Brothers Fund,[92] which in June 2018 authorized the Tides Center to give a $160,000 grant to AJP.[93]

OSF and its well-funded proxies, such as Human Rights Watch (HRW) and Amnesty International, promote the "elimination of Israel as the nation-state of the Jewish people" by supporting the Palestinians' bogus claim of the "right of return."[94] In July 2020, The Begin-Sadat (BESA) Center for Strategic Studies and Bar-Ilan University published a report exhibiting Human Rights Watch's "fundamental and consistent bias against Israel."[95]

HRW's local branches continue to side and collaborate with Palestinian groups, clearly disregarding the evidence that these groups promote BDS and collaborate with the PFLP, Hamas, and the Palestinian Islamic Jihad (PIJ), an Iranian-funded and run[96] group—all U.S.-designated terrorist groups.[97] The OSF, which denies supporting BDS groups directly or indirectly, disregards this evidence.

Despite widely available information,[98] including official statements linking these and other Palestinian NGOs to terrorist groups designated by the U.S., EU, Israel, and Canada, the EU and several European nations, the UN and other American and European foundations never stopped funding PFLP and PFLP-linked NGOs.

Dream Defenders', al-Haq, the Palestinian Center for Human Rights, and Adalah's anti-Israel activities are no secret. They have been publicizing them for years. And the OSF often hypes these groups on its "Grantee Spotlight" page.

A feeble attempt at plausible deniability was made by Soros spokesperson Michael Vachon, who, in 2019, while denying Soros's organizations' support of BDS groups, admitted that at times they simply don't know how their support is used: "The foundation cannot track every project connected to every organization that it has supported over the decades" he stated.[99]

Such indifference is not a defense for giving money to organizations with known links, including financial ties, with terrorist groups. It is time the OSF, Soros, his family members, and his foundations' boards of directors, as well as their affiliated NGOs and INGOs, are held accountable, especially since Soros, a well-known micromanager, has stated clearly, "I run one of the largest foundations in the world and I am personally, deeply involved."[100]

Because of the advocacy veneer of "human rights," environmentalism, and other popular causes, NGOs' investment, more accurately, "support" of terrorist groups, is particularly pernicious. Professionals, businesses, and financial institutions can be attacked as succumbing to simple "greed." Not so the NGOs whose unquenchable thirst for funding is exploited by Soros to further his agenda.

Moreover, the OSF and its well-funded proxies never fail to condemn Israel for its effort to curb the activities of Palestinian terrorist groups masquerading as human-rights charities, including, as already shown, those designated as "terrorists." Like parrots, they repeat the Palestinians' lies about Israel. Their phrasing is then used by the UN, the EU, Germany, and Biden's State Department to further criticize Israel.

Many countries, international organizations, and large foundations have been duped over the decades by Palestinian leaders and organizations who misuse vocabularies used in non-Arabic-speaking countries and Western democracies to mislead, whitewash, and mask their real mission and intentions to eliminate the Jewish State. However, their statements in Arabic reveal their true agenda. Yet, for more than seven decades, political interests of anti-Israel, and pro-Palestinian entities have bred willful blindness that has allowed the masquerading Palestinian leaders and NGOs to raise billions of dollars.

In addition to the Open Society Institute (OSI), funders of this PFLP network include the EU, the European Commission, the World Bank, UNDP, Austria, Belgium, Italy, Sweden, Norway, Ireland, France, Spain, the Netherlands, Switzerland, Japan, and the Basque Government, together with a long list of U.S. and foreign foundations, NGOs and private organizations.[101]

In 1965, shortly after Yasser Arafat founded the Palestine Liberation Organization, he established the Martyr Fund to pay individual terrorists to attack Israeli civilians. This strategy continued after the Palestinian Authority (PA) was established in September 1993.[102] The PA never stopped paying monthly "salaries" (several times the average monthly Palestinian wage[103]), even to dead Palestinian terrorists and their families.

This "pay for slay" strategy did not stop even after President Donald Trump signed into law the Taylor Force Act (2018), which blocks U.S. funding to the PA as long as they pay the terrorists and their families. The PA refused to comply with the law and lost $165 million in U.S. aid.[104] Moreover, PA chief Mahmoud Abbas, in a speech to PLO's Central Council, which aired on the official PA TV, cursed U.S. President Donald Trump: "May your house be destroyed."[105] He was followed by the Palestine Liberation Organization (PLO) Executive Committee member, the longtime darling of the progressive anti-Israel Democrats in the U.S., Hanan Ashrawi, who accused the Trump administration of using "cheap blackmail as a political tool." She declared, "The Palestinian people and leadership will not be intimidated and will not succumb to coercion."[106] Soros-funded J Street joined them, condemning the Trump administration's move as a "moral outrage and a major strategic blunder."[107]

Israel's 2020 anti-terror legislation, like all countries with similar laws, prohibits banks from banking transactions whose purpose is to pay a reward for an act of terror, and it was met with a similar reaction.[108] PA head Abbas, as other Palestinian leaders have on several occasions, reiterated that the PA will not stop paying the terrorists. "They are our martyrs and prisoners and the injured, and we will continue to pay them, as we have done since 1965," Abbas said.[109] In 2020, in an apparent effort to elude detection, the PA transferred over a billion Israeli shekels (approximately $400 million at the time) to the PLO, which paid the terrorists $157 million.[110]

As soon as President Biden took office in January 2021, he decided to reverse his predecessor's policies, including blocking aid to the Palestinians. To get around the Taylor Act, the heavily Soros-influenced Biden administration, with state secretary Anthony Blinken as his chief foreign policy advisor, found a way to continue to fund Palestinian terrorism with $130 million indirectly. This despite the General Accounting Office (GAO) report, published on March 31, 2021, which did not reverse its finding that "the U.S. government," since 1993, . . "has provided more than $6.3 billion" of American tax dollars in assistance to Palestinians in the West Bank and Gaza, [but] "had not properly vetted all the recipients to ensure they were in compliance with the U.S. anti-terrorism laws."

On January 17, 2022, Adam Kredo of the *Washington Free Beacon* reported on the State Department's admission "to Congress in March 2021 that the Palestinian government spent at least $151 million in 2019 on the pay-to-slay program." In addition, "$191 million was spent on 'deceased Palestinians referred to as "martyrs.""""[111]

However, the GAO report did little to diminish the Biden administration's eagerness to fund the Palestinians, especially since it reversed former President Trump's decision to comply with the 2018 bipartisan law, the Anti-Terrorism Clarification Act (ATCA), known as the Taylor Force Act, which "bars the federal government from providing taxpayer aid" to the PA directly or through the United Nations Relief and Works Agency (UNRWA) for Palestinian refugees in the Near East,[112] as long as the PA continues paying terrorists to kill Israelis.

The PA refused to change its policy of providing stipends to Palestinian terrorists "who are serving out sentences in Israeli jails . . . in accordance with the severity of their crime—the more Israelis they murdered, the more money they and their families receive."[113]

In early April 2021, a few days after the GAO report was published, U.S. Secretary of State Antony Blinken announced the U.S. was restarting its funding to the Palestinians, giving $75 million in U.S. "economic and development assistance in the West Bank and Gaza; $10 million for peacebuilding programs through the U.S. Agency for International Development (USAID) (and) $150 million to UNRWA." But in late May, while visiting the PA headquarters in Ramallah, Blinken announced, "We are in the process of providing $360 million in urgent support to the Palestinian people." That includes $5.5 million in immediate relief to Gaza, which Hamas rules. His announcement will mean $32 million of "global emergency" aid to UNRWA,[114] thus violating the Taylor Force Act but boosting the PA's legendary corruption and facilitating the activities of Palestinian NGOs against Israel.

On March 27, 2022, Blinken, on yet another pilgrimage to visit PA president Abbas in Ramallah, emphasized the Biden administration's desire to revitalize US relations with the PA and "pledged to continue American financial aid to the PA," as well as " $500 million annually" for humanitarian assistance.[115]

On February 1, 2022, the London-based Amnesty International posted one of its most unfounded malicious slanders against the Jewish state of Israel: "Israel's Apartheid Against Palestinians: Cruel System of Domination and Crime Against Humanity."[116]

In response, the International Legal Forum tweeted:

> The Amnesty International report accuses Israel of 'apartheid,' just as the Human Rights Watch report, which preceded it, is just the latest intensified attack in these organizations' longstanding & relentless campaign of lawfare and vilification against the State of Israel.

Written under the guise of 'international law and human rights,' this baseless report, which whitewashes Palestinian terror and blatantly calls for the dismantlement of the Jewish state, is replete with malicious lies, gross distortions of truth, and fabrications of law while peddling unhinged hate, incitement, and racism.

In short, this report is tantamount to a 'blood libel' against the Jewish state and deserves to be placed in the dustbin of antisemitic history.

At the end of the day, a lie told a thousand times, is still a lie.

Perhaps Amnesty International, which has been beleaguered by charges of institutionalized racism, would be better served getting its own house in order first, instead of casting aspersions against Israel.

—Arsen Ostrovsky, Chair & CEO
International Legal Forum[117]

The organization's secretary-general, Agnès Callamard, also serves as director of the OSF-sponsored Columbia University Global Freedom of Expression, and special advisor to Columbia's president, Lee Bollinger. Columbia did not fire her despite her false claim in a 2013 tweet that Israel murdered Yasser Arafat.[118] It took Amnesty eight years "to back down from this serious and baseless accusation."[119] But neither Callamard nor Twitter deleted her lie.

Callamard does not like the U.S., either. In 2020, in her role as a UN special rapporteur on an extrajudicial summary, or arbitrary executions (August 2016–March 2021),[120] she accused the U.S. of unlawfully killing Qaseem Soleimani, the Iranian arch-terrorist who led the Islamic Revolutionary Guard Corps (IRGC), which killed hundreds of Americans and others.[121]

A day before Callamard released her claims, Israel's Ministry of Foreign Affairs issued a statement condemning the report. Here is an excerpt: "The report consolidates and recycles lies, inconsistencies, and unfounded assertions that originate from well-known anti-Israeli hate organizations, all with the aim of reselling damaged goods in new packaging. Repeating the same lies of hate organizations over and over does not make the lies reality, but rather makes Amnesty illegitimate."[122]

The statement pointed out that Amnesty is using "double standards and demonization in order to delegitimize Israel . . . Amnesty criticizes the very existence of the State of Israel as the nation-state of the Jewish people, and effectively denies its right to exist at all . . . Amnesty's report effectively serves as a green light for the perpetrators and others to harm not only Israel, but Jews around the world."[123]

Moreover, it condemned the report for denying "the State of Israel's right to exist as the nation state of the Jewish people. Its extremist language and distortion of historical context were designed to demonize Israel and pour fuel onto the fire of antisemitism."[124]

The Israeli NGO Monitor website has been listing and regularly updating the identities of contributors and donations made to all Palestinian and pro-Palestinian Israeli organizations for decades.[125] For example, on October 22, 2021, Israeli defense minister Benny Gantz designated six Palestinian NGOs as terrorists.[126] According to Israel's counterterrorism office, the U.S. was notified in advance and "received intelligence information about the matter." Yet, the State Department's spokesperson not only denied that Israel had given an "advance warning" of the designation but also implied these PFLP-affiliated NGOs are indeed working for "human rights, fundamental freedoms, and a strong civil society [which] are critically important to responsible and responsive governance." He also used this opportunity to condemn the Israeli government, yet again, for its plans to build new homes for its Jewish citizens in the West Bank[127] while conspicuously ignoring the government's allocation of 1,600 housing units for Palestinians in the same region.

The designation was not the first to identify these misleadingly called NGOs' ties with the PFLP, PIJ, and Hamas, all internationally designated terrorist groups. In 2019, Israel's Ministry of Strategic Affairs published the abovementioned report, "Terrorists in Suits," which showed how these NGOs have been masquerading as civil society organizations. This report provided detailed information on "the ties between NGOs promoting BDS and terror organizations."[128]

A good example is the Gaza-based NGO Palestinian Center for Human Rights (PCHR), which claims to be "dedicated to protecting human rights, promoting the rule of law and upholding democratic principles in the Occupied Palestinian Territories."[129] Raji Sourani, PCHR founder and director, "served 'a three-year sentence [1979–1982]'" for his membership in the PFLP.[130] In 2012, he was denied a US entry visa.[131]

In 2020, NGO Monitor exhaustively documented the PCHR's activities in delegitimizing the Jewish State of Israel. These are coordinated with the Palestinians' efforts toward promoting anti-Israel propaganda, disinformation, economic warfare, and Lawfare to criminalize Israeli businesses and current and former Israeli government officials and officers of the Israeli Defense Forces. The PCHR is a major actor in the Palestinian efforts to delegitimize Israel, using Lawfare to "galvaniz[e] international pressure and punitive measures against Israel in the legal realm."[132] It "has multiple links" to PFLP.[133]

In July 1976, together with members of the German Revolutionary Cells (*Revolutionäre Zellen*)[134]—a particularly violent Leftist terrorist group—the PFLP's External Operation (PFLP-EO) group, which was used for terrorist attacks outside Israel, hijacked Air France Flight 139 on its way from Tel-Aviv to Athens and Paris. The terrorists boarded the plane in Athens and seized it, along with 254 passengers and crew, of whom 106 were Jews and Israelis. They flew to Entebbe, Uganda's capital,[135] where dictator Idi Amin welcomed the hijackers. There, the terrorists released 148 non-Israelis/Jews. The rest of the passengers, the Israelis/Jews and the Air France crew, were kept as hostages at the airport terminal and "threatened with death." The airport was raided by Israeli Defense Forces' commandos, who killed the Palestinian and German terrorists. Yonatan (Yoni) Netanyahu, who commanded the raid, was killed. His brother Benjamin (Bibi) Netanyahu, later became Israel's prime minister.

In 2001, PFLP terrorists assassinated Israel's tourism minister,

Rehavam Zeevi,[136] and in 2014 attacked by stabbing and shooting thirty worshipers wearing prayer shawls and phylacteries during the morning prayers at the Har Nof synagogue in Jerusalem, killing six. The police killed the two PFLP terrorists.

These PFLP's terrorist attacks against Israelis were widely reported by the international media, as were the PCHR's organizational and staff members' links with the terror group.[137] Yet, two of Soros's foundations have been funding the PCHR, whose website lists the Foundation to Promote Open Society among its funders,[138] and its 2017 annual report lists "Foundation Open Society" as a contributor.[139] Not surprisingly, the amount was undisclosed.

The October 2021 designation of six Palestinian NGOs as terrorists highlighted their fraud and identified them as "an arm of the [PFLP] leadership" that works for "the liberation of Palestine and destruction of Israel."[140] Israel's security forces investigations revealed that "the six NGOs provide a place of employment for PFLP agents, including militants, who get paid regular salaries." Under the directive of the Popular Front's leadership, "their offices serve as quarters for the terrorist organization's missions and activities."[141]

Moreover, these "organizations forged documents to raise money and to continue raising them. . . . The organizations represent a lifeline for the Popular Front."[142] They are raising money to finance terrorist attacks against Israeli civilian targets, as well as to reward the terrorists and their families, pay for propaganda, recruit operatives willing to join the fight physically, and enlist others to raise and launder money for the PFLP.

Using open sources, including social media, the NGO Monitor identified 13 Palestinian NGOs linked to the PFLP and more than "70 staff and board members, as well as other officials who hold positions in both the NGOs and the PFLP."[143]

"The EU and European governments have provided more than $200 million to these groups during this time without conducting proper due diligence or adherence to counter-terror regulations," remarked Anne Herzberg, legal adviser for NGO Monitor.[144]

As soon as Israel announced the new designations, the vast anti-Israel media network echoed the propaganda of the newly designated Palestinian NGOs' accusations against Israel's "occupation and oppression," calling the designation "a sinister, unprecedented, and blanket attack on Palestinian human rights defenders and civil society organizations," accusing Israel of trying to silence criticism of its [alleged] human rights abuses.

Such statements were made immediately after the designation was announced by Amnesty International, HRW, and FIDH, vilifying the Israeli government for its "appalling and unjust decision" and "an attack on the international human rights movement."[145]

Another OSF grantee, the Israeli pro-Palestinian B'Tselem, condemned Israel for designating the "Palestinian human rights organizations as 'terror organizations,'" claiming "It is an act characteristic of totalitarian regimes, with the clear purpose of shutting down these organizations." [146]

In the U.S., the Soros-funded J Street called the Israeli designation "a deeply repressive measure that seems designed to outlaw and persecute important Palestinian human rights groups" and called on the Biden administration to "make clear to the Israeli government that this is totally unacceptable and anti-democratic, and call on them to reverse the decision." Other Jewish and Israeli Left-leaning, progressive organizations followed suit, as did the virulently anti-Israel, pro-Palestinian Rep. Ilhan Omar. She tweeted, "There must be immediate consequences from the US and the international community for this brazen act."[147] Other pro-Palestinian progressive Democrats in Congress followed suit, even introducing a draft "resolution condemning Israel's actions as 'a repressive act' designed to criminalize and persecute important Palestinian human rights organizations."[148]

On October 26, 2021, shortly after the Israeli designation of the six NGOs as terrorists was announced, the United Nations' human rights high commissioner, Michelle Bachelet, condemned Israel and demanded an immediate reversal of the designation. She claimed the designation was "an attack on human rights defenders, on the rights to freedoms of association, opinion, and expression, and on the right to public participation."[149]

A few days later, Bachelet used the opportunity of presenting the HRC's annual report to double down her harsh criticism of Israel.

Countering the false accusations, Israel's ambassador to the U.S. and the United Nations, Gilad Erdan, lambasted the body's Human Rights Council (HRC) in remarks at the special session that was held to present an annual report that included severe criticism of Israel. "The voices of the victims of the terrible crimes against humanity that we have already seen in the first decades of this century cannot be heard over the obsession of the so-called Human Rights Council with targeting Israel," Erdan said.[150]

After tearing up the UNHRC's annual report to all UN member states, Erdan said, "Since the establishment of the council 15 years ago, it has decided to blame and condemn Israel, not 10 times like Iran, or 35 times like Syria. No, the Human Rights Council has attacked Israel with 95 resolutions. Compared to 142 against all other countries combined."[151]

HRC president Nazhat Shameen Khan presented the report, noting that the forum had held three special sessions in the past year on Myanmar, Afghanistan, and the Israeli-Palestinian issue.

"The Council decided to urgently[152] establish an ongoing independent, international commission of inquiry to investigate in the occupied Palestinian territory, and in Israel, all alleged violations of international humanitarian law and all alleged violations and abuses of international human rights law leading up to and since 13 April 2021," Khan said.

She also recognized the group of nations that were elected to serve on the Human Rights Council: Argentina, Benin, Cameroon, Eritrea, Finland, Gambia, Honduras, India, Kazakhstan, Lithuania, Luxembourg, Malaysia, Montenegro, Paraguay, Qatar, Somalia, the United Arab Emirates, and the US.

In his remarks, Erdan argued that the HRC inquiry on Israel and the Palestinian territories "completely disregarded the hostilities of one party to the conflict—Hamas—while shifting all the blame to the other party—Israel."[153]

"It was on this stage, at this very body, that the very right of the Jewish people, to have a national home, was itself declared to be racist," Erdan concluded, recounting the 1975 General Assembly speech by Israel's then-UN ambassador, Chaim Herzog, who physically tore up a copy of a resolution condemning Zionism that was later revoked.[154]

"This is exactly what should be done to this antisemitic, distorted, one-sided report," Erdan said. "For just as that 1975 resolution, equating Zionism with racism, was itself a gross form of anti-Jewish racism, which has no place in this international body, so too, the Human Rights Council's obsessive anti-Israel bias, embodied, once again, by this report, should have no place in anybody concerned with human rights, security or peace."[155]

Since Biden took office, the anti-Israel voices at the UN, in the Biden administration, and in the U.S. Congress have gotten louder. In December 2021, HRW ranked "Israel's apartheid and persecution against millions of Palestinians" at the top of their report.[156] It was ranked even higher than "Philippine Pres Duterte's 'drug war' executions," "China's mass detention of Uyghur Muslims in Xinjiang," and the "Taliban attack on women's rights," according to a tweet from HRW executive director Kenneth Roth.[157]

"Human Rights Watch has previously been accused of bias, lax fact-checking, collusion with the US government and accepting donations from foreign governments," the *Jerusalem Post* reported. In addition to funding from Soros, according to the *Intercept* in 2020, "HRW accepted a $470,000 donation from a Saudi real estate magnate they 'had previously identified as complicit in labor rights abuse'—under the condition that the donation not be used to support LGBT advocacy in the Middle East and North Africa."[158]

HRW had to return the money. In the summer of 2014, Hamas increased its attacks against Israel, firing thousands of rockets from the Gaza Strip on Israeli civilian targets. Israel responded. The war lasted

51 days, during which Roth published more than 400 tweets filled with vitriol, labeling Israel's defensive activities "unlawful" and "war crimes." He even retweeted an advertisement published in the *New York Times* and the *Guardian* equating "Nazi genocide" with "the massacre of Palestinians in Gaza."[159] And like his benefactor, George Soros, Roth blamed Israel, on Twitter, for the rise in European anti-Semitism, which he claimed was "in response to Israel's conduct in Gaza war."[160] Roth's anti-Israeli stance was no secret. In 2009, Roth's virulent anti-Israel advocacy led HRW's founder Robert L. Bernstein, to denounce its leadership (Roth) in the *New York Times*[161]. Bernstein criticized HRW for condemning Israel, "the repeated victim of aggression," (with) "far more" human rights abuses than in other countries in the Middle East ruled by "authoritarian regimes with appalling human rights records." When Roth announced his resignation in May 2022[162], Gerald M. Steinberg, a professor of politics at Bar Ilan University, and president of NGO Monitor, told the *Jerusalem Post*, "In his 30-year reign as head of H.R.W., Ken Roth has obsessively distorted and exploited human rights to demonize Israel." Steinberg pointed out that Roth's "language reflects a deeply personal hostility to Judaism and Jewish self-determination, regardless of policies, and he has hired many staffers who share this antipathy, amplifying the structural bias against Israel in the UN and other institutions."[163]

Israel also played a role in internal friction in Mr. Roth's group. Its founder, Robert L. Bernstein, wrote an op-ed for the *New York Times* in 2009, distancing himself from the organization because of what he called its portrayal of Israel as a "pariah state."

After decades of hostile, deceitful, and fabricated HRW, Amnesty, and associated anti-Israel NGOs reports on Israel, these groups should have been discredited because of unswerving political bias. Furthermore, their reports on other countries should also be questioned. But that is unlikely to happen as long as Soros and other anti-Israel, and often anti-U.S., entities keep funding them. Meanwhile, their false reporting strengthens the UN Human Rights Council's baseless accusations of Israel's made-up violations against Palestinians. Such accusations contributed to the HRC's resolution to urgently establish its first-ever, open-ended "commission of inquiry,"[164] targeting Israel for alleged "all alleged violations of international humanitarian law and all alleged violations and abuses of international human rights law," and also "all underlying root causes of recurrent tensions, instability and protraction of conflict, including systematic discrimination and repression based on national, ethnic, racial or religious identity," aka "apartheid" against the Palestinians. And in the best UN tradition, Navanethem "Navi" Pillay, a bitter critic of Israel, was appointed to head the inquiry.

Previously, the UN had appointed Pillay, a South African jurist and radical pro-abortion activist, as the UN high commissioner for human rights (2008–2014)![165]

In. 2014, when Israel responded to Hamas's bombardment of its cities and towns with thousands of rockets it fired from civilian areas (schools, hospitals, markets, etc.) in Gaza, Pillay, a fanatical Israel-hater, incredibly declared Israel was "guilty of not sharing Iron Dome (The Iron Dome, "an effective, truck-towed, multi-mission mobile air defence system developed by Rafael Advanced Defence Systems[166]) with Hamas in order to protect Palestinian civilians."[167] Accusations from hypocrites such as Pillay that Israel's response to Hamas's attacks was "disproportionate"[168] were repeated by the usual anti-Israel, Soros-funded groups, such as Amnesty International, B'tselem, and Human Rights Watch.

The Geneva-based UN Watch protested Pillay's appointment, saying she "has been actively campaigning against Israel, signing letters to President Biden urging him to end Israeli 'oppression,' and signing boycott appeals that call to 'Sanction Apartheid Israel!'"[169]

U.N. Watch and 42 members of Congress from both parties asked State Secretary Blinken to prioritize efforts to shut down the UN's first-ever open-ended investigation targeting one country, Israel.[170] They are not holding their breath.

OSF's and other Soros entities' direct and indirect support and direct and indirect funding of Palestinian individuals and groups that make no secret of their resolve to destroy the Jewish state of Israel indicates a disregard for U.S. and international laws banning support of terrorists. But neither Soros nor his foundations, nor many other governments and organizations funding known Palestinian terrorist groups, seem to care. Why should they? Most large international donors have never been held accountable for funding internationally designated Palestinian terrorist groups.

Soros's assistance to the Palestinian cause seemed to have influenced State Secretary Blinken's decision to drop the Trump administration's demand that the PA stop paying salaries to terrorists serving time in Israeli prisons for murdering Israelis as a condition for aid.[171]

Tom Nides, Biden's ambassador to Israel, openly displays his sympathy for the Palestinians. In a webinar with a pro-BDS group, he told the audience, "Your agenda is where my heart is," and according to *Front Page Magazine,* stated that "the real problem with the Palestinian Authority funding terrorism is that 'it gives the "haters" an excuse not to support the PA based on the argument that it is 'paying for people who killed Jews.'"[172] Nides is affiliated with the Soros-funded J Street and the pro-Palestinian Americans for Peace Now. He opposes the Jewish presence in the east part of Jerusalem, the nation's historic capital, and is "infuriate[d]" by Israeli cities and towns in Judea and Samaria.[173]

The Soros effect on Soros's lackey Blinken and Soros's staffed State Department was highlighted in February 2022, when the Bureau of Democracy, Human Rights and Labor (DRL) announced a NOFO [notice of funding opportunity] of $987,654 for projects reporting human rights violations by Israel in West Bank and Gaza to "collect, archive and maintain human rights documentation to support justice and accountability and civil society-led advocacy efforts, which may include documentation of legal or security sector violations and housing, land, and property rights. Local organizations with a proven ability to implement programs"[174] will be the recipients of the funds. This project could not have been better tailored to select the radical-Left, anti-Israel, Soros-affiliated groups.

On March 16, 2022, as the barbaric Russian invasion of Ukraine was advancing, the negotiations on a new nuclear deal with Iran were advancing, and China was about to sign a security deal with the Solomon Islands to increase its military buildup in the South Pacific, State Secretary Blinken found it necessary to talk with the two leading anti-Israel, Soros-affiliated NGOs. In his tweet about his talk with HRW's Ken Roth and Amnesty International's Agnes Callamard, Blinken wrote, "Human rights are central to U.S. foreign policy. We support the important work of human rights defenders."[175] What was the urgency? Was it to coordinate increasing pressure on Israel to not retaliate for increased Palestinian terrorist attacks?

7

SOROS IS NO DREYFUS

*It's a mitzvah (a righteous act)—not "anti-Semitism"—
to castigate George Soros for his radical attempts to
undermine public safety and the American republic.*[1]

—RABBI DOV FISCHER, FEB 1, 2022

*There is an actual, genuine international conspiracy against me. So, when
I am challenging… issues for an Open Society throughout the world, like
discrimination, racial exclusion, totalitarian regimes, I am not conspiring,
I am openly bringing forward the mission of my life. And my enemies
learn from each other. And they attack together using similar techniques.*[2]

—GEORGE SOROS, AUGUST 11, 2020

GYÖRGY SCHWARTZ was born in Budapest, Hungary, in 1930 to an
assimilated Jewish family. According to Robert Slater's 1997 unauthorized
biography of Soros, the blue-eyed and blond young György would "beam"
when other children would tell him, "You don't look Jewish."[3] In 1936,
as anti-Semitism grew in Hungary, the family name changed to Soros[4]

Soros, the self-proclaimed agnostic,[5] stated, "I am proud of being a Jew—although I must admit it took me practically a life-time to get there."[6] This is not surprising since he grew up in an assimilated home with an "anti-Semitic mother" who was "ashamed of being Jewish," he told the *New Yorker*. "Being Jewish was a clear-cut stigma, a disadvantage, a handicap—and, therefore, there was always the desire to transcend it, to escape it," he said.[7] Elsewhere, Soros wrote that in his early life, he had "suffered from the low self-esteem that is the bane of the assimilationist Jew. This is a heavy load that I could shed only when I recognized my success," he noted.[8]

His youngest son, Alexander, told the *New York Times Magazine* that for "many years," his father was "not eager to advertise his Judaism." but "had always "identified firstly as a Jew." His father's philanthropy," he claimed, "was ultimately an expression of his Jewish identity."[9]

His son's claim sounds a bit odd, considering Soros's lavish funding of pro-Palestinian, anti-Israel, and BDS groups to exclusively demonize and delegitimize the Jewish State of Israel by fabricating slanderous reports they widely disseminate in the media and submitting them to international organizations that use the falsity to denounce Israel. (As described earlier.) At the same time, Soros and his many followers cynically weaponized the Jewish religion he was born into to cast him as the victim of worldwide anti-Semitism.

In 1995, Soros told Connie Bruck: "I don't think that you can ever overcome anti-Semitism if you behave as a tribe . . . The only way you can overcome it is if you give up the tribalness." However, as Soros explained, he gave up his tribalness a long time ago by choosing the universal concept of "open society."[10]

With this attitude, one would expect Soros to be not only tolerant but also forthright and inclusive of Jews and judge them, to paraphrase Martin Luther King, "by the content of their character." Not so.

When looking for people for the board of his Moscow foundation in the early 1990s, he took a trip with the most promising of them, only to find out "they were all too old and too Jewish! And not acceptable."

He laughed as he added, "I mean, you can't be that Jewish in Russia. So I told them, 'You can't have more than one-third Jews on the board.'"[11]

But as criticism for Soros's meddling in the domestic affairs of independent countries, including the U.S., grew, Soros chose to exploit the religion he was born into—which he renounced—repeatedly declaring he's agnostic. Yet, he has been using the religion he was born into as a flag of convenience, claiming "victimhood" whenever he could exploit it one way or another. And the more he seems to indulge in his alleged victimhood, the more he prompts anti-Semitism.

His narcissistic impulses have been honed into a very effective and reliable weapon to discredit opponents and intimidate potential critics while trivializing and stoking anti-Semitism.

Here are but a few of many examples:

Former New York City mayor Rudy Giuliani, an ardent supporter of Israel, tweeted in December 2019 (before his Rudy Giuliani @RudyGiuliani was canceled), "Soros has funded many enemies to the State of Israel, including groups that support BDS, who's [sic] ultimate goal is to destroy the Jewish homeland.

"Those who oppose these groups are not only better Jews, but better people than him. Most certainly not anti-Semitic."[12] Giuliani's statement was accurate. But the Left-leaning media and Soros propagandists in the U.S. and elsewhere instantly attacked Giuliani, labeling his speech "dangerous," "antisemitic, and "racist," among many other things.[13] In August 2020, as BLM hoodlums were rioting in the streets of American cities; looting and burning stores; attacking police officers, police stations, and courts; and wreaking havoc everywhere, Giuliani appeared on Martha MacCallum's *The Story* and dared to condemn Black Lives Matter (BLM), whose co-founder Patrisse Cullors, boasted in a July 2015 video "we are trained Marxists. We are super-versed on, sort of, ideological theories."[14]

Giuliani likened BLM's defacing of national monuments and destruction of statues of American leaders and heroes to tactics used by

Lenin and Mao to rewrite history. Giuliani was right.

Detailing BLM's violent activities, Giuliani noted their calls to murder police officers and their organized looting. He argued: "This is an illegal organization, and their intent is to overthrow our government," and he called on President Trump to declare BLM a "domestic terrorist organization." Trump should have listened to Giuliani, but either did not understand the threat posed by BLM or was too busy fighting the trojan horses who had penetrated the White House and the administration.

Giuliani also admonished the Democrats and Soros for supporting the Leninist anarchist group. "I can't understand why major American corporations are giving money to Black Lives Matter, which is run by three Communists who are avowed terrorists," he said. He called Soros for "wanting to destroy America so we become socialists because it's all part of a socialist theory to bring down this country."[15] Giuliani was promptly vilified as an anti-Semite.

When Giuliani directly addressed Soros for "using a religion you don't seem to accept as a shield and a sword against all criticism," the media frenzy that followed proved Giuliani right. He was labeled "racist" and accused of spreading "classic antisemitic tropes."[16] Giuliani was not intimidated and continued making similar public statements until CNN, Fox News, and most TV and other media outlets banned him from the air.

In another instance, during the heated 2021 election race in Virginia, where the race for governor and other office holders was fueled by millions of dollars from Soros, when the Republican gubernatorial nominee, Glenn Youngkin, commented on the New York-based billionaire's meddling in the state's politics, he was instantly accused of anti-Semitism. A Democrat Congresswoman's tweet, "Evoking George Soros as a shadowy funder is an anti-Semitic conspiracy theory," made it to the Leftist major U.S. media outlets and was widely cited by the international media.[17]

In response to the Democrats' progressive-Left dog whistle "criticizing Soros is anti-Semitic,' the president of Caucus for America, Rabbi Aryeh

Spero, issued a statement saying that Soros is used by the Left "not because he is Jewish but because he is Soros, Soros being the most high profile and effective opponent today of American traditional values . . . As is well documented," the Rabbi continued, "he is by far the primary funder of radical Leftist candidates and groups vowing to transform America into a transnational entity." Moreover, he added that it is "ironic and disingenuous casting Mr. Soros as a symbol of Jewish peoplehood when, in fact, Mr. Soros has spent a lifetime working against Israel's defense and Jewish survival and needs. He has been proud of his disassociation from the Jewish community." The Rabbi also noted, "No person is beyond criticism simply because he is a member of a minority community."[18]

Yet, anyone daring to criticize Soros's policies and funding of organizations and individuals who promote his agendas is guaranteed the Leftist media's Pavlovian condemnation as an anti-Semite.

That happened to Senator Marco Rubio (R-FL)[19], on August 7, 2022, when he twitted, "The democrats just blocked my effort to try & force Soros backed prosecutors to put dangerous criminals in jail." Mentioning Soros—who just a week earlier boasted in the *Wall Street Journal* of his backing "reform-minded prosecutors"—was enough to create a barrage of criticism: "Marco Rubio, what is a Soros-backed prosecutor? Do you mean Jewish?"[20] Rubio's "assertion that Soros, who is Jewish, secretly controls a network of powerful decision-makers," was promoting an anti-Semitic conspiracy theory" was a typical comment, one of many labeling Rubio as an anti-Semite.

Tom Cotton (R-AR) was also labeled anti-Semitic after he gave an important speech on the alarming rise of anti-Semitic attacks on the floor of the U.S. Senate. The Senator had the hutzpah to point out that anti-Semitism "festers even on elite college campuses, which incubate the radical Boycott, Divestment, and Sanctions movement—a movement to wage economic warfare against the Jewish state." Furthermore, he pointed out that anti-Semitism is festering "in so-called Washington think tanks like the Quincy Institute (QI)." (QI was discussed in

Chapter 6.) Senator Cotton did not mention Soros by name, but the media got the message. The headline of *Haaretz*, the Israeli Left-leaning daily—and *New York Times'* partner—screeched, "Sen. Tom Cotton accuses Soros-funded think tank of fostering antisemitism."[21]

The Senator was right to point out that the Soros-funded QI—an isolationist, "blame-America-first" money pit for so-called scholars—has been asserting "that American foreign policy could be fixed if only it were rid of the malign influence of Jewish money." He was also right to point out that QI is not only promoting anti-Israel and anti-Semitic policies but also employing known pro-Iran and Israel haters, such as QI's cofounder and executive vice president, Trita Parsi, [22, 23, 24] whom we discussed in Chapter 6.

More recently, as the opposition to his well-funded political agenda for a globalist progressive socialist world—especially support of illegal immigration into Europe and the United States—has increased, so have his son and heir Alexander, and his supporters (some funded by him) allegations[25] and surrogates' allegations that his opponents are anti-Semites. In April 2017, after the Orban government amended a law tightening regulations on foreign universities operating in Hungary, which restricted the activities of Soros's Central European University in Hungary, Soros initiated a massive international media campaign accusing the government of limiting "free-speech and liberalism," and lobbied the EU Commission to launch "an infringement procedure against Hungary."

The Commission "referred Hungary to the court of justice."[26] Hungary's minister of human capacities, Zoltan Balog, declared, "We are committed to use all legal means at our disposal to stop pseudo-civil society spy groups such as the ones funded by George Soros."[27] Soros protested, as did the U.S. Department of State, American politicians, and the international media. In October 2020, after three years of a relentless campaign against the new regulations, the European Court of Justice (ECJ) ruled in favor of the CEU, declaring, "The conditions introduced by Hungary to enable foreign higher education institutions to carry out their activities in its territory are incompatible with EU law."[28] By then, however, the CEU had relocated to Vienna. Throughout this time, Soros's many supporters and beneficiaries claimed that the motive behind the Orban government's actions against the CEU and the OSF was anti-Semitism.[29]

While anti-Semitism is not new in Hungary or elsewhere, Soros and his entourage have been using the tactic of victimhood, claiming anti-Semitism whenever his well-publicized activities and policies face opposition. By doing so, he has contributed to cheapening anti-Semitism.

Frustrated by his failed efforts to defeat Hungary's Fidesz Party; the reelection of its leader and antagonist, Viktor Orban, as prime minister; and the new laws to curb his political influence through his OSF and his Central European University, Soros has conducted a massive media propaganda campaign[30] denouncing Orban and his government, as corrupt and "Anti-Semitic!" and complaining that the Orban government opposes Soros's activities and plans mainly because he is Jewish.[31] No wonder when Orban was reelected in April 2022, he gleefully declared victory over the "International Left, Soros Empire, and the Mainstream Media"![32]

Captain Alfred Dreyfus was one of the few Jewish officers in the French military. He was a secular, assimilated, patriotic French Jew who loyally served his country. In 1894, he fell victim to an anti-Semitic conspiracy that falsely accused and convicted him of treason. Exposés of evidence that Dreyfus was a victim of prevalent antisemitism in the French military caused a public outcry, which Emile Zola led. It took 12 years until Dreyfus was exonerated, reinstated, promoted, and knighted. "Dreyfus reenlisted and fought as a reservist for the French army in World War One."[33]

Soros, unlike Dreyfus, is loyal only to himself. His tremendous wealth has allowed him to buy politicians and influence domestic and international politics, which he advances through various organizations. The religion he was born into has nothing to do with his political actions.

Soros personifies his agenda and should be held responsible for his efforts to force his globalist, neo-Socialist plan on the U.S., Israel, and a host of other countries. Acknowledging his meddling has nothing to do with anti-Semitism. But you can count on him and his coterie to claim victimhood and to further trivialize anti-Semitism.

8

CALLING THE TUNE

He who pays the piper calls the tune

SOROS'S FUNDING OF THE ELECTIONS of Democratic candidates for local and national offices, including presidential candidates, has become legendary, allowing him to influence their decisions. However, as Hillary Clinton's and the Biden family's corruption has revealed, he was not alone.

According to the *Federalist*, the 2020 IRS tax filings of the Soros-funded Democracy Integrity Project listed a payment of close to a million dollars to a former British intelligence agent who concocted the "Steele dossier" used to promote President Donald Trump's "Russia collusion" hoax.[1] Earlier, in April 2019, the *Daily Caller* revealed that Democracy Integrity Project's 2017 tax filling showed it paid $3.8

million to Fusion GPS and Christopher Steele, "more than three times what the DNC and the Clinton campaign paid Fusion GPS and Steele during the 2016 presidential campaign to investigate Donald Trump's possible ties to Russia."[2]

The 2016 leaked documents, discussed in a previous chapter, show that in addition to his personal, business, and family contributions, Soros has also been channeling money through the complex network under his Open Society umbrella to dozens of 501(c)(3) and (c)(4) charities to promote his political agenda. The documents detailed how he poured "hundreds of millions of dollars . . . into the effort to transform the legal and media environment touching on elections."[3]

Soros, his family's, and their foundations' enormous direct contributions, as well as those made through nonprofit organizations supporting the elections of Hillary Clinton, John Kerry, Barack Obama, Joe Biden, Kamala Harris, and other Democratic candidates, have been widely covered by the media.[4] However, by miscalculating Donald Trump's successful run to the White House, Soros shorted the equity market and lost nearly $1 billion.[5] (You probably won't see *that* trumpeted by the liberal media.) Add this humiliation to Soros's vehement opposition to Trump, whom he has called an "imposter" and his administration a "Danger to the World," as Soros's impetus to use all available means to depose Trump while he was in office and to ensure that he never returns to the Oval Office.[6]

Accurate information about the total amount of the Soros empire's direct and indirect funding of elections in the U.S. (and elsewhere) is unavailable. For reasons unknown, the IRS seems to agree with Soros that restrictions on campaign contributions do not apply to his political investments, aka his political philanthropy. By 1995 the *New Yorker* had already written that Soros was "a consummate gamesman, adept at finding tax loopholes and operating in gray areas where oversight is scant and maneuverability wide. Indeed, the sums he managed *not* to pay the I.R.S. for many years put his present giving in a slightly different light. And the fact that he is perceived by many who have dealt with him as an autocratic master manipulator does, of course, make his spending many hundreds of millions of dollars to promote the cultivation of open society a heady paradox."[7]

The IRS code forbids nonprofits from intervening "directly or indirectly . . ., in any political campaign on behalf of (or in opposition to) any candidate for elective public office.[8] So, until not long ago, OSI/OSF website stated, "George Soros' private political activities are wholly separate from the Open Society Institute." It claimed, "OSI is a nonpartisan, nonpolitical entity in accordance with U.S. laws for tax-exempt organizations. Soros, as a private individual, is entitled to use his after-tax personal funds to support political candidates or parties within the parameters of U.S. election law. Any public statements on political issues are also made solely in his personal capacity. The Open Society Institute is not consulted or otherwise involved, and OSI is neither able nor permitted to comment."[9] (By 2021, the OSF had revamped and scraped the website, updating, changing, and deleting older postings.) But as Soros had on occasions implied, nothing in his life is wholly separate from everything else. "There can't be two George Soroses, right?" he asked Connie Bruck. "There can only be one, right?"[10]

While Soros invested heavily in the election of past and current Democratic office holders, he also lavishly donated to establish a chain of nonprofit progressive-Left organizations that served as "echo chambers" for appeasement and "America Last" abroad and radical neo-Marxist policies at home.

Soros invested millions of dollars in supporting the "defund the police" movement and a garden variety of "social justice" initiatives, individuals, and groups, increasing their visibility and influence. Paying homage to Soros, Democrat presidential candidate Joe Biden, in an interview on *NowThis News*, on July 8, 2020, called for defunding the police.[11] On June 9, 2020, Democratic senator Kamala Harris praised Los Angeles's mayor's efforts to defund the police. "I applaud Eric Garcetti," she reassured George Stephanopoulos on ABC's *Good Morning America*.[12] On the same day, Harris even promoted raising funds for the Minnesota Freedom Fund to bail out George Howard, a forty-eight-year-old black from Minneapolis, who was out on a $1,500 bond in a domestic assault and whose previous conviction barred him from carrying firearms, who was "charged with . . . second-degree murder for allegedly shooting Luis Damian Martinez Ortiz, 38, during a road-rage incident on I- 94." Harris tweeted, "If you're able to, chip in now to the @MNFreedomFund to help post bail for those protesting on the ground in Minnesota." The *New York Post* detailed Harris's help in raising the bail-out money. Howard was released, only to be charged two months later with "two counts of second-degree murder."[13] Her since-deleted tweet was archived for posterity.[14]

***

Arabella Advisors is one example of how Soros and his friends circumvent reporting their political investments/contributions. However, Capital Research Center was able to document Arabella's $1.7 billion distribution for the 2020 election.[15] According to the CRC report: "A 2018 document reveals the Leftist billionaire granted $300,000 to Co-Equal Action via Sixteen Thirty Fund (one of Arabella's "sister" organizations) to "support work to enhance congressional effectiveness and oversight" from his 501(c)(4) Open Society Policy Center—almost certainly referring to Co-Equal's alleged campaign to illegally fund House Democrats' climate witch hunt."

Arabella Advisors, a for-profit consulting firm established in 2005, also operates as an intermediary, distributing contributions to Left-leaning organizations and individuals.[16] In February 2020, Arabella's CEO, Sampriti Ganguli, clarified the role of intermediary organizations: "It is hard for very large foundations to give money to grassroots organizations. Sometimes a large foundation will need three years of audited financials in order to make its governance requirements. When foundations work via an intermediary, those intermediaries can more effectively get money to, say, a changemaker at a school in rural Mississippi," she said.

Moreover, the company's "four nonprofits known as the 'sisters,' all run from its swanky headquarters in downtown Washington." Through these four groups—the Sixteen Thirty Fund, the New Venture Fund, the Hopewell Fund, and the Windward Fund—Arabella oversaw the distribution of at least $3.3 billion to untold numbers of Leftist activist groups "that fight for the Left on a wide array of public policies, including court-packing, environmentalism, gun control, and abortion."[17]

In 2018, for example, "Demand Justice" was established as a non-profit by Brian Fallon, the former spokesperson of Hillary Clinton's 2016 presidential campaign, specifically to defeat Trump's Supreme Court nominees. "Mr. Fallon sowed the seed of Demand Justice by speaking at a 2018 meeting of the Democracy Alliance; a secretive donor group co-founded by George Soros, who pledged millions in support." Instead, as Walter Scott, the president of the Capital Research Center, described in the *Wall Street Journal,* Arabella's Advisors were used as the intermediary to transfer the money to Demand Justice. "Such politicized nonprofits defy the average American's understanding of philanthropy, but Left-wing donors have for years invested $100 million or more in 501(c)(3)s every cycle to register Democratic-leaning voters." Scott explained how using Arabella's services allows "liberal donors to bypass "the tax regime" and its "constraints" on charitable giving, presumably including limits on political activity and financial disclosure requirements."[18]

Also, in 2018, Soros, who holds "environmental justice" high on his agenda, "granted $300,000 to Co-Equal Action via Sixteen Thirty Fund to 'support work to enhance congressional effectiveness and oversight' from his 501(c)(4) Open Society Policy Center—almost certainly referring to Co-Equal's alleged campaign to illegally fund House Democrats' climate witch hunt."[19]

In November 2021, Politico reported that Arabella's sole 501(c)(4), the Sixteen Thirty Fund—which according to the IRS, "provides for the exemption of two very different types of organizations . . . Social welfare organizations: Civic leagues or organizations not organized for profit but operated exclusively for the promotion of social welfare, and Local associations of employees, the membership of which is limited to the employees of a designated person(s) in a particular municipality, and the net earnings of which are devoted exclusively to charitable, educational or recreational purposes"[20]—assisted "Democratic efforts to unseat then-President Donald Trump and win back control of the Senate" using "massive get-out-the-vote and issue advocacy campaigns" as well as "attack ads against Trump and vulnerable Republican senators."[21]

Hayden Ludwig, CRC's senior investigative researcher, reported on January 25, 2022, that Soros's funding caused the watchdog group Government Accountability & Oversight to file "ethics complaints alleging that House Democrats broke a prohibition on private financing of official congressional business." He said that "Arabella's goal appears to be to help the U.S. Justice Department prosecute climate 'crimes,' according to the complaints."[22]

Ludwig reminded us that because a "clean energy revolution" was on the agenda of presidential candidate Joe Biden, he promised to "pursue [polluters] to the fullest extent permitted by law and . . . seek additional legislation to hold corporate executives personally responsible—including jail time when merited."[23]

"Soros has spent on district attorney campaigns in Florida, Illinois, Louisiana, Mississippi, New Mexico, and Texas through a network of state-level super PACs and a national '527' unlimited-money group, each named a variation on 'Safety and Justice,'" wrote business and marketing strategist Eliyohu Mintz. "(Soros has also funded a federal super PAC with the same name.) Each organization received most of its money directly from Soros, according to public state and federal financial records, though some groups also got donations from nonprofits like the Civic Participation Action Fund, which gave to the Safety and Justice group in Illinois."[24] Soros's various organizations routinely used passthrough schemes to indirectly fund organizations that advanced his agenda while circumventing transparency and feigning ignorance of how his contribution was used.

In June 2022, more than 1,800 individuals hired by the Biden administration were identified as linked to Soros's funded organizations. Here are but a few examples of folks who are influencing the Biden administration:

Judge Ketanji Brown Jackson is Biden's promised black female nominee to the Supreme Court, who, during her confirmation hearing at the Senate on March 23, 2022, could not or would not define "a woman" because she is "not a biologist," and her judicial philosophy is "methodology."[25] Jackson's memory failed her often when asked about her lenient ruling, especially in sex-offender cases. Like Soros, President Biden, and members of his administration, Jackson has mastered the art of denial, deflection, and contradicting statements. The radically progressive-Left, soft-on-crime, pro-criminal activist judge, noted for disregarding the law to force her political views, had several of her decisions overturned by the appellate court. Though she is on record agreeing with and endorsing critical race theory, she feigned ignorance. She exemplifies the judicial pragmatism that Soros and the radical Left are pining for. She was confirmed so her radical-Left views will sway the Supreme Court's decisions on cases involving an expanding catalog of the "justice reform" agenda.

Her nomination has been backed by "dark money" progressive-Left organizations that Soros funded, including Demand Justice, Arabella Advisors, and Sixteen Thirty Fund.[26]

Anthony Blinken, Biden's secretary of state, and his wife are close to Soros. Blinken's father, Donald, a Left-leaning banker, gave enough to the Democrats and Clinton's election to get the ambassadorship to Hungary (1994-1997). He and his wife supported Soros's Central European University (CEU) in Budapest and his Open Society Archives. After they gifted a permanent (undisclosed) endowed fund to the organization, it was renamed the Vera and Donald Blinken Open Society Archives."[27] Tony Blinken's Soros connections and views while serving in the Clinton and Obama administrations were no secret. Upon his confirmation as Biden's state secretary, the Hungarian Newspaper

Magyar Nemzet's headline read: "Great News for George Soros."

Robert Malley, whom we discussed in Chapter 5, is Biden's special envoy and lead negotiator of Biden's worrying negotiations with Iran. Remember that Malley is the former president and CEO of the Soros-funded, anti-Israel, pro-Hamas International Crisis Group and demonstrated "markedly pro-Palestinian"[28] attitudes when he served under President Bill Clinton. He was Obama's lead negotiator on the 2015 Iran nuclear deal (or JCPOA), which Soros actively supported. And don't forget his "contributions" to the terrorist-designated Islamic Republic of Iran (again, see Chapter 1).[29]

Wendy Sherman, deputy secretary of state, served on the Soros-funded anti-American anti-Israel International Crisis Group board.

Victoria Nuland is the undersecretary of state for political affairs. As assistant secretary for European and Eurasian affairs during the Obama administration, she is on record helping the Soros Fund Management in Ukraine, and his Renaissance Foundation supports the Euromaidan "revolution." Soros publicly supports the revolution.[30]

Sarah Margon: Up until July 26, 2022, her appointment as assistant secretary of state for democracy, human rights, and labor[31] was still in limbo. It has been held up in the Senate following her responses to Senator James Risch's (R-Idaho) questions regarding her tweet in support of AirBnB's initial boycott of Judea and Samaria (AirBNB later retracted it) and her November 19, 2018, re-tweet of Peter Beinart's article "I No Longer Believe in a Jewish State," delegitimizing the Jewish State of Israel. Her attempts to whitewash her tweets did not sway Senator Risch: "With all due respect, ma'am, I don't believe it. . ... Saying it over and over again just doesn't square with your actions," and "doesn't make it true," he said.[32]

Margon headed the Soros-funded Human Rights Watch (HRW) office in Washington, DC, and was director of foreign policy advocacy at the Open Society Foundation. She often described Israel as a "repressive government" and accused it of committing "crimes against humanity."[33]

However, she seems the perfect choice for Biden's policy toward

Israel. In mid-February 2022, the State's Bureau of Democracy, Human Rights, and Labor issued a solicitation to "nonprofit groups to apply for grant money up to $987,654 to strengthen "accountability and human rights in Israel and the West Bank and Gaza."[34]

"The Biden administration wants to use American taxpayer money to subsidize the international NGO campaign to demonize and isolate Israel, which then serves as a basis for anti-Semitic efforts to boycott and wage economic warfare against Israeli Jews," Senator Ted Cruz told Adam Kredo of the *Washington Free Beacon*, who exposed the program, "Congress did not appropriate funds for this purpose and has repeatedly condemned such campaigns." He went on to say that the State Department "should immediately cancel this program and investigate how it was approved."[35]

Alvaro Bedoya, a Georgetown law professor, and the founding director of the Soros-funded Center on Privacy & Technology at Georgetown Law, is a progressive-Left propagator of the Democrats' false accusations against President Trump and was picked by the Biden administration to head the Federal Trade Commission (FTC).[36]

Gigi Sohn has deep ties to Soros and, like him, advocates net neutrality and is avidly pro-censorship.[37] She is Biden's nominee for one of the most important regulators in government, the Federal Communications Commission (FCC), which oversees the largest US industries: technology, telecommunications, and media.[38] Biden appointed her in October 2021, but she faced the Republican members of the Commerce Department opposition, which also included "ethical concerns" for "her involvement with the Locast settlement, conflicts of interest, lack of candor, and secret recusal agreements."[39] But Biden was eager to have her, so he renominated her. In early March 2022, the Committee sent her nomination to the full Senate for a vote. But on August 5, 2022,[40] she was still waiting for confirmation. If confirmed, she will reinstate net neutrality, which was repealed by the former President, Donald Trump. Soros will be pleased.

The *Wall Street Journal* editorial "A Media Censor for the FCC?"

documented Sohn's "long history of Left-wing bias against conservative media" as co-founder and former president of the Leftist group Public Knowledge, which "has long sought more government control of the internet and media."[41] Influence Watch reported that Public Knowledge is a "staunch supporter of expanded regulations on internet businesses and technology companies, backing so-called 'net neutrality regulations against internet service providers."[42] Public Knowledge received at least $1,148,984 between 2016 and 2020 from Soros's Open Society Foundations.[43]

On several occasions, Sohn conveyed her support for deploying the agency's regulatory power to censor conservative media and revive a version of its mooted fairness doctrine. Moreover, before and during her confirmation hearing before the Senate Commerce Committee, she repeatedly attacked Fox News as "state-sponsored propaganda" and said Sinclair Broadcast Group's license should be pulled.[44]

Even more telling, in 2017, Sohn was a Fellow of the OSF's "Leadership in Government.[45] Sohn celebrated via her old, verified Twitter account: "On Jan 16, I start a Leadership in Government Fellowship @OpenSocietyFoundations. I'll be speaking, writing, etc."[46]

The *Wall Street Journal* Editorial Board warned that Sohn has "hinted at deploying the agency's regulatory power to censor conservative media and revive a version of its mooted fairness doctrine." Sohn's "strident partisanship should disqualify her from serving as an officer of an independent agency with so much power to control the public airwaves," the *Journal* declared.[47]

Maher Bitar, senior director for intelligence at the National Security Council, has a long history of anti-Israel activity.[48] According to a senior reporter for Israel365 News, "Her anti-Israel activism has even stepped over into outright anti-Semitism. When President Trump signed Executive Order 13899 on Combating Anti-Semitism at colleges, Margon complained that it 'ostensibly addresses antisemitism. But in reality, it's a bogus initiative geared to stifle free speech & go after those who might criticize Israel.'"[49]

Ur Jaddou, director of U.S. Citizenship and Immigration Services at the Biden administration, came directly from America's Voice (AV).[50] From 2016 to 2019, Soros's Open Society Foundations granted America's Voice $2.64 million for immigration-related policy action and education, as well as for "general support."[51]

America's Voice, previously known as the Coalition for Comprehensive Immigration Reform, teams with other progressive organizations to push the "goal of citizenship rights for illegal immigrants," according to the Capital Research Center, an investigative think tank that monitors nonprofit groups on their Influence Watch profile for AV. *America's Voice signed a letter urging American CEOs not to hire anyone from the Trump administration involved in the forty-fifth president's immigration policy.*[52]

Tyler Moran. Special assistant to the president for immigration on the Domestic Policy Council was a co-founder and executive director of the Immigration Hub, a project of the Emerson Collective, a Left-leaning grantmaking institute founded by Laurene Powell Jobs, widow of Apple founder Steve Jobs.[53] The Immigration Hub has worked with America's Voice and FWD.US through the steering committee of another pro-amnesty nonprofit, We Are Home.[54]

Moran previously worked for the National Immigration Law Center,[55] which received financial support from the Soros-funded Open Society Foundations.

As executive director of the Immigration Hub, Moran was critical of the Trump administration's immigration policy. "President Trump's strategy has always been clear: weaponize immigration to energize his base and appeal to swing voters," Morgan said in a public statement in June 2020. "But it didn't work in the 2018 midterms, and it's not working now. Voters across the spectrum have consistently supported a humane and fair solution for Dreamers, not chaotic or cruel policymaking."[56]

Moran was deputy policy director for immigration at the White House Domestic Policy Council during the Obama administration and helped develop DACA in 2012.

Esther Olavarria, deputy director for immigration of the White House's Domestic Policy Council, was previously director of policy and oversight at the Immigration Hub, working with Moran.[57] Olavarria also worked for John Podesta's Soros-funded Center for American Progress.[58]

Emmy Ruiz, the White House's director of political strategy and outreach,[59] worked as a political strategist for the Soros-funded America's Voice, which seeks to promote "comprehensive" immigration reform that includes amnesty for illegal aliens.

Vanita Gupta, associate attorney general, Department of Justice, was a 2001 Soros Justice Fellow.[60] Gupta developed a comprehensive environmental justice enforcement strategy, "consistent with President Biden's Executive Order on Tackling the Climate Crisis at Home and Abroad," to guide the Justice Department's "litigators, investigators, and U.S. Attorneys' Offices nationwide to advance the cause of environmental justice through the enforcement of federal laws.[61] The Office of Environmental Justice, with an initial budget of $1.4 million, was created to oversee the enforcement of Biden's fiat. During Obama's second term, Gupta served as the head of the Civil Rights Division and the chief civil rights prosecutor at the Department of Justice and worked with the ACLU and the NAACP.

Jennifer Daskal is the Disinformation Governance Board leader and the principal deputy general counsel at the Department of Homeland Security (DHS).[62] She has several connections to Soros. First, she was an Open Society Institute fellow from 2016–2017. She also served as senior counterterrorism counsel for the Soros-funded Human Rights Watch (HRW) and as founding editor of the *Just Security* blog, based out of the Reiss Center on Law and Security at New York University School of Law,[63] which between 2017 and 2019 received $675,000 from Soros.[64]

Nina Jankowicz, another darling of the Biden administration, though not a former direct beneficiary of Soros's foundations, has been affiliated with StopFake, an "anti-disinformation" organization established after the 2014 Maidan Revolution.

According to the *Nation*'s investigative piece about Jankowicz, "the 'grand wizards' of battling fake news, StopFake, have even dabbled with Holocaust distortion, downplaying WWII-era paramilitaries who slaughtered Jews as mere 'historical figures' and Ukrainian nationalist leaders, while attacking members of the US Congress who had denounced Ukraine's glorification of Nazi collaborators."[65] Jankowicz was discussed briefly in Chapter 5. She was appointed as Biden's disinformation czarina, despite her social media postings being riddled with disinformation she was pushing over the years. On May 18, 2022, after intense public criticism of the Disinformation Governance Board, planned by DHS, and a strong push-back from the Republicans, Janowicz resigned.[66]

Patrick Gaspard, former OSF president, though not currently serving in the Biden administration, is now the president of what Politico claims is "the most influential think tank of the Biden era," the Soros-funded Center for American Progress (CAP). At least alums are working in the Biden administration.[67] Gaspard is there to ensure Soros's agenda is not overlooked. Judging by the anti-constitutional, anti-American policies of Biden and his administration and the progressive-Left Democrat representatives in Congress, Gaspard is doing an excellent job. He is proving Soros hasn't lost his touch and assures that the tunes Soros paid for to change America reach an epic climax during the billionaire's lifetime.

9

JUST A TALENTED HUNGARIAN?

ON JULY 4, 2022, as America celebrated its 246th Independence Day, Soros published his call to arm, demanding, "throw the Republican Party out of office in a landslide." The one-party Democrat Congress would then "protect through legislation" Soros's agenda of turning the U.S. into *Sorostan*. In his tirade, *US Democracy Under Concerted Attack*[1], he accused the Republicans of everything he and the illiberal-progressive Left have been doing to subvert America's unique democratic system. Later, he declared he would not stop funding "sensible reform-minded candidates"[2] whom he expects would fulfill his dream to change America. Judging by the policies they enforce, they are already turning

America into a chaotic, racist, lawless, doped, confused, poor, and a weak country.

Soros is right; America is under attack; its Constitution, independence, and democracy are under attack by Soros and his army. Succeeding in changing—more accurately - shattering the U.S. legal system, as he set out to do when he opened his Open Society office in New York, would affirm his childhood fantasy that he's God.

In his splendid address to the Conservative Political Action Conference (CPAC) on August 4, 2022, Hungarian Prime Minister, Viktor Orban[3] cautioned his audience of "talented Hungarians." Orban, of course, meant Soros. Orban warned against Soros and his army of "progressive liberals" who are set on destroying America's Judeo-Christian-based Constitution, sovereignty, independence, and the freedom of its citizens.

As the Hungarian premier predicted, the mostly Left media headlines criticized him and his speech, labeling him, as they always do to anyone critical of Soros, a far-right, racist, antisemitic strongman. He was also called "Trojan horse of Putin."[4] and "Russia's Trojan Horse in Europe."[5] Orban remarked that Soros failed in Hungary because his policies and intimidation tactics reminded Hungarians of their previous oppressors, the Nazis and the Communists. "But Communists are tough to beat," he warned, "Communists rose from the ashes and joined forces with progressive liberals, and they are stronger than ever, and they have to be defeated again,"[6] he stated.

Soros's success was possible because most Americans have not lived under Communist, Nazi, or Islamic tyrannies. Soros took advantage of their naivete and ignorance and bamboozled them with flowery liberal-sounding concepts and language. And many, especially among the Left, fell for it. But it's time to wake up and counter the sweeping web he spawned of globalist, racist, woke elitists who are destroying the United States, ruining its economy, attacking both its religious and secular traditions, dividing its populace, and creating havoc and fear. By choosing to undermine the U.S. criminal law system, he succeeded in weakening what until recently was the most successful, prosperous, and powerful nation. Stopping the decline of the U.S. would be possible only by patriotic, brave, charismatic, sophisticated, and well-funded leadership with a new strategy to counter Soros's and the Left's neo-Marxist utopian agenda for America so that it could celebrate at least 246 more years of independence. My early warning that "unchallenged Soros would change the political landscape in America"[7] was ignored. Soros turned out to be not just a megalomanic, wealthy, "talented Hungarian" but a political virtuoso who managed to undermine the freest, most powerful country in the world. On whose behalf?

EPILOGUE

SOROS'S AGENDA to reshape the U.S. legal system continues. For example, on the eve of the midterm elections, "President Biden issued a presidential proclamation that pardons federal convictions for simple marijuana possession offenses."[1] Some 6,500 people with federal convictions of simple marijuana possession and thousands more charged locally in the District of Columbia were affected[2] by Soros's push for decriminalizing drug offenses.

Another example is the Biden administration's adherence to Soros's open-borders policy. By October 2022, less than two years into the Biden administration, more than 5.5 million illegal migrants[3] entered the U.S. through the "canceled" border with Mexico. The Federation for American Immigration Report (FAIR) reported, "98 known or suspected terrorists in fiscal year 2022." How many more terrorists and criminals were among the millions of gotaways that flooded the country?

Soros funded the elections of additional "woke" DAs and State Secretaries, as well as other progressive-Left officeholders around the country, guaranteeing the further spread of his "reform" policies.

Soros was the largest contributor to the Democrats for the 2022 midterm elections, spending more than $128.5 million through different PACs.[4] While the Republicans won narrowly in the House of Representatives, they failed to win the majority in the Senate.

And Soros is not done. While he is around, he will continue his targeted funding for spreading his woke revolutionary agenda, increasing cultural, racial, political, social, and economic discord in the U.S. and beyond. The billions of dollars in his foundations' coffers ensure his woke legacy continues long after he is gone.

ACKNOWLEDGMENTS

I THANK MY AGENT, Alexander Hoyt, for his literary presentation and friendship. My valiant publishers Alfred S. Regnery and Eric Kampmann, of Republic Book Publishers, for taking on this complex project. Special thanks to the expert team at Republic Book Publishers for their patience and help.

I owe special thanks to Kenneth S. Abramowitz for his constant support and encouragement, as well as to "Ranger" for his readiness to help and provide sound advice, and to Brendan Healey for his counsel.

I am also grateful to all supporters of my work, who must remain anonymous.

ENDNOTES

INTRODUCTION

1   Rachel Ehrenfeld, "An Evening At Soros's, Insight on the News (ceased publications in May 2008) February 1995; Pros and Cons of Drug Legalization, Decriminalization, and Harm Reduction: Hearing Before the Subcommittee on Criminal Justice, Drug Policy, and Human Resources of the Committee on Government Reform, 106th Cong. (Washington, DC: U.S. Government Printing Office, 2000), 246, https://archive.org/details/gov.gpo.fdsys.CHRG-106hhrg63346.

2   Christopher Wren, One Million Gift for Needles Is a Lifesaver, Financier Says, Not a Ruse to Legalize Drugs, *New York Times*, August 17, 1997, p.20.; Also: Mr. George Soros was recently interviewed by TIME magazine, issue, April 21, 1997. He stated the following: "I firmly believe the war on drugs is doing more harm to our society than drug abuse itself." And, George Soros, "Why I Support Legal Marijuana, *Wall Street Journal*, October 26, 2010.

3   Ehrenfeld, "An Evening at Soros's."

4   Ehrenfeld.

5   Ehrenfeld.

6   Rachel Ehrenfeld, "ObamaCare's Medical Marijuana," Forbes, August 13, 2009, https://www.forbes.com/2009/08/13/george-soros-marijuana-legalization-opinions-contributors-rachel-ehrenfeld.html?sh=728607fb2b72,

7   George Soros, "The Drug War Cannot Be Won," *Washington Post*, February 2, 1997, reprinted on the George Soros website, https://www.georgesoros.com/1997/02/02/the-drug-war-cannot-be-won/.

8   Transparify, How Transparent Are Think Tanks about Who Funds Them 2016?, transparify.org, June 29, 2016, https://static1.squarespace.com/static/52e1f399e4b06a94c0cdaa41/t/5773022de6f2e1ecf70b26d1/1467154992324/Transparify+2016+Think+Tanks+Report.pdf, p. 16,

9   Christian Datoc, "George Soros' 'Open Society Foundations' Named 2016's LEAST Transparent Think Tank," Daily Caller, July 6, 2016, https://dailycaller.com/2016/07/06/george-soros-open-society-foundations-named-2016s-least-transparent-think-tank/.

10   Rachel Ehrenfeld and Shawn Macomber, "Soros: The Man Who Would Be Kingmaker, Part I," Front Page Magazine, October 28, 2004, reprinted on the website of the American Center for Democracy, https://acdemocracy.org/the-man-who-would-be-kingmaker-part-i/.

11   See Matjaz Kuntner, "Web Gigantism in Darwin's Bark Spider, a new species from Madagascar," Journal of Arachnology 38 (September 2010): 346–56, http://dx.doi.org/10.1636/B09-113.1.

12   "Naches" in Leo Rosten, The New Joys of Yiddish, rev. Lawrence Bush (New York: Harmony/Rodale, 2010). ebook.

1: THE ONE-EYED KING

1   Rachel Ehrenfeld, "Can We Afford to Give Up the Drug War?" *Wall Street Journal*, February 7, 1996, reprinted by the American Center for Democracy, https://acdemocracy.org/can-we-afford-to-give-up-the-drug-war/.

2   George Soros, The Bubble of American Supremacy: Correcting the Misuse of American Power (New York: PublicAffairs, 2003), 87.

3   See Karl Popper, The Open Society and Its Enemies, Routledge Classics ed. (London: Routledge, 2011).

4   Karl Popper, *Unended Quest: An Intellectual Autobiography*, Routledge Classics 2nd ed. (London: Routledge, 2002), 36.

5   Stefan Kanfer, "A Look at the Dystopian Vision of the Connoisseur of Chaos, George Soros," Swarajya magazine, January 28, 2017, https://swarajyamag.com/world/a-look-at-the-dystopian-vision-of-the-connoisseur-of-chaos-george-soros.

6   George Soros, The Alchemy of Finance: Reading the Mind of the Market (New York: John Wiley & Sons, 1994), 362.

7   Gail Counsell, "The Billionaire Who Built on Chaos—George Soros," Independent (UK), June 3, 1993.

8   A good example is New York City, where, by the end of June 2022, as Kyle Schnitzer reported in the *New York Post*, "NYC Murders, Shootings Spiked in July as Part of 40% Jump in Major Crimes in 2022," https://nypost.com/2022/08/01/nyc-murders-shootings-spiked-in-july-as-part-of-40-jump-in-major-crimes-in-2022/

9   Christopher F. Rufo, In Portland, the Sexual Revolution Starts in Kindergarten, July 27, 2022, City Journal, https://www.city-journal.org/in-portland-the-sexual-revolution-starts-in-kindergarten

10   Danielle Kurtzleben, Top General Defends Studying Critical Race Theory In The Military, NPR, June 23, 2021 https://www.npr.org/2021/06/23/1009592838/top-general-defends-studying-critical-race-theory-in-the-military

11   Doug Carlin, 15 Cities with Highest Homeless in the US [Report of 2022], USA by Numbers, JUNE 17, 2022 -

12   See, for example, Tucker Higgins, "PHILANTHROPY: George Soros Just Gave Almost 80 Percent of His Wealth to His Charity," CNBC, October 17, 2017, https://www.cnbc.com/2017/10/17/philanthropist-george-soros-donates-most-of-his-net-worth-to-charity.html.

13   Elena Schneider, "Soros Pours $125M into Super PAC ahead of Midterms," Politico, January 28, 2022, https://www.politico.com/news/2022/01/28/soros-pours-125m-into-super-pac-ahead-of-midterms-00002847.

14   World Policy Journal, The Pursuit of Truth: A Talk with George Soros, World Policy Journal Vol. 23, No. 3 (Fall, 2006), pp. 59-63, Duke University Press.

15   George Soros, The Pursuit of Truth: A Talk with George Soro, World Policy Journal Vol. 23, No. 3 (Fall, 2006), pp. 59-63, Duke University Press, https://www.jstor.org/stable/40210033; Soros claimed the Founding Fathers, "did not fully recognize how imperfectly we understand the world, how our own perceptions of reality actually change that reality."

16 "60 Minutes—George Soros Interview," YouTube video, 11:20, posted January 30, 2022 by Local 6 News, https://www.youtube.com/watch?v=Or9pYKMKgr0.

17 Jake Wallis Simons, Revealed: The Hungarian 'Schindler' who saved George Soros from Nazi death squads during the occupation by hiding him behind a cupboard, Daily Mail.com, November 26, 2018. https://www.dailymail.co.uk/news/article-6415189/Revealed-Hungarian-Schindler-hid-George-Soros-Gestapo-death-squads.html

18 "60 Minutes—George Soros Interview."

19 WABC-Radio News Team, "Cities Will Set Murder Records Because of 'Soros Effect'," December 15, 2021, RealClearPolitics, https://www.realclearpolitics.com/articles/2021/12/15/cities_will_set_murder_records_because_of_soros_effect_146884.html/

20 Ehrenfeld and Macomber, "Soros: The Man Who Would Be Kingmaker, Part I" (see intro., n. 9).

21 Robert Slater, Soros: The Life, Times & Trading Secrets of the World's Greatest Investor (n.p.: Irwin Professional, 1996), 186.

22 Kaufman, Soros, 56.

23 Byron Wien, quoted in Glenn Beck, "Radio Clips: The Glenn Beck Program," Glenn, November 11, 2010, https://www.glennbeck.com/content/articles/article/198/47856/.

24 Noreena Hertz, The Silent Takeover: Global Capitalism and the Death of Democracy (New York: Free Press, 2001), 156.

25 TIME—In the Path of a Killer (n.p.: n.p., 1997), 54.

26 David Litterick, "Billionaire Who Broke the Bank of England," Telegraph (UK), September 13, 2003, https://www.telegraph.co.uk/finance/2773265/Billionaire-who-broke-the-Bank-of-England.html *See Chapter 6.

27 Ploughshares Fund, for example, served as a major "echo chamber" to spread disinformation in support of Obama's bad Iran deal in different media outlets. The $100,000 from Soros's Open Society Foundations, and Policy Center in 2015, were given to help in this effort. See: Rachel Ehrenfeld, "Plowing the American Mind," May 21, 2016, American Center for Democracy https://acdemocracy.org/plowing-the-american-mind/ Also see, https://www.ploughshares.org/sites/default/files/resources/Ploughshares-AR-2015-web-version.pdf

28 See Richard A. Epstein, "Obama's Disastrous Iran Deal," Hoover Institution, July 20, 2015, https://www.hoover.org/research/obamas-disastrous-iran-deal; Kiyoko Metzler and David Rising, "UN Agency: Iran Violating All Restrictions of Nuclear Deal," ABCNews, June 5, 2020, https://abcnews.go.com/International/wireStory/agency-iran-violating-restrictions-nuclear-deal-71090757.

29 Washington Examiner, "Iran Irradiates Biden's Credibility," Washington Examiner, June 15, 2022, https://www.washingtonexaminer.com/opinion/editorials/iran-irradiates-bidens-credibility.

30 Emily Tamkin, "George Soros Is Trying to Change the System That Made Him Rich," Washington Post, July 6, 2020, https://www.washingtonpost.com/outlook/2020/07/06/george-soros-influence-excerpt/.

31 "The CEU Lectures: Lecture Four, George Soros on Capitalism versus Open Society," Central European University, October 30, 2009, https://www.ceu.edu/article/2009-10-30/ceu-lectures-lecture-four-george-soros-capitalism-versus-open-society.

32 See George Soros, "The Capitalist Threat," Atlantic, February 1997, https://www.theatlantic.com/magazine/archive/1997/02/the-capitalist-threat/376773/.

33 George Soros, Soros on Soros: Staying Ahead of the Curve (New York: John Wiley & Sons, 1995), 196.

34 Soros, "The Capitalist Threat."

35 Soros, The Bubble of American Supremacy, 169.

36   Soros, 94.

37   George Soros, on Charlie Rose, December 22, 1998, https://charlierose.com/videos/16590.

38   Soros, Soros on Soros, 196.

39   Soros, "The Capitalist Threat."

40   Daisy Luther, "George Soros in Forgotten Interview: 'I cannot and do not look at the social consequences of what I do,'"

41   Chris Hedges, "Honoring Investing That Paid," New York Times, October 15, 1990, https://www.nytimes.com/1990/10/15/world/honoring-investing-that-paid.html.

42   Connie Bruck, "The World According to George Soros," New Yorker, January 23, 1995, https://www.newyorker.com/magazine/1995/01/23/the-world-according-to-soros.

43   See Robert Slater, SOROS: The Life, Times and Trading Secrets of the World's Greatest Investor (UK: Irwin Professional, 1996).

44   Robert E. Kaplan, The Soros Connection: George Soros—An Agent for Germany in Its Third Attempt to Rule the World? (n.p.: Robert E. Kaplan, 2012).

45   See Gary Weiss et al., "The Man Who Moves Markets," Business Week, August 23, 1993, posted at Study Mode Research, https://www.studymode.com/essays/Man-Who-Moves-Markets-71639038.html.

46   Excerpt from a case study conducted by Stanford University on institutional investors, in Savio Rodrigues, "Twitter, New York Times: Global Economic Terrorist George Soros Launches 'Operation to remove Modi'," Samhati Samvad, July 7, 2021, https://samhatisamvad.com/2021/07/07/twitter-new-york-times-global-economic-terrorist-george-soros-launches-operation-to-remove-modi/.

47   Slater, Soros, 251.

48   Bruck, "The World According to George Soros."

49   Dailymail.com Reporter, "Billionaire Democratic Donor George Soros Told an Ally of Hillary Clinton He Regretted Supporting President Obama over Her in the 2008 Presidential Primary," Daily Mail, January 1, 2016, https://www.dailymail.co.uk/news/article-3381033/Billionaire-Democratic-donor-George-Soros-told-ally-Hillary-Clinton-regretted-supporting-President-Obama-2008-presidential-primary.html.

50   See the Open Society Policy Center website: https://www.opensocietypolicycenter.org/.

51   "Products Made from Oil and Natural Gas," https://www.energy.gov/sites/prod/files/2019/11/f68/Products%20Made%20From%20Oil%20and%20Natural%20Gas%20Infographic.pdf

52   Timothy H.J. Nerozzi, Biden administration endorses transgender youth sex-change operations, 'top surgery,' hormone therapy, March 31, 2022, Fox News, https://www.foxnews.com/politics/biden-administration-transgender-agenda-youth-sex-change-hormone-therapy; Also, Youth. Gov,, Resource: Gender-Affirming Care and Young People, https://youth.gov/announcements/resource-gender-affirming-care-and-young-people.

53   Daniel Patrick Moynihan, "Defining Deviancy Down: How We"ve Become Accustomed to Alarming Levelsof Crime and Destructive Behavior," American Educator (Winter 1993/1994): 12, https://nation.time.com/wp-content/uploads/sites/8/2012/03/defining-deviancy-down-amereducator.pdf.

54   Bruck, "The World According to George Soros."

55   Soros, "The Capitalist Threat."

56   "George Soros," Open Society Foundations website, https://www.opensocietyfoundations.org/george-soros, accessed June 22, 2022.

ENDNOTES

57 George Soros, "The Danger of Reagan's 'Imperial Circle,'" Financial Times, May 23, 1984, reposted on the George Soros website, https://www.georgesoros.com/1984/05/23/the-danger-of-reagans-imperial-circle/.

58 Soros, quoted in Bruck, "The World According to George Soros."

59 Soros, "The Danger of Reagan's 'Imperial Circle.'"

60 Soros, "The Danger of Reagan's 'Imperial Circle.'"

61 "Full text: bin Laden's 'letter to America',"

62 Soros, "The Capitalist Threat."

63 Robert J. Samuelson, "George Soros, Don't Give Up Your Day Job," Washington Post, March 5, 1997, https://www.washingtonpost.com/archive/opinions/1997/03/05/george-soros-dont-give-up-your-day-job/45cae1c2-cacd-46de-9e91-b15a63dca562/.

64 Robert J. Samuelson, "Crackpot Prophet," Newsweek, March 9, 1997, https://www.newsweek.com/crackpot-prophet-170568.

65 Soros, "The Capitalist Threat."

66 Samuelson, "Crackpot Prophet."

67 "60 Minutes—George Soros Interview."

68 A. T. (Andrew Tobias), "Offshore Funds," Andrew Tobias, September 11, 1997, https://andrewtobias.com/offshore-funds/.

69 Tobias, "Offshore Funds."

70 Bruck, "The World According to George Soros."

71 George Soros, 1994, quoted in Jonas E. Alexis, Kevin MacDonald's Metaphysical Failure: A Philosophical, Historical, and Moral Critique of Evolutionary Psychology, Sociobiology, and Identity Politics (Bloomington, IN: AuthorHouse, 2022), 101.

72 Kaufman, Soros, 135

73 Kaufman, 135.

74 Bruck, "The World According to George Soros." https://www.newyorker.com/magazine/1995/01/23/the-world-according-to-soros

75 Bruck, "The World According to George Soros."

76 John Tagliabue, "French Court Fines Soros for Insider Trading," New York Times, December 20, 2002, https://www.nytimes.com/2002/12/20/international/french-court-fines-soros-for-insider-trading.html.

77 Rachel Ehrenfeld and Shawn Macomber, "Soros: The Man Who Would Be Kingmaker, Part II," Front Page Magazine, October 29, 2004, reprinted on the website of the American Center for Democracy, https://acdemocracy.org/the-man-who-would-be-kingmaker-part-ii/.

78 Risks That Hedge Funds Pose to the Banking System: Hearing Before the Committee on Banking, Finance, and Urban Affairs, House of Representatives, One Hundred Third Congress, Second Session, April 13, 1994 (Washington, DC: Government Printing Office, 2004), 46

79 Risks That Hedge Funds Pose to the Banking System, 39, 40, 45, 53.

80 Risks That Hedge Funds Pose to the Banking System, 38.

81 Risks, 38.

82 Ehrenfeld and Macomber, "Soros: The Man Who Would Be Kingmaker, Part II."

83 Jeffrey T. Kuhner, "KUHNER: The Soros Empire: Billionaire Megalomaniac Undermines American Values," Washington Times, October 28, 2010, https://www.washingtontimes.com/news/2010/oct/28/the-soros-empire/.

84 Soros, "The Capitalist Threat."

85 Soros, "The Capitalist Threat."

86   See the Justice Initiative's website at https://www.justiceinitiative.org/.

87   Rachel Ehrenfeld and Shawn Macombe, Soros: The Man Who Would be Kingmaker, Part IV, FrontPageMagazine.com, October 28th, 2004, and https://acdemocracy.org/soros-the-man-who-would-be-kingmaker-part-iv/

88   George Soros, in a presentation at the Secretary" Open Forum, Washington, DC, September 16, 2003, U.S. Department of State Archive, https://2001-2009.state.gov/s/p/of/proc/24381.htm.

89   Soros, Soros on Soros, 138.

90   George Soros, Underwriting Democracy (New York: Free Press, 1991), 91.

91   Open Society Justice Initiative, "International Justice," accessed June 23, 2022, https://www.justiceinitiative.org/topics/international-justice.

92   The Text is no longer available since it has been removed. Statements that appeared on than OS website, are no longer available, since changes were made to the organization and the OSF's website, especially by the end of 2021. See Rachel Ehrenfeld and Shawn Macombe, Soros: The Man Who Would be Kingmaker, Part IV, FrontPageMagazine.com, October 28th, 2004, and https://acdemocracy.org/soros-the-man-who-would-be-kingmaker-part-iv/

93   See Rachel Ehrenfeld and Shawn Macomber, Soros: The Man Who Would be Kingmaker, Part IV....PageMagazine.com, October 28th, 2004, and https://acdemocracy.org/soros-the-man-who-would-be-kingmaker-part-iv/

94   See Christine Hauser and Greg Myre, "World Court Says Israeli Barrier Violates International Law," New York Times, July 9, 2004, https://www.nytimes.com/2004/07/09/international/middleeast/world-court-says-israeli-barrier-violates.html.

95   David S. Broder, "Wealthy Benefactors Stoke Campaigns for Medical Marijuana," Washington Post, October 20, 1998, https://www.washingtonpost.com/wp-srv/politics/campaigns/keyraces98/stories/ballot102098.htm.

96   Rachel Sandler, "MacKenzie Scott, Michael Bloomberg Among the Biggest Billionaire Donors to Abortion-Rights Groups," Forbes, May 12, 2022, https://www.forbes.com/sites/rachelsandler/2022/05/12/mackenzie-scott-michael-bloomberg-among-the-biggest-billionaire-donors-to-abortion-rights-groups/?sh=4f6db99d7081.

97   Joe Schoffstall, Soros Pours $5.1 Million Into New 2020 PAC, The Washigton Free Beacon, August 1, 2019, https://freebeacon.com/politics/soros-pours-5-1-million-into-new-2020-pac/

98   Ruth King, "My Say: There Is an Insurrection but Who Are the Real Culprits?," Ruthfully Yours: The Right News, Front and Center (blog), October 3, 2021, http://www.ruthfullyyours.com/2021/10/03/my-say-there-is-an-insurrection-but-who-are-the-real-culprits/.

99   See Bryan Magee , Popper (n.p.: Woburn, 1974), 86.

100 New York Times, https://dealbook.nytimes.com/2007/01/27/george-soros-backs-obama-but-hedges-his-bets/. No longer accessible. See Jim Geraghty, "Obama Backer Soros Declares America Needs 'to Go through a Certain De-Nazification Process'," National Review, https://www.nationalreview.com/the-campaign-spot/obama-backer-soros-declares-america-needs-go-through-certain-de-nazification/.

101 George Soros, "On Israel, America and AIPAC," New York Review of Books, April 12, 2007, https://www.georgesoros.com/2007/04/12/on_israel_america_and_aipac/.

102 Joshua Muravchik, "The Mind of George Soros," Wall Street Journal, March 3, 2004, https://www.wsj.com/articles/SB122721445670545291.

ENDNOTES

103 NGO Monitor, "Rule of Law and Due Process: NGO Campaigns to Discredit the Israeli Justice System : NGO Monitor Submission to the UN Human Rights Council Commission of Inquiry on the 2014 Gaza Conflict," January 30, 2015, http://www.ngo-monitor.org/data/images/File/NGO_Monitor_Submission_to_the_Commission_of_Inquiry_on_Gaza.pdf,

104 Nadine Epstein, "Soros: A Small Sacrifice for Netanyahu," Moment magazine, March–April 2019, https://momentmag.com/soros-a-small-sacrifice-for-netanyahu/.

105 Kaufman, Soros, 118.

106 George Soros, "The Burden of Consciousness" (unpublished essay), quoted in Kaufman, Soros, 113.

107 Soros, "Burden of Consciousness."

108 Kaufman, Soros, 290–93.

109 Kroft, 60 Minutes, . https://www.scribd.com/document/455566069/CREC-2006-09-29-pt1-PgE1917#from_embed

110 "The Guilt-Free Record of George Soros," Congressional Record 152, no 125 (September 29, 2006), E1917–18, https://www.govinfo.gov/content/pkg/CREC-2006-09-29/html/CREC-2006-09-29-pt1-PgE1917.htm.

111 Kaufman, Soros, 48.

112 Kaufman, 75.

113 Kaufman, 140.

114 Soros, "The Capitalist Threat."

115 Kaufman, Soros, 292.

116 Ehrfeld and Macomber, "Soros: The Man Who Would Be Kingmaker, Part II."

117 Popper, Unended Quest, 133.

118 Popper, 133.

119 Popper, 131.

120 Kaufman, Soros, 73.

121 Popper, Unended Quest, 36.

122 Knowledge at Wharton Staff, "George Soros Takes on George Bush," Knowledge at Wharton (business journal from the Wharton School of the University of Pennsylvania), April 24, 2002

123 Eduardo Andino, quoted in Matt Palumbo, The Man Behind the Curtain: Inside the Secret Network of George Soros (New York: Liberatio Protocol, 2022), ch. 1.

124 "George Soros Has Enemies. He's Fine with That," New York Times, October 25, 2019, https://www.nytimes.com/2019/10/25/business/dealbook/george-soros-interview.html.

125 George Soros, "My Philanthropy," in Chuck Sudetic, The Philanthropy of George Soros: Building Open Societies (New York: PublicAffairs, 2011), 51.

126 Soros, in Sudetic, 51.

127 Antonio Gramsci, "Audacia e Fede," Avanti May 22, 1916, reprinted in Sotta la Mole: 1916–1929 (Turin: Einaudi, 1960), 148, author's translation; and Gramsci, cited in Damien , "What's Left of Western Culture? Just about Everything," Spectator, October 9, 2017, https://www.spectator.com.au/2017/10/whats-left-of-western-culture-just-about-everything/; both requoted in Robert S. Smith, "Cultural Marxism: Imaginary Conspiracy or Revolutionary Reality?" Themelios 44, no. 3 (December 2019): 443

128 Cover copy. Hegemony and Revolution: Antonio Gramsci's Political and Cultural Theory, by Walter Adamson, Echo Point Books & Media, LLC, 2014. Used with permission.

129 Antonio Gramsci, The Modern Prince and Other Writings (n.p.: International, 1959). N.p.

ENDNOTES

130 Antonio Gramsci, April 10, 1920, reprinted at "An Address to the Anarchists—Antonio Gramsci, 1920," libcom.org, https://libcom.org/article/address-anarchists-antonio-gramsci-1920.

131 See "Tides Center," Influence Watch, https://www.influencewatch.org/non-profit/tides-center/.

132 See Dream Defenders home page https://dreamdefenders.org, and "JOB OPPORTUNITIES," Dream Defenders website, accessed June 24, 2022, https://dreamdefenders.org/jobs/.

133 Soros, Soros on Soros, 145.

134 Eduardo Andino, "George Soros, Karl Popper, and ironies of 'The Open Society,'" Philanthropy Daily, March 7, 2017, https://www.philanthropydaily.com/george-soros-karl-popper-and-the-ironies-of-the-open-society/.

135 "The George Soros Philosophy—and Its Fatal Flaw," Guardian, July 6, 2018, https://www.the-guardian.com/news/2018/jul/06/the-george-soros-philosophy-and-its-fatal-flaw.

136 See George Soros, "My Philanthropy," New York Review of Books, June 22, 2011, reprinted on George Soros's website, https://www.georgesoros.com/2011/06/22/my_philanthropy/.

137 Open Society Foundations, "George Soros Launches Global Network to Transform Higher Education," press release, January 23, 2020, https://www.opensocietyfoundations.org/newsroom/george-soros-launches-global-network-to-transform-higher-education.

138 David Dawkins, "Billionaire George Soros Pledges $1 Billion University Fund to Fight 'Would-Be Dictators'," Forbes, January 24, 2020, https://www.forbes.com/sites/david-dawkins/2020/01/24/billionaire-george-soros-pledges-1-billion-university-fund-to-fight-would-be-dictators/?sh=52d164fd39d2.

139 "George Soros Has Enemies. He's Fine with That."

140 "Special Report: George Soros: Godfather of the Left," Media Research Center, accessed June 27, 2022, https://www.mrc.org/special-report-george-soros-godfather-left.

141 Zoltán Kovács, "George Soros Plans to Give the World What It "Really Needs" in a New Global, Educational Network," About Hungary (blog), January 24, 2020, https://abouthungary.hu/blog/george-soros-plans-to-give-the-world-what-it-really-needs-in-a-new-global-educational-network.

142 See "George Soros Launches $1bn Move to Educate against Nationalism," Financial Times, https://www.ft.com/content/1d683f18-3e35-11ea-a01a-bae547046735.

143 Open Society Foundations, "George Soros Launches Global Network to Transform Higher Education."

144 Al-Quds Bard College's Program Fair-2022 - Al-Quds University, March 6, 2022, https://www.alquds.edu/en/news/announcement/25631/al-quds-bard-colleges-program-fair-2022/

145 See the website of Brillantmont International School Lausanne at https://www.brillantmont.ch/.

146 See "Voices from Russia's Cold War 'Friendship' University," BBC News, last updated February 6, 2010, http://news.bbc.co.uk/2/hi/europe/8498904.stm.

147 StudyLandRus Group, "Peoples' Friendship University of Russia, accessed June 27, 2022, https://www.studylandrus.com/rudn.

148 See Rachel Ehrenfeld, Funding Evil: How Terrorism Is Financed and How to Stop It, upd. ed. (New Rochelle, NY: MultiEducator, 2011).

149 Stephen Koch,, "Lying for the truth: Münzenberg & the Comintern", The New Criterion, re-trieved 27 July 2011

150 Sean McMeekin, The Red Millionaire: A Political Biography of Willy Münzenberg, Moscow's Se-cret Propaganda Tsar in the West, 1917-1940, Yale University Press; 1St Edition , January 1, 2004

151 Kent Clizbe, Willing Accomplices: How KGB Covert Influence Agents Created Political Correct-ness and Destroyed America (Ashburn, VA: Andemca, 2011), 224.

152 Susanna Schrobsdorff, "Soros on American Fallibility," *Newsweek*, June 27, 2006, https://www. *newsweek*.com/soros-american-fallibility-110647; George Soros, In Defense of Open Society (New York: PublicAffairs, 2019).

153 See Stephen Koch, Double Lives: Stalin, Willi Münzenberg, and the Seduction of the Intellectuals (New York: Enigma, 2004).

154 See Fredrik Petersson, Willi Münzenberg, the League Against Imperialism, and the Comintern, 1925–1933: Conceiving the Anti-Colonial Project (n.p.: Queenston, 2013); and Kasper Braskén, The International Workers' Relief, Communism, and Transnational Solidarity: Willi Münzenberg in Weimar Germany (UK: Palgrave Macmillan, 2015).

155 SNAC (Social Networks and Archival Context), "League of American Writers," accessed June 27, 2022, https://snaccooperative.org/view/41168682.

156 Franklin Folson, Days of Anger, Days of Hope: A Memoir of the League of American Writers, 1937–1942 (University Press of Colorado, 1994), 93.

157 Hugh Wilford, The Mighty Wurlitzer: How the CIA Played America (Cambridge, MA: Harvard University Press, 2009),12.

158 Monica Showalter, Lenin Used Cultural Propaganda To Create A 'New Soviet Man', Investor Business Daily, October 2, 2013. https://www.investors.com/politics/commentary/lenins-failed-policies-led-to-economic-collapse/

159 Rephael Ben-Ari, "International Nongovernmental Organizations: 'Global Conscience' or Power-ful Political Actors?," Jerusalem Issue Briefs 13, no. 13 (July 15, 2013), https://jcpa.org/article/international-nongovernmental-organizations-global-conscience-or-powerful-political-actors/.

160 Ben-Ari, "International Nongovernmental Organizations."

161 Ben-Ari, "International Nongovernmental Organizations."

162 Saul Alinsky, Rules for Radicals, Random House, 1971

163 George Soros, "From Karl Popper to Karl Rove—and Back," Project Syndicate, November 8, 2007, https://www.project-syndicate.org/commentary/from-karl-popper-to-karl-rove---and-back-2007-11?barrier=accesspaylog.

164 Soros, "From Karl Popper to Karl Rove."

165 George Soros, The Age of Fallibility: Consequences of the War on Terror (New York: PublicAffairs, 2007), xvi.

166 See Victor Davis Hanson, The Dying Citizen: How Progressive Elites, Tribalism, and Globalization Are Destroying the Idea of America (New York: Basic Books, 2001), title page.

167 David P. Goldman, "The World No Longer Believes in American Democracy, and Neither Do We," PJ Media, November 6, 2021, https://pjmedia.com/news-and-politics/david-p-gold-man/2021/11/06/the-world-no-longer-believes-in-american-democracy-neither-do-we-n1530393.

2: SOROS'S DRUG LEGACY

1 Phil Davison, "Soros Slams Drug War as $17bn Flop," *Guardian*, June 6, 1998, https://www. independent.co.uk/news/soros-slams-drug-war-as-17bn-flop-1163425.html.

2 Steven Nelson, "House Votes to Legalize Marijuana Despite Biden Opposition," *New York Post*, April 1, 2022, https://nypost.com/2022/04/01/house-votes-to-legalize-marijuana-despite-biden-opposition/.

3 See Niall Ferguson and Jonathan Schlefler, "Who Broke the Bank of England?" (September 9, 2009). Harvard Business School BGIE Unit Case No. 709-026, available at SSRN: https://ssrn.com/abstract=1485674.

4   Phil Davison, "Soros Slams Drug War as $17bn Flop," *Guardian*, June 6, 1998, https://www. independent.co.uk/news/soros-slams-drug-war-as-17bn-flop-1163425.html.
5   U.S. Department of Justice, Office of Justice Programs, Promising Strategies to Reduce Substance Abuse, title page, https://www.ojp.gov/sites/g/files/xyckuh241/files/media/document/psrsa.pdf.
6   AIM Report (United States: Accuracy in Media, 2003).
7   This was Bill Weinberg, interview of Ethan A Nedelmann,, in High Times, on October 1, 1995, https://archive.hightimes.com/article/1995/10/1/ethan-a-nadelmann,
8   Rachel Ehrenfeld, "An Evening at Soros's, Insight on the News, February 1995. The magazine stopped publications in 2008, but the article is available on the UKCIA - The Cannabis Internet Activist- The Cannabis Information Site on the page titled: Various pieces about George Soros 1995-97. http://www.ukcia.org/research/argue/soros.htm
9   Rachel Ehrenfeld, "An Evening at Soros's"
10   See Drug Enforcement Administration, U.S. Department of Justice, Drugs of Abuse: A DEA Resource Guide, 2020 ed., https://www.dea.gov/sites/default/files/2020-04/Drugs%20of%20 Abuse%202020-Web%20Version-508%20compliant-4-24-20_0.pdf.
11   Rachel Ehrenfeld, Can we afford to give up the drug war? The *Wall Street Journal*, Feb 7, 1996, Also at https://acdemocracy.org/can-we-afford-to-give-up-the-drug-war/
12   Reed Irvine and Cliff Kincaid, "'60 Minutes' Ignores the Soros' Drug Ties," Accuracy in Media, January 12, 1999, https://www.aim.org/media-monitor/60-minutes-ignores-the-soros-drug-ties/.
13   Connie Bruck, The World Accordhttps://www.newyorker.com/magazine/1995/01/23/the-world-according-to-soros
14   Bruck, "The World According to Soros, https://www.newyorker.cm/magazine/1995/01/23/the-world-according-to-soros
15   Bruck, "The World According to Soros" (see chap. 1, n. 35).
16   Support for Legal Marijuana Holds at Record High of 68%
17   "Support for Legal Marijuana Holds at Record High of 68%," Gallup, November 4, 2021, https://news.gallup.com/poll/356939/support-legal-marijuana-holds-record-high.aspx.
18   See Camille Furst, "House Votes to Decriminalize Marijuana," *Wall Street Journal*, April 1, 2022, https://www.wsj.com/articles/house-votes-to-decriminalize-marijuana-11648849628.
19   Nelson, "House Votes to Legalize Marijuana Despite Biden Opposition."
20   See Department of Health and Human Services, Substance Abuse and Mental Health Services Administration, FY 2022 Harm Reduction Program Grant (Short Title: Harm Reduction): (Modified Announcement), https://www.samhsa.gov/sites/default/files/grants/pdf/fy22-harm-reduction-nofo.pdf.
21   Patrick Hauf, "Biden Admin to Fund Crack Pipe Distribution to Advance 'Racial Equity,'" *Washington Free Beacon*, February 7, 2022, https://freebeacon.com/biden-administration/biden-admin-to-fund-crack-pipe-distribution-to-advance-racial-equity/.
22   Morgan Phillips, "Liberal Drug Group Now Criticizes Biden Administration for NOT Giving Out Free Crack Pipes in Safe Smoking and Harm Reduction Kits That Include 'Lip Balm, Alcohol Swabs, Fentanyl Testing Strips and Clean Syringes'—and Have Infuriated Republicans, DailyMail. com, February 10, 2022, https://www.dailymail.co.uk/news/article-10499799/Liberal-drug-group-criticizes-Biden-administration-NOT-giving-free-crack-pipes.html.
23   Harm Reduction International and coAct, "Harm Reduction for Stimulant Use," briefing paper, April 2019, p. 2., https://www.hri.global/files/2019/04/28/harm-reduction-stimulants-coact.pdf.
24   Phillips, "Liberal Drug Group Now Criticizes Biden Administration."
25   Hauf, "Biden Admin to Fund Crack Pipe Distribution to Advance 'Racial Equity.'"

26   Fox News Staff, "Senator Rips White House for Failing to Be 'Candid' on Alleged Crack Pipe Distribution," Fox News, February 9, 2022, https://www.foxnews.com/media/senator-white-house-crack-distribution-plan.

27   Patrick Hauf, "Yes, Safe Smoking Kits Include Free Crack Pipes. We Know Because We Got Them," *Washington Free Beacon*, May 12, 2022, https://freebeacon.com/biden-administration/yes-safe-smoking-kits-include-free-crack-pipes-we-know-because-we-got-them/.

28   Liz Longley, "Soros in Baltimore: Lessons from 20 Years of Place-Based Giving," OSI Baltimore, October 2, 2019, https://www.osibaltimore.org/2019/10/inside-philanthropy-looks-back-on-20-years-of-osi-baltimore/.

29   See, for example, Brie Stimson, "Marilyn Mosby, Baltimore's Top Prosecutor, Pleads Not Guilty to Perjury Charges," Fox News, February 6, 2022, https://www.foxnews.com/politics/marilyn-mosby-baltimore-states-attorney-not-guilty-perjury-corruption.

30   "Baltimore City, MD Drug-Related Crime Rates and Maps: Drug-Related Crime per Capita in Baltimore City," CrimeGrade.org, accessed June 29, 2022, https://crimegrade.org/drug-crimes-baltimore-city-area-md/.

31   See Charm City Care Connection, "About Us," https://www.charmcitycareconnection.org/aboutus.

32   See Hauf's photo at https://freebeacon.com/wp-content/uploads/2022/03/IMG_2083-scaled.jpeg.

33   Hauf, "Yes, Safe Smoking Kits Include Free Crack Pipes."

34   Hauf, "Yes, Safe Smoking Kits Include Free Crack Pipes."

35   Morgan Phillips, Liberal drug group now criticizes Biden administration for NOT giving out free crack pipes in safe smoking and harm reduction kits that include 'lip balm, alcohol swabs, fentanyl testing strips and clean syringes' - and have infuriated Republicans, *Daily Mail*, February 22, 2022. https://www.dailymail.co.uk/news/article-10499799/Liberal-drug-group-criticizes-Biden-administration-NOT-giving-free-crack-pipes.html

36   ibid

37   Phillips, "Liberal Drug Group Now Criticizes Biden Administration."

38   Fox News Staff, "Senator Rips White House."

39   Patrick Hauf, These Harm-Reduction Facilities Are Slated for Biden Administration Grants. They're Also Distributing Crack Pipes. *Washington Free Beacon*, Aug 3, 2022. https://freebeacon.com/biden-administration/these-harm-reduction-facilities-are-slated-for-biden-administration-grants-theyre-also-distributing-crack-pipes/

40   See Global Drug Policy Program, "Who We Are," Open Society Foundations, accessed June 29, 2022, https://www.opensocietyfoundations.org/who-we-are/programs/global-drug-policy-program; Holly Catania and Joanne Csete, "Drug Courts and Drug Treatment: Dismissing Science and Patients' Rights," Open Society Foundations, January 10, 2014, https://www.opensocietyfoundations.org/voices/drug-courts-and-drug-treatment-dismissing-science-and-patients-rights; and Alexandra Kirby-Lepesh, "Reducing the Harm of Drug Use—and of Drug Policies," Open Society Foundations, May 10, 2010, https://www.opensocietyfoundations.org/voices/reducing-harm-drug-use-and-drug-policies.

41   See Melissa Schiller, "Drug Policy Alliance Leads 50+ Organizations in Calling on Congress to Finally Remove D.C. Marijuana Rider," Cannabis Business Times, March 4, 2022, https://www.cannabisbusinesstimes.com/article/drug-policy-alliance-leads-organizations-calling-on-congress-to-remove-dc-marijuana-rider/; "Drug Policy Alliance Biennial Conference," Open Society Foundations, accessed June 29, 2022, https://www.opensocietyfoundations.org/events/drug-policy-alliance-biennial-conference.

42   See Drug Policy Alliance, "Marijuana Legalization and Regulation," DrugPolicy.org, accessed June
      29, 2022, https://drugpolicy.org/issues/marijuana-legalization-and-regulation?ms=5B1_21Grant&
      cid=7011K000001Rr6yQAC.

43   See Jacob Fischler, U.S. House Votes to Decriminalize Marijuana in Federal Law," The Pulse (NC
      Policy Watch blog), April 1, 2022, https://pulse.ncpolicywatch.org/2022/04/01/u-s-house-votes-
      to-decriminalize-marijuana-in-federal-law/#sthash.hQanzNkI.dpbs.

44   Steven Nelson, "Biden 'Committed' to Freeing Inmates with Marijuana Convictions, Psaki Says,"
      New York Post, April 20, 2022. https://nypost.com/2022/04/20/joe-biden-committed-to-freeing-
      convicts-locked-up-for-marijuana/.

45   George Soros, "Remarks Delivered at the World Economic Forum," Davos, Switzerland, January
      25, 2018, George Soros website, https://www.georgesoros.com/2018/01/25/remarks-delivered-at-
      the-world-economic-forum/.

46   Soros, "Remarks Delivered at the World Economic Forum."

47   Soros, "Remarks Delivered at the World Economic Forum."

48   "Booker Statement on Marijuana Legalization Mark-Up," Cory Booker website, November 20,
      2019, https://www.booker.senate.gov/news/press/booker-statement-on-marijuana-legalization-
      mark-up.

49   Soros, The Bubble of American Supremacy, 27 (see chap.1, n. 2).

50   Soros, Soros on Soros, 197 (see chap. 1, n. 26).

51   Soros, The Bubble of American Supremacy, 27.

52   Soros, Soros on Soros, 198.

53   Matt Sledge, "The DEA Would Like You to Be Aware of Billionaire George Soros's Scary
      Plans," The Blog (HuffPost), April 11, 2013, https://www.huffpost.com/entry/dea-george-
      soros_b_3063849.

54   Rachel Ehrenfeld, Narco-Terrorism, Basic Books, 1990, p.xv; Sovetskaya Voyenna Entsiklopedia,
      vol. 7 (1979), 493; S. Pope, "Diversion: An Unrecognized Element of Intelligence?" Defense
      Analysis 3, no. 2 (1987): 133–51. See also Victor Suvorov, "Spetsnaz: The Soviet Union's Special
      Forces," International Defense Review, September 1983, 1210. In addition, see the Russian texts of
      the Soviet Military Encyclopedia Dictionary of 1986, s.v. "special reconnaissance." This informa-
      tion was also verified by consulting with experts on Soviet strategy, among them Dr. Leon Goure
      from SAIC, McLean, Virginia, in December 1989.

55   John M. Kramer, "Drug Abuse in the Soviet Union," Problems of Communism 37 (January–Feb-
      ruary 1988): 40. Rachel Ehrenfeld," Narco-Terrorism: The Kremlin Connection." The Heritage
      Foundation, January 28, 1987. https://www.heritage.org/europe/report/narco-terrorism-the-krem-
      lin-connection

56   Edward Codey, "Castro Ties to Drugs Suggested," The Washington Post, May 1, 1983. https://www.
      washingtonpost.com/archive/politics/1983/05/01/castro-ties-to-drugs-suggested/242170fe-a930-
      4bc4-b30c-18016f794497/

57   Aldous Huxley, Brave New World, Harper Perennial Modern Classics ed. (New York: HarperCol-
      lins, 2006), 53.

58   Huxley, 75, 80–81.

59   Huxley, 238, 77.

60   OSF, Gender-Affirming Medical Treatment and Change of Sex on Identity Documents, https://
      www.opensocietyfoundations.org/publications/gender-affirming-medical-treatment-and-change-
      sex-identity-documents

ENDNOTES

61   David Callahan, The Givers: Wealth, Power, and Philanthropy in a New Gilded Age (New York: Knopf, 2017), 275.

62   Sean Williams, "Residents in These 8 States Are Set to Vote on Marijuana This November," The Motley Fool, July 10, 2016, https://www.fool.com/investing/2016/07/10/residents-in-these-8-states-are-set-to-vote-on-mar.aspx

63   Joseph A. Califano Jr., "Devious Efforts to Legalize Drugs," Washington Post, December 4, 1996, https://www.washingtonpost.com/archive/opinions/1996/12/04/devious-efforts-to-legalize-drugs/d71996ac-faaf-4e1e-a2e2-a177b31d7afa/.

64   David S. Broder, "Wealthy Benefactors Stoke Campaigns for Medical Marijuana," Washington Post, October 20, 1998, https://www.washingtonpost.com/wp-srv/politics/campaigns/keyraces98/stories/ballot102098.htm.

65   N. Aisbett, "The Billionaire, Drugs and Us," West Australian, November 30, 2002.

66   George Soros, Remarks delivered at the World Economic Forum, January 25, 2018, https://www.georgesoros.com/2018/01/25/remarks-delivered-at-the-world-economic-forum/

67   See Ron DeSantis (@RonDeSantisFL), "The Soros-funded radical Left is running a scheme to manipulate local media in Florida to push their Marxist agenda on voters," Twitter, June 6, 2022, 6:35 p.m., https://twitter.com/rondesantisfl/status/1533955785901985792?s=21&t=JKaX3Txwf OhtiubFVrGZVQ.

68   George Soros, "Why I Support Legal Marijuana," Wall Street Journal, October 26, 2010, https://www.wsj.com/articles/SB10001424052702303467004575574450703567656.

69   NIDA, Drug Facts, Nationwide Trends, 2014, p.2. https://nida.nih.gov/sites/default/files/drug-factsnationwidetrends1.pdf

70   Christian Gunadi, Bin Zhu, and Yuyan Shi, "Recreational Cannabis Legalizatin and Transitions in Cannabis Use: Findings from a Nationally Representative Longitudinal Cohort in the United States," Addiction, July 22, 2021, https://onlinelibrary.wiley.com/doi/epdf/10.1111/add.15895.

71   Yadira Galindo, "More Young People Begin Recreational Cannabis Use Illegally in States That Legalize It," UC San Diego News Center, May 26, 2022, https://ucsdnews.ucsd.edu/pressrelease/more-youth-begin-recreational-cannabis-use-illegally-in-states-that-legalize-it?utm_source=syndication.

72   Soros, "Why I Support Legal Marijuana."

73   [1] Narcofornia- How Progressives Sold Out Rural Towns to Foreign Drug Lords. Daily Caller, https://narcofornia.com

74   See "California Medical Marijuana Laws," Medical Marijuana, accessed June 30, 2022, https://www.medicalmarijuana.com/law/california-medical-marijuana-laws/.

75   NIDA, RFP Announcement: Production, Analysis, & Distribution of Cannabis & Marijuana Cigarettes, NOT-DA-09-031, August 21, 2009. https://grants.nih.gov/grants/guide/notice-files/NOT-DA-09-031.html

76   Nick Chiles, "Holder Pushes Plan to Reduce Sentences for Drug-Dealing Crimes," Atlanta Black Star, March 13, 2014, https://atlantablackstar.com/2014/03/13/holder-pushes-plan-reduce-sentences-drug-crimes/.

77   See Sean Williams, "Residents in These 8 States Are Set to Vote on Marijuana This November," The Motley Fool, July 10, 2016, https://www.fool.com/investing/2016/07/10/residents-in-these-8-states-are-set-to-vote-on-mar.aspx; Tony Newman, "Looking Back: President Obama's Historic Efforts to Roll Back the Drug War and Tackle Mass Incarceration," Drug Policy Alliance, January 18, 2017, https://drugpolicy.org/blog/looking-back-president-obamas-historic-efforts-roll-back-drug-war-and-tackle-mass-incarceration;

78   Theodore Dalrymple, "Don't Legalize Drugs," City Journal (Spring 1997), https://vdocuments.site/dont-legalize-drugs.html.

79   Andrea Noble, "DEA to Decide within Months Whether to Change Federal Status of Marijuana," *Washington Times*, April 6, 2016, https://www.washingtontimes.com/news/2016/apr/6/dea-decide-within-months-whether-change-federal-st/.

80   Noble, "DEA to Decide within Months Whether to Change Federal Status of Marijuana.

81   Peter Suciu, "Marijuana May Cause Schizophrenia-Like Brain Changes," RedOrbit, December 16, 2013, https://www.redorbit.com/news/health/1113028919/marijuana-effects-on-the-brain-similar-to-schizophrenia-121613/.

82   "Marijuana," MedicineNet, last reviewed October 6, 2008, https://www.medicinenet.com/script/main/art.asp?articlekey=148793.

83   "Marijuana Abuse Facts," Marijuana Abuse, accessed June 30, 2022, https://www.marijuana-abuse.org/Marijuana_Abuse_Facts.htm.

84   Marijuana Effects on the Heart and the Lungs. https://clearga.org/marijuana-effects-on-the-heart-and-the-lungs/,

85   American Heart Association Rapid Access Journal Report, Marijuana use may increase heart complications in young, middle-aged adults, April 23, 2014 http://newsroom.heart.org/news/marijuana-use-may-increase-heart-complications-in-young-middle-aged-adults,

86   Hazeldon Betty Ford Foundation, "Marijuana Addiction," accessed June 30, 2022, https://www.hazeldenbettyford.org/addiction/types-of-addiction/marijuana.

87   "Marijuana Abuse Facts."

88   The National Institute on Drug Abuse Media Guide, https://nida.nih.gov/sites/default/files/mediaguide_web_3_0.pdf

89   James M. Cole, Office of the Deputy Attorney General, Memorandum for All State Attorneys, August 29, 2013, https://www.dfi.wa.gov/documents/banks/cole-memo-08-29-13.pdf.

90   George Soros, Soros on Soros, Wiley; 1st edition (August 18, 1995), p. 198.

91   Carlton E. Turner, "'Medical' Marijuana a Con," American Center for Democracy, November 19, 2016, https://acdemocracy.org/medical-marijuana-a-con/.

92   Jeremy Berke, Shayanne Gal, and Yeji Jesse Lee, "Marijuana Legalization Is Sweeping the US. See Every State Where Cannabis Is Legal." Business Insider, updated May 27, 2022, https://www.businessinsider.com/legal-marijuana-states-2018-1.

93   CDC Press Release, U.S. Overdose Deaths In 2021 Increased Half as Much as in 2020—But Are Still Up 15%, May 11, 2022,https://www.cdc.gov/nchs/pressroom/nchs_press_releases/2022/202205.htm .

94   Naveed Jamali and Tom O'Connor, "Chinese Chemicals in Mexican Cartel Hands Feed Deadly U.S. Fentanyl Crisis," *Newsweek*, May 5, 2021. https://www.*newsweek*.com/chinese-chemicals-mexican-cartel-hands-feed-deadly-us-fentanyl-crisis-1588948

95   Patrick Hauf, Yes, Safe Smoking Kits Include Free Crack Pipes. We Know Because We Got Them, The *Washington Free Beacon*, May 12, 2022. https://freebeacon.com/biden-administration/yes-safe-smoking-kits-include-free-crack-pipes-we-know-because-we-got-them/

96   Rachel Ehrenfeld, Crack Pipe Dreams, *Washington Times*, Dec,15, 1997, http://www.mapinc.org/drugnews/v97/n698/a06.html

97   Christopher Rufo, Safe Injection Sites' Don't Work Well. Just Ask Canada, The Daily Signal, Oct.2, 2020. https://www.dailysignal.com/2020/10/02/safe-injection-sites-dont-work-well-just-ask-canada/. Also see, Rachel Ehrenfeld, Selling Syringes: The Swiss Experiment, The *Wall Street Journal*, Sept 6, 1995, p. A18, https://acdemocracy.org/selling-syringes-the-swiss-experiment/,

98 Amy Larson, San Francisco's new DA vows to shut down open-air drug market, July 12, 2022, https://www.kron4.com/news/bay-area/san-franciscos-new-da-vows-to-shut-down-open-air-drug-market/

99 Liza Rozner, Some Chelsea residents say drug use in the area is completely out of control, and they're hiring private security. CBS New York, July 31, 2022, https://www.cbsnews.com/newyork/news/some-chelsea-residents-say-drug-use-in-the-area-is-completely-out-of-control-and-theyre-hiring-private-security/

100 St. Michael's Hospital, Emergency care and hospitalizations higher among cannabis users, study finds, ScienceDaily, June 28, 2022, https://www.sciencedaily.com/releases/2022/06/220628083257.htm

101 World Drug Report 2022, UN Office on Drugs and Crime, June 27, 2022. https://www.unodc.org/unodc/frontpage/2022/June/unodc-world-drug-report-2022-highlights-trends-on-cannabis-post-legalization--environmental-impacts-of-illicit-drugs--and-drug-use-among-women-and-youth.html

102 James Reinl, "A 5.8% rise in car crashes, a spike in addictions and children as young as NINE interested in trying marijuana: Studies lay bare the cost of legalizing cannabis as Democrats try to lift federal ban," Daily Mail, July 22, 2022. https://www.dailymail.co.uk/ushome/index.html.

103 Erik Robinson," Cannabis products demonstrate short-term reduction in chronic pain, little else," OHSU News, June 6, 2022. https://news.ohsu.edu/2022/06/06/cannabis-products-demonstrate-short-term-reduction-in-chronic-pain-little-else

104 Dwight K. Blake, "Marijuana Statistics 2020, Usage, Trends and Data," American Marijuana, last updated on September 17, 2020, https://americanmarijuana.org/marijuana-statistics/.

105 US Drug Enforcement Administration, "Drug Scheduling," DEA website, accessed July 2, 2022, https://www.dea.gov/drug-information/drug-scheduling.

106 "Five Reasons Eating Marijuana Is Actually Good for Your Health," Cannabis.net, June 29, 2018, https://cannabis.net/blog/medical/five-reasons-eating-marijuana-is-actually-good-for-your-health.

107 Nora Volkow, "COVID-19: Potential Implications for Individuals with Substance Use Disorders," Nora's Blog, National Institute on Drug Abuse, April 6, 2020, https://nida.nih.gov/about-nida/noras-blog/2020/04/covid-19-potential-implications-individuals-substance-use-disorders.

108 Mauro Maccarone, Tribute to Professor Raphael Mechoulam, The Founder of Cannabinoid and Endocannabinoid Research, Molecules. 2022 Jan; 27(1): 323. https://www.ncbi.nlm.nih.gov/pmc/articles/PMC8746417/ 10.3390/molecules27010323

109 Seth Wong, "Cannabis Research in Israel: Meeting with Dr. Raphael Mechoulam," Cannabis Industry Journal, January 27, 2016, https://cannabisindustryjournal.com/column/cannabis-research-in-israel-meeting-with-dr-raphael-mechoulam/.

110 Endocannabinoids, Roger G. Pertwee Ed., Handbook of Experimental Pharmacology, Volume 231, (Cham: Springer International Switzerland, 2015) preface, viii-ix, https://link.springer.com/content/pdf/bfm%3A978-3-319-20825-1%2F1

111 See "April 3, 2022 'Cannabis & Childhood Cancer' - Dr. Stuart Reece," We the People Radio, https://www.wethepeopleradio.us/archives/2022-04-03/.

112 Regina LaBelle, "U.S. National Statement to the 64th Session of the CND," April 2021, https://www.unodc.org/documents/commissions/CND/CND_Sessions/CND_64/Statements/13April/USA.pdf; see Executive Office of the President, Office of National Drug Control Policy, "The Biden-Harris Administration's Statement of Drug Policy Priorities for Year One," https://www.whitehouse.gov/wp-content/uploads/2021/03/BidenHarris-Statement-of-Drug-Policy-Priorities-April-1.pdf.

113   Stephan M. Hann, "Better Data for a Better Understanding of the Use and Safety Profile of Cannabidiol (CBD) Products," https://www.fda.gov/news-events/fda-voices/better-data-better-understanding-use-and-safety-profile-cannabidiol-cbd-products

114   Stephen M. Hahn, "Better Data for a Better Understanding of the Use and Safety Profile of Cannabidiol (CBD) Products," U.S. Food and Drug Administration, content current as of January 8, 2021, https://www.fda.gov/news-events/fda-voices/better-data-better-understanding-use-and-safety-profile-cannabidiol-cbd-products.

115   Geoffrey A. Dubrow et al., "A Survey of Cannabinoids and Toxic Elements in Hemp-Derived Products from the United States Marketplace," Journal of Food Composition and Analysis 97 (April 2021), https://www.sciencedirect.com/science/article/abs/pii/S0889157520315052.

116   Albert Stuart Reece and Gary Kenneth Hulse, A geospatiotemporal and causal inference epidemiological exploration of substance and cannabinoid exposure as drivers of rising US pediatric cancer rates." BMC Cancer 21, no. 197 (2021), 1, 2, https://bmccancer.biomedcentral.com/track/pdf/10.1186/s12885-021-07924-3.pdf/.

117   "April 3, 2022," We the People Radio.

118   "Times letters: The Jury System and the Colston Statue Case," Times, accessed July 2, 2022, https://www.thetimes.co.uk/article/times-letters-the-jury-system-and-the-colston-statue-case-xpjl82jp2.

3: JUSTICE, SOROS-STYLE

1   George Soros, Why I support Reform Prosecutors, Wall Street Journal, July 31, 2022. https://www.wsj.com/articles/why-i-support-reform-prosecutors-law-enforces-jail-prison-crime-rate-justice-police-funding-11659277441

2   Sen. Tom Cotton, George Soros Gets Criminal Justice All Wrong, Wall Street Journal, Aug 3, 2022. https://www.wsj.com/amp/articles/george-soros-tom-cotton-crime-progressive-prosecutor-justice-11659476488

3   See The Sentencing Project, "Drug Policy and the Criminal Justice System," 2001, https://static.prisonpolicy.org/scans/sp/5047.pdf.

4   "JOB OPPORTUNITIES," Dream Defenders website, accessed July 2, 2022, https://dreamdefenders.org/jobs/.

5   American Civil Liberties Union, "ACLU Awarded $50 Million by Open Society Foundations to End Mass Incarceration," press release, November 7, 2014, https://www.aclu.org/print/node/48907.

6   See Sean Murphy, "Election 2022: Sizable Soros-Backed Contribution Stirs Up Cumberland County DA Race," Spectrum News, June 8, 2022, https://spectrumlocalnews.com/me/maine/news/2022/06/08/soros-backed-super-pac-campaigning-for-cumberland-da-hopeful; and David Sharp, Andrew Demillo and Geoff Mulvihill, "National Groups Flooding Local Prosecutor Races with Money," Midland Daily News, June 10, 2022, updated June 13, 2022, https://www.ourmidland.com/news/article/National-groups-flooding-local-prosecutor-races-17232780.php.

7   See Associated Press, "76,000 California Inmates to Be Eligible for Earlier Release," NBC News, April 30, 2021, https://www.nbcnews.com/news/us-news/76-000-california-inmates-be-eligible-earlier-release-n1266044; WAND (Decatur, IL), "Gov. Pritzker Addresses Release of 4,035 Inmates from State Prisons," WAND, April 30, 2020, updated May 1, 2020, https://www.wandtv.com/news/gov-pritzker-addresses-release-of-4-035-inmates-from-state-prisons/article_ffa549f4-8b54-11ea-86d1-a73779ba8bce.html.

ENDNOTES

8   Leonardo Antenangeli and Matthew R. Durose, "Recidivism of Prisoners Released in 24 States in 2008: A 10-Year Follow-Up Period (2008–2018)," U.S. Department of Justice Special Report, September 2021, 1, https://bjs.ojp.gov/BJS_PUB/rpr24s0810yfup0818/Web%20content/508%20 compliant%20PDFs.

9   Antenangeli and Matthew R. Durose, 8, 4.

10 Antenangeli and Matthew R. Durose, 16, 9

11 WABC-Radio News Team, "Cities Will Set Murder Records Because of 'Soros Effect," RealClear Politics, December 15, 2021, https://www.realclearpolitics.com/articles/2021/12/15/cities_will_ set_murder_records_because_of_soros_effect_146884.html.

12 John H. Johnson, "Black on Black Crime: the Cause, the Consequences, the Cures," Ebony, August 1979, p. 35, https://books.google.com/books?id=K3bfmTebrYQC&pg=PA32&lpg=PA32&d q#v=onepage&q&f=false.

13 Michael Javen Fortner, Black Silent Majority: The Rockefeller Drug Laws and the Politics of Punishment, Harvard University Press; Illustrated edition (September 28, 2015) https://www.amazon. com/gp/product/0674743997/ref=as_li_qf_asin_il_tl?ie=UTF8&tag=manhattani03b-20&crea tive=9325&linkCode=as2&creativeASIN=0674743997&linkId=a77422d6758cd4806d0cecf-0c64627b1.

14 Julio Rosas, Jaw-Dropping: Police Chief Association Releases Number of Officers Injured During Violent Riots, Townhall, Nov 30, 2020, https://townhall.com/tipsheet/juliorosas/2020/11/30/ police-chief-association-releases-jawdropping-numbers-of-injured-officers-during-n2580844.

15 FBI Dallas, FBI Releases Statistics for Law Enforcement Officers Assaulted and Killed in the Line of Duty, October 22, 2021, https://www.fbi.gov/contact-us/field-offices/dallas/news/press-releases/ fbi-releases-statistics-for-law-enforcement-officers-assaulted-and-killed-in-the-line-of-duty

16 Police Officer Deaths in 2020, March 12, 2021, American Police Officers Alliance. https://ameri-canpoliceofficersalliance.com/police-officer-deaths-in-2020/.

17 Rachel Herzing, ""Let's Reduce, Not Reform, Policing in America," Open Society Foundation Voices, October 6, 2016, https://www.opensocietyfoundations.org/voices/let-s-reduce-not-reform-policing-america.

18 Stefan Kanfer, "Connoisseur of Chaos: The Dystopian Vision of George Soros, Billionaire Funder of the Left," City Journal, Winter 2017, https://www.city-journal.org/html/connoisseur-cha-os-14954.html.

19 Open Society Foundations, "Awarded Grants," accessed July 2, 2022, https://www.opensociety-foundations.org/grants/past?filter_keyword=community+resource+hub.

20 Joe Schoffstall, "Soros Bankrolls Dark Money Hub for Activists Pushing to Dismantle Police, Grants Show," Fox News, accessed July 2, 2022, https://www.foxnews.com/politics/soros-bank-rolls-dark-money-hub-activists-dismantle-police.

21 Schoffstall, "Soros Bankrolls Dark Money Hub for Activists Pushing to Dismantle Police, Grants Show."

22 See Federal Election Commission, FEC Form 1: Statement of Organization, for Lead the Way 2022, January 1, 2022, https://docquery.fec.gov/cgi-bin/forms/C00782151/1576269/.

23 Joe Schoffstall, "Soros Family Quietly Bankrolls Committees Supporting 'Defund the Police' Candidates," Fox News, April 8, 2022, https://www.foxnews.com/politics/soros-family-quietly-bankrolls-defund-the-police-candidates.

24 Dan Springer, "Oregon's Drug Decriminalization Effort a 'Tragedy,'" Fox News, accessed July 2, 2022, https://www.foxnews.com/us/portland-drug-decriminalization-effort-tragedy.

25   Elise Hammond, et al., Derek Chauvin sentenced for violating George Floyd's civil rights, CNN, July 7, 2022. https://www.cnn.com/us/live-news/derek-chauvin-federal-sentencing-07-07-22/index.html.

26   Paul Vercammen and Steve Almasy, Derek Chauvin sentenced to 21 years in federal prison for depriving George Floyd of his civil rights, CNN, July 7, 2022.https://www.cnn.com/2022/07/07/us/derek-chauvin-federal-sentencing/index.html.

27   Danielle Wallace, Ex-Minneapolis cop Thomas Lane sentenced to 3 years for manslaughter in George Floyd death, Fox News, September 21, 2022, https://nypost.com/2022/09/21/thomas-lane-sentenced-for-manslaughter-in-george-floyd-death/.

28   "Most Voters Want Congress to Investigate the 574 Violent Riots in 2020 That Resulted in over 2,000 Injured Police Officers as Well as the January 6th Riot at the US Capitol," National Police Association. Accessed July 2, 2022, https://nationalpolice.org/most-voters-want-congress-to-investigate-the-574-violent-riots-in-2020-that-resulted-in-over-2000-injured-police-officers-as-well-as-the-january-6th-riot-at-the-us-capitol/.

29   Fola Akinnibi, Sarah Holder and Christopher Cannon, "Cities Say They Want to Defund the Police. Their Budgets Say Otherwise," Bloomberg, January 12, 2021, https://www.bloomberg.com/graphics/2021-city-budget-police-funding/.

30   Constitutional Nobody, "NYPD blues: 'It will take 20 years to fix this mess' as record 1,596 officers quit over 'low pay, inferior benefits and constant abuse'," USSA News, June 14, 2022, https://ussanews.com/2022/06/14/nypd-blues-it-will-take-20-years-to-fix-this-mess-as-record-1596-officers-quit-over-low-pay-inferior-benefits-and-constant-abuse/.

31   Tim Balk and Chris Sommerfeldt, "Poll: More Than 75% of New Yorkers Worry They Will Be Victims of Violent Crime," MSN, June 7, 2022, https://www.msn.com/en-us/news/us/poll-more-than-75percent-of-new-yorkers-worry-they-will-be-victims-of-violent-crime/ar-AAYbtGt.

32   M. Dowling, "Nearly 500,000 Flee New York Crime and Taxes," Independent Sentinal, May 31, 2022, https://www.independentsentinel.com/quarter-million-people-flee-new-york-crime-and-taxes/.

33   "George Soros's Foundation Pours $220 Million into Racial Equality Push," New York Times, July 13, 2020, https://www.nytimes.com/2020/07/13/us/politics/george-soros-racial-justice-organizations.html?action=click&module=Top%20Stories&pgtype=Homepage.

34   "George Soros's Foundation Pours $220 Million into Racial Equality Push,"

35   See "What We Do," Open Society Foundations, accessed July 2, 2022, https://www.opensocietyfoundations.org/what-we-do.

36   "Open Society Foundations (OSF)," Influence Watch, accessed July 2, 2022, https://www.influencewatch.org/non-profit/open-society-foundations/.

37   Christopher F. Rufo, "Critical Race Theory: What It Is and How to Fight It," Imprimis 50, no. 3 (March 2021), https://imprimis.hillsdale.edu/critical-race-theory-fight/.

38   See Debora Guidetti and Clara Grosset, "Slavery and Reparation in France," Open Society Foundations Voices, May 9, 2013, https://www.opensocietyfoundations.org/voices/slavery-and-reparation-france.

39   See Melissa Klein and Jon Levine, "Groups Tied to George Soros Pump Cash into NYC's John Jay College," New York Post, February 12, 2022, https://nypost.com/2022/02/12/george-soros-groups-pump-cash-into-nycs-john-jay-college/.

40   Melissa Klein, Jon Levine and Conor Skelding, "John Jay College Think Tank Is Ground Zero for Woke Das," New York Post, February 5, 2022, https://nypost.com/2022/02/05/manhattan-college-think-tank-is-ground-zero-for-woke-das/.

ENDNOTES

41 Astead W. Herndon, George Soros's Foundation Pours $220 Million Into Racial Equity Push, *The New York Times*, July 13, 2020. https://www.nytimes.com/2020/07/13/us/politics/george-soros-racial-justice-organizations.html?action=click&module=Top Stories&pgtype=Homepage.

42 Crime and Justice News, "Soros Providing New Funds for Criminal Justice Reform," The Crime Report, July 13, 2020, https://thecrimereport.org/2020/07/13/soros-providing-new-funds-for-criminal-justice-reform/.

43 Crime and Justice News, "Soros Providing New Funds for Criminal Justice Reform."

44 Crime and Justice News, "Soros Providing New Funds for Criminal Justice Reform."

45 Morgan Phillips, "Biden Says Some Funding Should 'Absolutely' Be Redirected from Police," Fox News, July 8, 2020, https://www.foxnews.com/politics/biden-says-some-funding-should-absolutely-be-redirected-from-police.

46 Joshua Rhett Miller, "Bail Fund Backed by Kamala Harris Freed Minneapolis Man Charged with Murder," *New York Post*, September 8, 2021, https://nypost.com/2021/09/08/bail-fund-backed-by-kamala-harris-freed-man-charged-with-murder/.

47 Roberto Roldan, "UPDATED: Louisville Community Bail Fund says it posted bail for accused shooter Quintez Brown,"89.3 WFPL, February 16, 2022 https://wfpl.org/louisville-community-bail-fund-says-it-will-post-bond-for-accused-shooter-quintez-brown/

48 See the Tides Center's 2020 Return of Organization Exempt from Income Tax form 990 at https://www.tides.org/wp-content/uploads/2021/11/2020_Tides-Center_Form-990-Public-Disclosure.pdf.

49 "Foundation to Promote Open Society (FPOS)," accessed July 6, 2022. https://www.influencewatch.org/non-profit/foundation-to-promote-open-society/.

50 Timothy H.J. Nerozzi, "Soros Donated $250,000 to Fiscal Sponsor of Louisville Group Who Bailed Out Attempted Murderer," Fox News, February 21, 2022, https://www.foxnews.com/politics/soros-donated-250000-fiscal-sponsor-louisville-bail-fund.

51 See Adam Kredo and Matthew Foldi, "Discover Card Cuts Ties with Palestinian Terror-Linked Organization," *Washington Free Beacon*, September 16, 2021, https://freebeacon.com/national-security/discover-card-cuts-ties-with-palestinian-terror-linked-organization/.

52 Nerozzi and Cawthorne, "Soros Donated $250,000 to Fiscal Sponsor of Louisville Group."

53 Hayden Ludwig, "'Dark Money' Networks on the Left Pulled In $3.7 Billion in 2020," Capital Research Center, May 12, 2022, https://capitalresearch.org/article/dark-money-networks-on-the-left-pulled-in-3-7-billion-in-2020/.

54 "Remarks of President Joe Biden—State of the Union Address as Prepared for Delivery," The White House, March 1, 2022, https://www.whitehouse.gov/briefing-room/speeches-remarks/2022/03/01/remarks-of-president-joe-biden-state-of-the-union-address-as-delivered/.

55 "Six Months after Mass Protests Began, What Is the Future of BLM?," Economist, December 10, 2020, https://www.economist.com/united-states/2020/12/10/six-months-after-mass-protests-began-what-is-the-future-of-blm?utm_campaign=editorial-social&utm_medium=social-organic&utm_source=twitter.

56 Maria Morava and Scottie Andrew, The Black Lives Matter foundation raised $90 million in 2020, and gave almost a quarter of it to local chapters and organizations, CNN, February 25, 2021, https://www.cnn.com/2021/02/25/us/black-lives-matter-2020-donation-report-trnd/index.html.

ENDNOTES

57   Kristin Harrison-Oneal, Black Lives Matter Of Greater Atlanta' Facebook Page Admin Indicted For Defrauding Donors, Shore News Network, March 15, 2021, https://www.shorenewsnetwork.com/2021/03/15/black-lives-matter-of-greater-atlanta-facebook-page-admin-indicted-for-defrauding-donors/; Huston Keene, Boston BLM leader and her husband hit with federal fraud, conspiracy charges, March 16, 2022, Fox News, https://www.foxnews.com/politics/boston-blm-leader-and-her-husband-hit-with-federal-fraud-conspiracy-charges.

58   See the various articles tagged "Black Lives Matter" on Spiked, https://www.spiked-online.com/tag/black-lives-matter/.

59   See Nicholas Kulish, "After Raising $90 Million in 2020, Black Lives Matter Has $42 Million in Assets," New York Times, May 17, 2022, https://www.nytimes.com/2022/05/17/business/blm-black-lives-matter-finances.html.

60   Houston Keene, "BLM Co-Founder's Consulting Firm Pulled in over $20K a mOnth as She Chaired LA Jail Reform Group," Fox News, April 14, 2021, https://www.foxnews.com/politics/black-lives-matter-patrisse-cullors-consulting-firm-paid-20k-month.

61   See "Introducing the 2012 Soros Justice Fellows," Open Society Foundations, May 17, 2012, https://www.opensocietyfoundations.org/publications/introducing-2012-soros-justice-fellows; and "Open Society Foundations Announce 2020 Soros Justice Fellows," Open Society Foundations, December 18, 2020, https://www.opensocietyfoundations.org/newsroom/open-society-foundations-announce-2020-soros-justice-fellows.

62   Kulish, "After Raising $90 Million in 2020, Black Lives Matter Has $42 Million in Assets."

63   See BLACK LIVES MATTER 2020 IMPACT REPORT, https://blacklivesmatter.com/wp-content/uploads/2021/02/blm-2020-impact-report.pdf.

64   Kulish, "After Raising $90 Million in 2020, Black Lives Matter Has $42 Million in Assets"; see also Sean Campbell, "Black Lives Matter Secretly Bought a $6 Million House Allies and Critics Alike Have Questioned Where the Organization's Money Has Gone," Intelligencer, April 4, 2022, https://nymag.com/intelligencer/2022/04/black-lives-matter-6-million-dollar-house.html.

65   See "Changing Public Attitudes Toward the Criminal Justice System," February 2002, Open Society Foundations, https://www.opensocietyfoundations.org/publications/changing-public-attitudes-toward-criminal-justice-system.

66   Christopher F. Rufo, "Crimes of Survival," ChristopherRufo.com, January 2, 2019, https://christopherrufo.com/crimes-of-survival/.

67   Rufo, "Crimes of Survival."

68   Paige St. John and Abbie Vansickle, "Here's Why George Soros, Liberal Groups Are Spending Big to Help Decide Who's Your Next D.A.," Los Angeles Times, May 23, 2018, https://www.latimes.com/local/california/la-me-prosecutor-campaign-20180523-story.html.

69   See "LELDF Original Research: Justice for Sale: How George Soros Put Radical Prosecutors in Power," Law Enforcement Legal Defense Fund, accessed July 6, 2022, https://www.policedefense.org/leldf-justice-for-sale/.

70   Charles Creitz, "AG Barr: Soros-Funded Dem Prosecutor Candidates Will Lead to Increased Crime, Fewer Police Officers," Fox News, December 20, 2019, https://www.foxnews.com/media/ag-barr-soros-funded-democratic-prosecutor-candidates-will-lead-to-increased-crime-police-department-vacancies.

71   Emma Tucker and Priya Krishnakumar, "Intentional Killings of Law Enforcement Officers Reach 20-Year High, FBI Says," CNN, January 13, 2022, https://www.cnn.com/2022/01/13/us/police-officers-line-of-duty-deaths/index.html.

72   Michael Wilson, "How a Calm Call for Help Led 2 N.Y.P.D. Officers into a Hail of Gunfire," *New York Times*, January 22, 2022, https://www.nytimes.com/2022/01/22/nyregion/nypd-officers-shot-harlem.html.

73   Farah Stockman, "How 'End Mass Incarceration' Became a Slogan for D.A. Candidates, *New York Times*, October 25, 2018, https://www.nytimes.com/2018/10/25/us/texas-district-attorney-race-mass-incarceration.html.

74   See Geoff Pursinger and Dirk VanderHart, "Soros-Tied Group Starts Up PAC in Oregon," Hillsboro NewsTimes, April 11, 2018, https://pamplinmedia.com/ht/117-hillsboro-tribune-news/392113-284284-soros-tied-group-starts-up-pac-in-oregon.

75   Stockman, "How 'End Mass Incarceration' Became a Slogan for D.A. Candidates."

76   See University of California Television (UCTV), "George Soros - The Bubble of American Supremacy," YouTube video, February 8, 2008, https://www.youtube.com/watch?v=Nnf62Uhl3ac.

77   Mike Gonzalez, "SOCIETYCOMMENTARY: Soros-Backed Media Consortium Is Buying, to Censor, Conservative Radio Stations," Daily Signal, June 9, 2022, https://www.dailysignal.com/2022/06/09/soros-backed-media-consortium-is-buying-to-censor-conservative-radio-stations/.

78   LELDF (Law Enforcement Legal Defense Fund), Justice for Sale: How George Soros Put Radical Prosecutors in Power (Alexandria, VA: LELDF, June 2022), 3, http://www.policedefense.org/wp-content/uploads/2022/06/Justice_For_Sale_LELDF_report.pdf.

79   LELDF, 4.

80   Amy Nelson, Recall Chesa Boudin founder says successful ousting a 'bittersweet victory': We didn't want to have to do this, Fox News, June 8, 2022. https://www.foxnews.com/media/san-francisco-district-attorney-chesa-boudin-recall-richie-greenberg-bittersweet-victory

81   Staff, Campaign to Recall George Gascón Turns in Petition Signatures, Santa Monica Mirror, July 12, 2022, https://smmirror.com/2022/07/campaign-to-recall-george-gascon-turns-in-petition-signatures/.

82   Emma Colton and Bill Melugin, "California Gang Member Pushes for Plea Deal ahead of Potential Gascon Recall," MSN, June 8, 2022, https://www.msn.com/en-us/news/crime/california-gang-member-pushes-for-plea-deal-ahead-of-potential-gascon-recall/ar-AAYdvvI.

83   See "Maine Justice & Public Safety PAC," Maine Ethics Commission, accessed July 6, 2022, https://mainecampaignfinance.com/index.html#!exploreCommitteeDetail/438206/0/0/38/2022.

84   David Sharp, Andrew Demillo, and Geoff Mulvihill, "National Groups Flooding Local Prosecutor Races with Money," AP News, June 10, 2022, https://apnews.com/article/2022-midterm-elections-maine-portland-government-and-politics-crime-2f8ad96c907729dffd2f112d3cf1703a.

85   See Parker Thayer, "Living Room Pundit's Guide to Soros District Attorneys," Capital Research Center, January 18, 2022, https://capitalresearch.org/article/living-room-pundits-guide-to-soros-district-attorneys/?blm_aid=45982721. A few updates have been added where appropriate.

86   Thayer, "Living Room Pundit's Guide to Soros District Attorneys."

87   Charles Stimson and Zack Smith, "George Gascón: A Rogue Prosecutor Whose Extreme Policies Undermine the Rule of Law and Make Los Angeles Less Safe," Heritage Foundation, January 28, 2021.

88   Stimson and Smith, "George Gascón."

89   Thayer, "Living Room Pundit's Guide to Soros District Attorneys."

90   Stimson and Smith, "George Gascón."

91   See City News Service, "LA Sees 12% spike in Homicides: 'Los Angeles Is Not Alone in This Trend,' Mayor Garcetti Says," ABC7, January 16, 2022, https://abc7.com/lapd-crime-homicides-statistics/11476915/. "CRIME: 14 Arrested over LA Smash-and-Grab Thefts, but All Released as Leaders Call for End to COVID No-Bail Policy," CBS News, December 3, 2021, https://www.cbsnews.com/news/los-angeles-theft-robberies-smash-and-grab-arrests/; Alex Caprariello and Cassie Buchman, "Looters Raiding LA Cargo Trains of Amazon, UPS Shipments," January 14, 2022, https://www.newsnationnow.com/us-news/west/looters-stealing-amazon-ups-packages-from-la-trains/.

92   Kathleen Cady, "A Preventable Murder," ADDA (Association of Deputy District Attorneys), accessed July 6, 2022, https://myemail.constantcontact.com/A-Preventable-Murder.html?soid=11200 11172453&aid=72cbHCAG7vw.

93   Stimson and Smith, "George Gascón."

94   Jason McGahan, "Law-Enforcement Unions Join Effort to Recall George Gascón," Los Angeles Magazine, February 8, 2022, https://www.lamag.com/citythinkblog/law-enforcement-unions-join-effort-to-recall-george-gascon/.

95   Association of Deputy District Attorneys (ADDA), "Gascón Refuses to Meet," ADDA, February 9, 2022, https://myemail.constantcontact.com/Gasc-n-Refuses-to-Meet.html?soid=1120011172453 &aid=s3toc-6TIUc.

96   MetNews Staff Writer, "Gascón's Special Directives Are Partially Unenforceable," Metropolitan News-Enterprise, June 3, 2022, http://www.metnews.com/articles/2022/Gascon_06032022.htm.

97   MetNews Staff Writer, "Gascón's Special Directives Are Partially Unenforceable."

98   Lee Brown and Marjorie Hernandez, Woke LA County DA George Gascón narrowly survives recall effort, New York Post, August 16, 2022. https://nypost.com/2022/08/16/woke-la-da-george-gascon-survives-recall-bid/

99   Thayer, "Living Room Pundit's Guide to Soros District Attorneys."

100   Thayer.

101   Julius Young , Nate Day, Jussie Smollett convicted of staging hate crime, lying to cops, New York Post, December 9, 2021, https://www.foxnews.com/entertainment/jussie-smollett-verdict-alleged-hate-crime-hoax-trial

102   Thayer.

103   Thayer.

104   Thayer.

105   Michelle Liu, Incoming Hinds County district attorney Jody Owens accused of sexual harassment by former colleagues, Mississippi Today, October 11, 2019, https://mississippitoday.org/2019/10/11/incoming-hinds-county-district-attorney-jody-owens-accused-of-sexual-harassment-by-former-colleagues/

106   Joshua Williams, Hinds County District Attorney denies pointing gun at man in conflict that involved staffer, Clarion Ledger, September 14, 2022, https://www.clarionledger.com/story/news/2022/09/14/jody-owens-hinds-county-district-attorney-gun-apartment-staffer/69493881007/

107   Editorial Board, Editorial: Kimberly Gardner appears to have trouble obeying laws she's sworn to uphold, St. Louis Post-Dispatch, July 27, 2020, https://www.stltoday.com/opinion/editorial/editorial-kimberly-gardner-appears-to-have-trouble-obeying-laws-shes-sworn-to-uphold/article_120a3f3f-4aab-52fc-aa21-b9586aa99fec.html

108 Doyle Murphy, St. Louis Circuit Attorney Kim Gardner Fined for Campaign Violations, River-Front Times (RFT), Jan 3, 2019, https://www.riverfronttimes.com/news/st-louis-circuit-attorney-kim-gardner-fined-for-campaign-violations-29222850.

109 Sam Clancy, St. Louis Circuit Attorney Kim Gardner pays fine after campaign finance investigation, 5OnYourSide, January 2, 2019, https://www.ksdk.com/article/news/politics/st-louis-circuit-attorney-kim-gardner-pays-fine-after-campaign-finance-investigation/63-05eb590d-6334-4bf5-93f4-7cf44a59be1a.

110 Jim Salter, Missouri Supreme Court reprimands prosecutor over Eric Greitens case, The Washington Times, August 30, 2022, https://www.washingtontimes.com/news/2022/aug/30/missouri-supreme-court-reprimands-kim-gardner-st-l/.

111 Rebecca Rivas, Missouri Supreme Court fines Kim Gardner $750 for professional misconduct, Missouri Independent, August 31, 2022. https://news.stlpublicradio.org/government-politics-issues/2022-08-31/missouri-supreme-court-fines-kim-gardner-750-for-professional-misconduct, Also, Alisha Shurr, MEC fines Gardner $63K for campaign violations, The Missouri Times, January 3, 2019, https://themissouritimes.com/mec-fines-gardner-63k-for-campaign-violations/.

112 Tristan Justice, Legal Docs: St. Louis Prosecutor Tampered With Evidence In McCloskey Gun Case, The Federalist, JULY 23, 2020, https://thefederalist.com/2020/07/23/legal-docs-st-louis-prosecutor-tampered-with-evidence-in-mccloskey-gun-case/.

113 Christine Byers, Tampering charge against Patricia McCloskey dropped, could face harassment misdemeanor, 10News, May 25, 2021, https://www.wbir.com/article/news/crime/special-prosecutor-drops-tampering-patricia-mccloskey-harassment-charge/63-2b617908-a10f-4f0f-a4e3-25cf55557a79.

114 Joel Currier, St. Louis judge disqualifies Gardner, her office from prosecuting McCloskey gun-waving case, St. Louis Post-Dispatch, December 10, 2020, https://www.stltoday.com/news/local/crime-and-courts/st-louis-judge-disqualifies-gardner-her-office-from-prosecuting-gun-waving-case/article_6dd89413-e92e-54a7-ab32-ab1775c7ec3e.html.

115 Jim Salter, Missouri Supreme Court reprimands prosecutor over Eric Greitens case, The Washington Times, August 30, 2022, https://www.washingtontimes.com/news/2022/aug/30/missouri-supreme-court-reprimands-kim-gardner-st-l/.

116 Thayer, also, Zack Smith, Meet Kimberly Gardner, the Rogue Prosecutor Whose Policies Are Wreaking Havoc in St. Louis, The Heritage Foundation, April 14, 2021, https://www.heritage.org/crime-and-justice/commentary/meet-kimberly-gardner-the-rogue-prosecutor-whose-policies-are-wreaking.

117 Thayer.

118 Thayer.

119 Brooke Singman, Manhattan DA Bragg suspended Trump investigation 'indefinitely,' stopped pursuing charges, Fox News, March 24, 2022. https://www.foxnews.com/politics/manhattan-da-bragg-suspended-trump-investigation-indefinitely-stopped-pursuing-charges.

120 Thayer.

121 Thayer.

122 Thayer.

123 Thayer.

124 Randy DeSoto, Texas DA Announces He Won't Prosecute Theft Crimes Valued Under $750, The Western Journal, April 23, 2019, https://www.westernjournal.com/texas-da-announces-wont-prosecute-theft-crimes-valued-750/.

125 Thayer.

126 Thayer.

127 Thayer.

128 Brad Johnson, Travis County District Attorney Releases Relaxed Bail and Sentencing Guidelines, The Texan, May 27, 2021, https://thetexan.news/travis-county-district-attorney-releases-relaxed-bail-and-sentencing-guidelines/.

129 FOX 7 Austin Digital Team, Austin, Austin man gets over 18 years in prison for robbing multiple convenience stores, FOX 7 Austin, June 10, 2022, https://www.fox7austin.com/news/austin-man-gets-over-18-years-in-prison-for-robbing-multiple-convenience-stores.

130 Thayer.

131 Thayer.

132 Ann Maher, "Recall Effort Aimed at Soros-Funded Progressive Prosecutor in Fairfax County," Legal Newsline, April 13, 2021, https://legalnewsline.com/stories/589012282-recall-effort-aimed-at-soros-funded-progressive-prosecutor-in-fairfax-county.

133 Josh Christenson, "WATCH: Soros Prosecutor Plays Dumb When Asked Why Attorneys Are Fleeing His Office," Washington Free Beacon, April 6, 2022, https://freebeacon.com/politics/watch-soros-prosecutor-plays-dumb-when-asked-why-attorneys-are-fleeing-his-office/.

134 Thayer, "Living Room Pundit's Guide to Soros District Attorneys."

135 Emma Colton, Loudoun County judge boots liberal DA from case of dad whose daughter was sexually assaulted in school, Fox News, September 13, 2022, https://www.foxnews.com/us/loudoun-county-judge-boots-liberal-da-case-dad-daughter-sexually-assaulted-school.

136 Thayer.

137 Thayer.

138 Tom Cotton, "Recall, Remove & Replace Every Last Soros Prosecutor," RealClear Politics, December 20, 2021, https://www.realclearpolitics.com/articles/2021/12/20/recall_remove__replace_every_last_soros_prosecutor_146914.html.

139 Cotton, "Recall, Remove & Replace Every Last Soros Prosecutor."

140 See Patrick Reilly, "Kim Foxx's Husband Calls 911 on Her, Claims She Slapped Him in Alleged Domestic Dispute," New York Post, June 10, 2022, https://nypost.com/2022/06/10/cops-called-to-chicago-da-kim-foxxs-home-after-alleged-domestic-dispute/; News Editors, "Corrupt Liberal DA Has Another Judgement Against Her After Being Found Guilty of over 100 Counts of Misconduct . . . Guess Who Funded Her Election," Soros.News, April 27, 2022, https://soros.news/2022-04-27-corrupt-liberal-da-has-another-judgement-against-her.html; Mark Wolf, "Soros-Funded Prosecutor Removed and Disqualified After Judge Realizes He's Been Misled," Long Island, NY website, June 14, 2022, https://www.longisland-ny.com/2022/06/14/soros-funded-prosecutor-removed-and-disqualified-after-judge-realizes-hes-been-misled/; and Michael Austin, "Soros-Backed Top Prosecutor Indicted on 4 Federal Charges," Western Journal, January 14, 2022, https://www.westernjournal.com/soros-backed-top-prosecutor-indicted-4-federal-charges/.

141 Cheryl K. Chumley, "Chesa Boudin, San Francisco's Newest 'Communist' D.A., Fires 7 Prosecutors," Washington Times, January 13, 2020, https://www.washingtontimes.com/news/2020/jan/13/chesa-boudin-san-franciscos-newest-communist-d-fir/?utm_source=GOOGLE&utm_medium=cpc&utm_id=chacka&utm_campaign=TWT+-+DSA&gclid=CjwKCAiAo4OQBhBBEiwA5KWu_zSOvSiZbsziusBBLYJXsnrwNWF--2oFoSTVZdXHSsV9fGy0PvPZNBoCvT8QAvD_BwE.

142 Michael Shellenberger, "Why Crime Is Out of Control in San Francisco," Wall Street Journal, November 28, 2021, reprinted on Substack.com, https://michaelshellenberger.substack.com/p/why-crime-is-out-of-control-in-san.

143 Post Editorial Board, "Clueless San Francisco DA Chesa Boudin Disses Law-Abiding Citizens," *New York Post*, March 1, 2022, https://nypost.com/2022/03/01/clueless-san-francisco-da-chesa-boudin-disses-law-abiding-citizens/.

144 Post Editorial Board, "Clueless San Francisco DA Chesa Boudin Disses Law-Abiding Citizens."; Harriet Alexander and Alex Hammer, Woke San Francisco DA Chesa Boudin blames 'right-wing billionaires and police officers' as he is RECALLED by voters in notoriously liberal city where murders have soared 11% and stores forced to shut due to brazen daylight robberies, Daily Mail. com, June 8,2022. https://www.dailymail.co.uk/news/article-10895407/Woke-San-Francisco-DA-Chesa-Boudin-LOSES-recall-election.html.

145 Mark Moore, "Sore Loser Chesa Boudin Blames 'Right-Wing Billionaires' for Recall Defeat," *New York Post*, June 8, 2022, https://nypost.com/2022/06/08/supporters-of-chesa-boudin-recall-rejoice/.

146 The Editorial Board, "Crime and Political Punishment in California," *Wall Street Journal*, updated June 8, 2022, https://www.wsj.com/amp/articles/crime-and-punishment-in-california-san-francis-co-chesa-boudin-rick-caruso-progressives-los-angeles-11654699499.

147 Cyrus Farivar, "Why Silicon Valley Investors Are Injecting Millions Into San Francisco's DA Recall Election," Forbes, January 28, 2022, https://www.forbes.com/sites/cyrusfarivar/2022/01/28/chesa-boudin-recall-silicon-valley/?sh=2490f80a6922.

148 Theodore Hamm, "A Life-Long Fight for Justice Spurred Alvin Bragg into the Manhattan DA Race," Alvin Bragg website, August 6, 2020, https://www.alvinbragg.com/news-1/a-life-long-fight-for-justice-spurred-alvin-bragg-into-the-manhattan-da-race.

149 Larry Celona, Manhattan DA to stop seeking prison sentences in slew of criminal cases, *New York Post*, January 4, 2022, https://nypost.com/2022/01/04/manhattan-da-alvin-bragg-to-stop-seeking-prison-in-some-cases/.

150 "Alvin Bragg: Day 1 Memo," Alvin Bragg website, accessed July 7, 2022, https://www.alvinbragg. com/day-one.

151 Joel B. Pollak, "Soros-linked Manhattan DA Alvin Bragg: No Incarceration Except for Homicide and a Few Other Cases," Jewish Voice, January 5, 2022, https://thejewishvoice.com/2022/01/so-ros-linked-manhattan-da-alvin-bragg-no-incarceration-except-for-homicide-and-a-few-other-cases/.

152 See, for example, "DA George Gascón Issues Special Directives," California Appellate Project Los Angeles, December 7, 2020, http://cap-la.org/news/2020/12/7/da-gascn-issues-special-directives.

153 Barry Latzer, "Alvin Bragg, the Prosecutor Who Won't Prosecute," National Review, February 7, 2022, https://www.nationalreview.com/magazine/2022/02/07/alvin-bragg-the-prosecutor-who-wont-prosecute/.

154 Joe Marino et al., "Knife-Wielding Suspect Has Felony Charge Reduced under Manhattan DA Alvin Bragg's Policies," *New York Post*, January 11, 2022, https://nypost.com/2022/01/11/manhat-tan-da-alvin-bragg-reduces-armed-robbers-felony-charge/.

155 Marino et al.

156 Elizabeth Rosner and Bruce Golding, "Warrant Issued for 'Lucky' NYC Defendant Who Caught a Big Break from DA Bragg," *New York Post*, January 14, 2022, https://nypost.com/2022/01/14/warrant-issued-for-lucky-nyc-defendant-who-caught-a-big-break-from-da-bragg/.

157 Marino et al., "Knife-Wielding Suspect Has Felony Charge Reduced."

158 Joe Marino et al., "Knife-Wielding Suspect Has Felony Charge Reduced under Manhattan DA Alvin Bragg's Policies," *New York Post*, January 11, 2022, https://nypost.com/2022/01/11/manhat-tan-da-alvin-bragg-reduces-armed-robbers-felony-charge/.

159 Georgett Roberts and Melissa Klein, "Manhattan DA Alvin Bragg Surprised by 'Push Back'—Defends Policies," *New York Post*, January 8, 2022 .

160 "The Biden Plan for Strengthening America's Commitment to Justice," https://joebiden.com/justice/.

161 The revised/updated OSF website has many pages discussing policies on "criminal justice," See for example, https://www.opensocietyfoundations.org/voices/getting-criminal-justice-right, and search for more.

162 Craig McCarthy, "Manhattan DA Alvin Bragg, Commish Sewell Have 'Productive' Policies Chat," *New York Post*, January 11, 2022, https://nypost.com/2022/01/11/manhattan-da-alvin-bragg-talks-policy-with-nypd-commish-sewell/.

163 Stephanie Pagones, "NYC Subway Crime up 65% as Mayor Adams backtracks on Dismissal of Public Concerns as 'Perception of Fear'," Fox News, January 18, 2022, https://www.foxnews.com/us/nyc-subway-crime-mayor-adams-perception-of-fear.

164 Carl Campanile and Bruce Golding, "Embattled Manhattan DA Alvin Bragg huddles with PR Pro, Preet Bharara over soft-on-crime uproar," *New York Post*, January 17, 2022, https://nypost.com/2022/01/17/alvin-bragg-huddles-with-pr-pro-prett-bharara-over-soft-on-crime-uproar/.

165 Brittany Bernstein, "New Manhattan DA Walks Back Memo Claiming Decriminalization 'Will Make Us Safer'," National Review, January 20, 2022, https://www.nationalreview.com/news/new-manhattan-da-walks-back-memo-claiming-decriminalization-will-make-us-safer/?utm_source=email&utm_medium=breaking&utm_campaign=newstrack&utm_term=26433724.

166 NYPD Announces Citywide Crime Statistics for January 2022, Feb. 3, 2022. https://www1.nyc.gov/site/nypd/news/p00036/nypd-citywide-crime-statistics-january- 2022.

167 Brian Stieglitz, "Manhattan DA Alvin Bragg doubles down on soft-on-crime approach with new division to oversee ALTERNATIVES to prison for some criminals - even after backtracking from controversial sentencing memo in the face of backlash,",Daily Mail.com, March 8, 2022. https://www.dailymail.co.uk/news/article-10589911/Manhattan-DA-creates-new-division-oversee-alternatives-prison-sentences-criminals.html.

168 NYPD Announces Citywide Crime Statistics for February 2022, NYPD, March 3, 2022. https://www1.nyc.gov/site/nypd/news/p00039/nypd-citywide-crime-statistics-february-2022

169 See Nolan Hicks, Craig McCarthy and Bruce Golding, "'This Is Gun That Killed Our Young Officer': Adams Vows to Get 'Trigger Pullers off Streets'," *New York Post*, January 24, 2022, https://nypost.com/2022/01/24/mayor-eric-adams-unveils-plan-to-get-guns-off-nyc-streets/.

170 Danielle Wallace, "NYPD Reports 51% Surge in Car Thefts, as 'Brazen' Criminals Boast of Stolen Vehicles on Social media," Fox News, June 13, 2022, https://www.foxnews.com/us/nypd-surge-car-thefts-brazen-criminals-social-media.

171 Amanda Woods and Kevin Sheehan, "First Wave of NYPD's New Anti-Gun Units Hits the Streets," *New York Post*, March 14, 2022, https://nypost.com/2022/03/14/first-wave-of-nypds-new-anti-gun-units-hits-the-streets/.

172 FOX 5 NY Staff, "NYC Crime: Murders Down, Overall Crime Up 30% in March," Fox News 5 New York. updated April 7, 2022, https://www.fox5ny.com/news/nyc-crime-stats-march-2022.

173 George Soros, Why I Support Reform Prosecutors, *Wall Street Journal*, July 31, 2022, https://www.georgesoros.com/2022/07/31/why-i-support-reform-prosecutors/.

174 See Ethan Stark-Miller, "Adams Meets with Both Democratic and GOP Albany Leaders to Tackle Crime," PoliticsNY, February 15, 2022, https://politicsny.com/2022/02/15/adams-met-with-both-democratic-and-gop-albany-leaders-to-tackle-crime/.

175 Jo Clifton, "Is Money Going to Decide Travis County Races?," Austin Monitor, July 10, 2020, https://www.austinmonitor.com/stories/2020/07/is-money-going-to-decide-travis-county-races/.

176 Armando Garcia, Migrant's arrest under 'Operation Lone Star' ruled unconstitutional, ABC News, January 14, 2022, https://abcnews.go.com/US/migrants-arrest-operation-lone-star-ruled-unconstitutional/story?id=82266611.

177 "Texas Judge Rules Man's Arrest Under Operation Lone Star Violates US Constitution," Patabook News, January 13, 2022, https://patabook.com/news/2022/01/13/texas-judge-rules-mans-arrest-under-operation-lone-star-violates-us-constitution/.

178 "About Jan," Jan Soifer website, accessed July 7, 2022, https://www.jansoifer.com/about/.

179 Jason Edelstein, Is J Street pro-peace? Ynetnews.com February 27, 2011, https://www.ynetnews.com/articles/0,7340,L-4034916,00.html.

180 George Soros, On Israel, America and AIPAC, The New York Review of Books, April 12, 2007, https://www.georgesoros.com/2007/04/12/on_israel_america_and_aipac/.

181 Marc Tracy, Soros Funding of J Street Revealed, Tablet Magazine, Sept. 27, 2010, https://www.tabletmag.com/sections/news/articles/soros-funding-of-j-street-revealed; Alexander H. Joffe,

182 Eli Lake, Soros revealed as funder of liberal Jewish-American lobby, The *Washington Times*, September 24, 2010, https://www.washingtontimes.com/news/2010/sep/24/soros-funder-liberal-jewish-american-lobby/.

183 Marc Tracy, Soros Funding of J Street Revealed, Tablet Magazine, Sept. 27, 2010, https://www.tabletmag.com/sections/news/articles/soros-funding-of-j-street-revealed; Alexander H. Joffe,

184 Marc Tracy, Soros Funding of J Street Revealed, Tablet Magazine, Sept. 27, 2010, https://www.tabletmag.com/sections/news/articles/soros-funding-of-j-street-revealed; Alexander H. Joffe.

185 JNS, J Street joins anti-Israel groups in support of Gaza amendment to defense bill, September 20, 2022. https://www.jns.org/j-street-joins-anti-israel-groups-in-support-of-gaza-amendment-to-defense-bill/.

186 Morton A. Kline et al., J Street Sides With Israel's Enemies & Works to Destroy Support for Israel, ZOA, 2018. https://zoa.org/wp-content/uploads/2018/02/J-Street-Full-Report-H.pdf .

187 Tony Plohetski and Katie Hall, "Texas AG Paxton to Appeal Austin Judge's Ruling That Operation Lone Star Is Unconstitutional," Austin American-Statesman, January 14, 2022, https://www.statesman.com/story/news/2022/01/14/operation-lone-star-ruling-texas-ken-paxton-vows-appeal-ruling/6525459001/.

188 See "TEXAS COURT OF APPEALS, THIRD DISTRICT, AT AUSTIN: NO. 03-22-00032-CR The State of Texas, Appellant v. Jesus Alberto Guzman Curipoma, Appellee, p. 2, https://cases.justia.com/texas/third-court-of-appeals/2022-03-22-00032-cr.pdf?ts=1645881696.

189 Brian C. Joondeph, "The Eyes Have It—Colorado's "Crime Tsunami,"The Villager (Villager Publishing blog), December 29, 2021, https://villagerpublishing.com/the-eyes-have-it-colorados-crime-tsunami/.

190 Vince Bzdek, "Colorado's 'Tsunami of Crime' Is in Need of a Levee," Denver Gazette, December 11, 2021, updated January 11, 2022, https://denvergazette.com/news/local/colorados-tsunami-of-crime-is-in-need-of-a-levee-vince-bzdek/article_7cf30368-1ec1-58c3-9906-e7be89c1ded1.html?utm_source=listrak&utm_medium=email&utm_campaign=alert.

191 Joey Bunch, "New report links Colorado's rising crime to criminal-friendly public policy," Gazette, December 9, 2021, updated April 23, 2022, https://gazette.com/news/crime/new-report-links-colorados-rising-crime-to-criminal-friendly-public-policy/article_025a69e2-3d24-5f76-aaf5-9d0c59511066.html.

192 Rav Arora, "EYE ON THE NEWS An Ongoing National Crisis," City Journal, March 9, 2022, https://www.city-journal.org/homicides-are-a-national-crisis.

193 David B. Mustard and John Lott, Crime, Deterrence, and Right-to-Carry Concealed Handguns (Coase-Sandor Institute for Law & Economics Working Paper No. 41, 1996), 4.

194 John R. Lott Jr., More Guns Less Crime: Understanding Crime and Gun-Control Laws, 3rd ed. (independently published, 2018), 21. "Before going out of print, the first three editions of this book [1998, 2000, and 2010] were published by The University of Chicago Press . . . This version of the book published through Amazon is identical to the third edition that was published by the University of Chicago Press." (front matter)

195 George Soros, Why I Support Reform Prosecutors, Wall Street Journal, July 31, 2022, https://www.wsj.com/articles/why-i-support-reform-prosecutors-law-enforces-jail-prison-crime-rate-justice-police-funding-11659277441.

196 Stefan Kanfer, "Connoisseur of Chaos: The Dystopian Vision of George Soros, Billionaire Funder of the Left," City Journal, Winter 2017, https://www.city-journal.org/html/connoisseur-chaos-14954.html.

197 Alex Seitz-Wald, How Democrats went from defund to refund the police, NBC News, Feb 8, 2022. https://www.nbcnews.com/politics/politics-news/democrats-went-defund-refund-police-rcna14796; After attacking cops, the D.C. mayor just quietly refunded the defunded Metropolitan Police Department by $30 million, Law Enforcement Today, Apr 12, 2022, https://duckduckgo.com/?q=mayors+calling+to+refund+the+police+2022&t=osx&ia=web.

198 Dillon Burroughs, "12 Police Officers Relocate to a Single Florida Police Department as Anti-Cop Sentiment' Grows, The Western Journal, Oct. 28, 2021, https://www.westernjournal.com/12-nypd-officers-relocate-single-florida-police-department-anti-cop-sentiment-grows/.

199 Changing Shopping habits, crime forces retailers to close in 2022.Metro Voice, January 2, 2022. https://metrovoicenews.com/changing-shopping-habits-crime-force-retailers-to-close-in-2022/

200 Anders Hagstrom, Florida Gov. Ron DeSantis suspends 'Soros-backed' state attorney who refused to enforce abortion ban, Fox News, August 4, 2022, https://www.foxnews.com/politics/florida-gov-ron-desantis-suspends-liberal-state-attorney-andrew-warren.

201 George Soros, Why I support Reform Prosecutors, Wall Street Journal, July 31, 2022. https://www.wsj.com/articles/why-i-support-reform-prosecutors-law-enforces-jail-prison-crime-rate-justice-police-funding-11659277441.

4: SOROS'S OPEN BORDERS: UNDERMINING NATIONAL SOVEREIGNTY

1 George Soros, "The People's Sovereignty," Foreign Policy, October 28, 2009, https://www.georgesoros.com/2009/10/28/the-peoples-sovereignty/.

2 David S. Broder, Washingtonpost.com: Wealthy Benefactors Stoke Campaigns for Medical Marijuana, October 20, 1988, p, 5. Washingtonpost.com: Wealthy Benefactors Stoke Campaigns for Medical Marijuana.

3 See Andrew Glass, "Clinton signs 'Welfare to Work' bill, Aug. 22, 1996," Politico, August 22, 2018, https://www.politico.com/story/2018/08/22/clinton-signs-welfare-to-work-bill-aug-22-1996-790321.

4 Eric Schmitt, "Philanthropist Pledges Help to Immigrants," New York Times, October 1, 1996, https://www.nytimes.com/1996/10/01/us/philanthropist-pledges-help-to-immigrants.html.

5 Dara Lind, "The Disastrous, Forgotten 1996 Law That Created Today's Immigration Problem," Vox, April 28, 2016, https://www.vox.com/2016/4/28/11515132/iirira-clinton-immigration.

6   Charles T. Clotfelter and Thomas Ehrlich, eds., Philanthropy and the Nonprofit Sector in a Changing America (Bloomington: Indiana University Press, 2001), 289.

7   D'Vera Cohn, "How U.S. Immigration Laws and Rules Have Changed Through History," Pew Research Center, September 30, 2015, https://www.pewresearch.org/fact-tank/2015/09/30/how-u-s-immigration-laws-and-rules-have-changed-through-history/.

8   NPR Staff, "A Reagan Legacy: Amnesty for Illegal Immigrants," WBUR (Boston), July 4, 2010, https://www.wbur.org/npr/128303672/story.php.

9   See "Statue of Liberty: Fast Facts," ABC News, https://abcnews.go.com/US/video/statue-liberty-fast-facts-42862940.

10 Rachel Ehrenfeld, "George Soros' Agenda for Drug Legalization, Death, and Welfare," American Center for Democracy, January 15, 1997, https://acdemocracy.org/george-soros-agenda-for-drug-legalization-death-and-welfare/.

11 Mike Ciandella, "Soros Boasts of Spending $100 Million on U.S. Immigration Reform Push," CNS News blog, October 24, 2013, https://www.cnsnews.com/mrctv-blog/mike-ciandella/soros-boasts-spending-100-million-us-immigration-reform-push.

12 Daniel Newton, "Leaked Documents Prove Soros Working with UN Supporting Illegal Migrant Crisis," Neon Nettle, October 129, 2018, https://neonnettle.com/news/5480-leaked-documents-prove-soros-working-with-un-supporting-illegal-migrant-crisis.

13 George Soros, "Why I'm Investing $500 Million in Migrants," Wall Street Journal, September 20, 2016, https://www.wsj.com/articles/why-im-investing-500-million-in-migrants-1474344001.

14 George Soros, "Why I'm Investing $500 Million in Migrants," Soros website, September 20, 2016, https://www.georgesoros.com/2016/09/20/why-im-investing-500-million-in-migrants/.

15 Giulia McDonnell Nieto del Rio and Miriam Jordan, "What Is DACA? And Where Does It Stand Now?" New York Times, June 14, 2022, https://www.nytimes.com/article/what-is-daca.html.

16 Julia Preston, "Federal Panel Lets Injunction Against Obama's Immigration Actions Stand," New York Times, May 26, 2015.

17 "The Way Forward on Immigration Reform," Open Society Foundations website, May 28, 2015, https://www.opensocietyfoundations.org/newsroom/way-forward-immigration-reform.

18 See "International Migration Initiative," Open Society Foundations website, accessed July 11, 2022, https://www.opensocietyfoundations.org/who-we-are/programs/international-migration-initiative.

19 Tyler Durden, "Soros Hack Reveals Plot Behind Europe's Refugee Crisis; Media Manipulation; Cash for 'Social Justice,'" ZeroHedge, August 16, 2016, https://www.zerohedge.com/news/2016-08-16/soros-hack-reveals-plot-behind-europes-refugee-crisis-media-funding-and-manipulation.

20 Aly Nielsen, "WikiLeaks Exposes Soros Millions Pushing to Undermine Catholics," NewsBusters, October 14, 2016, https://www.newsbusters.org/blogs/business/aly-nielsen/2016/10/14/wikileaks-exposes-soros-millions-pushing-undermine-catholics.

21 Erwin de Leon and Robert Roach, "Immigrant Legal-Aid Organizations in the United States," Urban Institute, 1, accessed July 11, 2022, https://www.urban.org/sites/default/files/publication/24066/412928-Immigrant-Legal-Aid-Organizations-in-the-United-States.PDF.

22 "The Emma Lazarus Campaign Executive Summary," Open Society Foundations, March 2021, https://www.opensocietyfoundations.org/publications/the-emma-lazarus-campaign-executive-summary.

23 "The Emma Lazarus Resilience Fund," Communities Foundation of Texas, accessed July 11, 2022, https://www.cftexas.org/nonprofits/apply-for-a-grant/funding-opportunities/closed-funding-opportunities/emma-lazarus-resilience-fund.

ENDNOTES

24   John Binder, "Soros-Linked Mass Migration Lobby: U.S. Must Open Borders to Ukraine Refu-
      gees," Breitbart, February 24, 2022, https://www.breitbart.com/politics/2022/02/24/soros-linked-
      mass-migration-lobby-u-s-must-open-borders-to-ukraine-refugees/.

25   Matthew O'Brien and Spencer Raley, "The Fiscal Cost of Resettling Refugees in the United States,"
      FAIR, February 5, 2018, https://www.fairus.org/issue/legal-immigration/fiscal-cost-resettling-
      refugees-united-states.

26   FAIR Research Team, "2021 Year in Review: Biden's Immigration Numbers Reveal Record Failures,
      Costs and Risks to Americans," FAIR, December 2021, https://www.fairus.org/issue/border-
      security/2021-year-review-biden-immigration-numbers-record-failures-costs.

27   Julian Resendiz, "Migrant Encounters Top 2 Million in Calendar Year 2021, on Pace for Repeat in
      2022," Border Report, January 24, 2022, https://www.borderreport.com/hot-topics/immigration/
      migrant-encounters-top-2-million-in-calendar-year-2021-on-pace-for-repeat-in-2022/.

28   The Post Editorial Board, More grim border numbers suggest Team Biden has simply given up,
      July 18, 2022, https://nypost.com/2022/07/18/more-grim-border-numbers-suggest-biden-has-
      simply-given-up/.

29   Resendiz, "Migrant Encounters Top 2 Million in Calendar Year 2021."

30   CDC Press Release, U.S. Overdose Deaths In 2021 Increased Half as Much as in 2020—But
      Are Still Up 15%, May 11, 2022,https://www.cdc.gov/nchs/pressroom/nchs_press_releas-
      es/2022/202205.htm.

31   Naveed Jamali and Tom O'Connor, "Chinese Chemicals in Mexican Cartel Hands Feed Deadly
      U.S. Fentanyl Crisis," Newsweek, May 5, 2021. https://www.newsweek.com/chinese-chemicals-
      mexican-cartel-hands-feed-deadly-us-fentanyl-crisis-1588948.

32   Christopher Rufo, Safe Injection Sites' Don't Work Well. Just Ask Canada, The Daily Signal, Oct.2,
      2020. https://www.dailysignal.com/2020/10/02/safe-injection-sites-dont-work-well-just-ask-can-
      ada/. Also see, Rachel Ehrenfeld, Selling Syringes: The Swiss Experiment, The Wall Street Journal,
      Sept 6, 1995, p. A18, https://acdemocracy.org/selling-syringes-the-swiss-experiment/.

33   Andrew R. Arthur, "January Border Numbers Reflect Ongoing Chaos," Center for Immigration
      Studies, February 22, 2022, https://cis.org/Arthur/January-Border-Numbers-Reflect-Ongoing-
      Chaos.

34   Arthur, "January Border Numbers Reflect Ongoing Chaos."

35   Miriam Jordan, "From India, Brazil and Beyond: Pandemic Refugees at the Border," The New
      York Times, June 7, 2021, https://www.nytimes.com/2021/05/16/us/migrants-border-coronavirus-
      pandemic.html.

36   Callie Patteson, Over 500,000 immigrant 'gotaways' at US border may be roaming the country:
      report, New York Post, July 25, 2022, https://nypost.com/2022/07/25/over-500k-immigrant-
      gotaways-at-border-may-be-in-us-report/.

37   Cision, FAIR Analysis: 4.9 Million Illegal Aliens Have Crossed our Borders Since President Biden
      Took Office, Federation for American Immigration Reform (FAIR) , August 16, 2022, https://
      www.prnewswire.com/news-releases/fair-analysis-4-9-million-illegal-aliens-have-crossed-our-
      borders-since-president-biden-took-office-301606980.html.

38   Luke Harding, "Angela Merkel Defends Germany's Handling of Refugee Influx," Guardian,
      September 15, 2015, https://www.theguardian.com/world/2015/sep/15/angela-merkel-defends-
      germanys-handling-of-refugee-influx.

39   Wesley Dockery, "Two Years Since Germany Opened Its Borders to Refugees: A Chronology," DW,
      April 9, 2017, https://www.dw.com/en/two-years-since-germany-opened-its-borders-to-refugees-a-
      chronology/a-40327634.

40 Imogen Calderwood, "Merkel's Open Door Policy Has Brought 'Chaos' to Europe, Claims George Soros as German Leader Is Blamed for Brexit over Her Failure to Deal with Migrant Crisis," DailyMail.com, June 29, 2016, https://www.dailymail.co.uk/news/article-3666511/Merkel-s-open-door-policy-caused-Britain-leave-EU-German-leader-blamed-Brexit-failure-deal-migrant-crisis-open-arms-immigration-policy.html.

41 Pablo Gorondi, "Hungary's Premier Rejects Immigration, Multicultural Society," Federal News Network, February 27, 2015, https://federalnewsnetwork.com/national-world-headlines/2015/02/hungarys-premier-rejects-immigration-multicultural-society/.

42 See, for example, "Europe Must Stand Up to Hungary and Poland," George Soros website, November 18, 2020, https://www.georgesoros.com/2020/11/18/europe-must-stand-up-to-hungary-and-poland/.

43 "Migration Data in the EU," Migration Data Portal, last updated on June 14, 2021, https://www.migrationdataportal.org/regional-data-overview/europe.

44 Judith Bergman, "The Terrorists Migrating into Europe," Gatestone Institute, February 15, 2020, https://www.gatestoneinstitute.org/15290/the-terrorists-migrating-into-europe.

45 Bergman, "The Terrorists Migrating into Europe."

46 f. William Engdahl, "Soros Plays Both Ends in Syria Refugee Chaos," Ron Paul Institute, Dec. 21, 2015. http://www.ronpaulinstitute.org/archives/featured-articles/2015/december/31/soros-plays-both-ends-in-syria-refugee-chaos/.

47 Robert Spencer, Kill yourselves, or else: EU sues Poland, Hungary, Czech Republic for not taking Muslim migrants, Jihad Watch, June 18, 2017, Jihad Watch, https://www.jihadwatch.org/2017/06/kill-yourselves-or-else-eu-sues-poland-hungary-czech-republic-for-not-taking-muslim-migrants.

48 Bergman, "The Terrorists Migrating into Europe."

49 Ayumi Davis, "Hungary Refuses to Change Immigration Policies, Faces Heavy Fines From EU," Newsweek, December 21, 2012, https://www.newsweek.com/hungary-refuses-change-immigration-policies-faces-heavy-fines-eu-1661804.

50 Associated Press, "Hungary Accepting All Ukraine Citizens and Legal Residents," NBC 10 Boston, February 26, 2022, https://www.nbcboston.com/news/national-international/hungary-accepting-all-ukraine-citizens-and-legal-residents/2655509/.

51 Robert Tait, "Hungary accused of inflating number of Ukrainian arrivals to seek EU funds," Guardian, March 31, 2022, https://www.theguardian.com/world/2022/mar/30/hungary-accused-of-inflating-number-of-ukrainian-arrivals-to-seek-eu-funds.

52 Opposition: "Viktor Orbán has become Putin's puppet, Hungary Today, https://hungarytoday.hu/putin-orban-meeting-moscow-russia-hungary-russian-hungarian-relations/.

53 Number of refugees from Ukraine crossing Central and Eastern European borders after Russia's invasion of Ukraine from February 24 to August 23, 2022, https://www.statista.com/statistics/1293403/cee-ukrainian-refugees-by-country/.

54 "Orban names Hungarian Government's 'Opponents'," RT, April 4, 2022, https://www.rt.com/news/553246-orban-soros-zelensky-opponents/.

55 Human Events Staff, "Biden Admin. Announces End to Title 42," Human Events, April 1, 2022, https://humanevents.com/2022/04/01/biden-admin-announces-end-to-title-42/.

5: THE STATELESS STATEMAN

1 Connie Bruck, The World According to George Soros, The New Yorker, Jan. 15, 1995. https://www.newyorker.com/magazine/1995/01/23/the-world-according-to-soros.

ENDNOTES

2   Bryan Bender, "George Soros and Charles Koch Take On the 'Endless Wars'," Politico, December 2, 2019, https://www.politico.com/news/2019/12/02/george-soros-and-charles-koch-take-on-the-endless-wars-074737; "Kelsey Piper, "George Soros and Charles Koch Team Up for a Common Cause: an End to "Endless War," Vox, July 1, 2019, https://www.vox.com/2019/7/1/20677441/soros-koch-end-interventionist-wars-military.

3   Armin Rosen, Washington's Weirdest Think Tank, Tablet Magazine, April 27, 2021, https://www.tabletmag.com/sections/news/articles/quincy-trita-parsi-soros-koch-armin-rosen

4   See their FAQ document to Congress at http://www.iraniansforum.com/Document/IIC/IICFAQ-Congress.pdf.

5   Staff Writer, "Iranian Regime's Lobby Group NIAC Under Scrutiny," NCRI (National Council of Resistance to Iran) Foreign Affairs Committee, January 17, 2020, https://www.ncr-iran.org/en/uncategorized/iranian-regimes-lobby-group-niac-under-scrutiny/.

6   See Hooshang Amirahmadi, memo to the AIC Board of Directors and Advisory Council, June 24, 2012, http://iraniansforum.com/Document/AICboardTP.pdf; American Iranian Council, accessed July 13, 2022, http://www.us-iran.org/.

7   See Thomas W. Lippman, "U.S. Defers Sanctions on Iran Gas Deal," Washington Post, October 4, 1997, https://www.washingtonpost.com/archive/politics/1997/10/04/us-defers-sanctions-on-iran-gas-deal/6f4a72cb-f760-4eaa-9ea6-bdf3c2de52f2/.

8   Hassan Dai, "How Trita Parsi and NIAC Used the White House to Advance Iran's Agenda," Tablet, June 28, 2017, https://www.tabletmag.com/sections/news/articles/parsi-niac-advance-irans-agenda. See also "Hoshang Amir Ahmadi in an Interview with Brokers," March 5, 2008, http://www.iraniansforum.com/Document/AsreNo-IranLobby.htm.

9   "History," American Iranian Council website, accessed July 13, 2022, http://www.us-iran.org/history.

10 "About NIAC," NIAC website, accessed July 13, 2022, https://www.niacouncil.org/about-niac/?locale=en.

11 Hassan Daioleslam,–Iran Politics Club: Hassan Daioleslam Index, https://iranpoliticsclub.net/authors/hassan-daioleslam/index.htm, and, Hassan Dai, How Trita Parsi and NIAC Used the White House to Advance Iran's Agenda, Tablet magazine, June 28, 2017. https://www.tabletmag.com/sections/news/articles/parsi-niac-advance-irans-agenda.

12 See Hassan Dai, "Iran's Oil Mafia Penetrating US Political System: Hezbollah IRI Lobby in USA," Iran Politics Club, 1st Edition: August 23, 2007; 2nd Edition: February 7, 2018, http://iranpoliticsclub.net/politics/oil-mafia/index.htm.

13 Hassan Daioleslam,–Iran Politics Club: Hassan Daioleslam Index, https://iranpoliticsclub.net/authors/hassan-daioleslam/index.htm.

14 Hassan Daioleslam, Trita Parsi and NIAC Lost Court Case to Hassan Daioleslam, Iran Politics Club, September 28, 2012, https://iranpoliticsclub.net/politics/trita-lost/index.htm.

15 Dai, "How Trita Parsi and NIAC Used the White House to Advance Iran's Agenda."

16 Tom Cotton, Ted Cruz, and Mike Braun, letter to William Barr, January 13, 2020, https://freebeacon.com/wp-content/uploads/2020/01/200113_NIAC-Letter-FINAL.pdf.

17 Hassan Dai, How Trita Parsi and NIAC Used the White House to Advance Iran's Agenda, Tablet Magazine, JUNE 28, 2017, https://www.tabletmag.com/sections/news/articles/parsi-niac-advance-irans-agenda

18 Majid Rafizadeh, "Iran Regime's Agents and Illegal Activities in the US," Gatestone Institute International Policy Council, January 30, 2021, https://www.gatestoneinstitute.org/17010/iran-agents-us.

19   JNS.org, "Report: Congress Calls for Investigation of Pro-Iran Lobbying Organization," Alge-
     meiner, January 16, 2020, https://www.algemeiner.com/2020/01/16/report-congress-calls-for-
     investigation-of-pro-iran-lobbying-organization/.

20   Adam Kredo, "Anti-Israel Soros Groups Cash In on Coronavirus Relief Funds," *Washington Free
     Beacon*, July 7, 2020, https://freebeacon.com/coronavirus/anti-israel-soros-groups-cash-in-on-
     coronavirus-relief-funds/.

21   Ruby Henley, "Update—America's Sovereignty Thrown Under the Bus—the Corrupt Iran Deal—
     George Soros Funded," Investment Watch, May 15, 2018, https://www.investmentwatchblog.com/
     update-americas-sovereignty-thrown-under-the-bus-the-corrupt-iran-deal-george-soros-funded/.

22   Associated Press, "Group That Pushed for Iran Nuclear Deal Gave NPR $100,000 to Support
     Reporting," *Guardian*, May 21, 2016, https://www.theguardian.com/media/2016/may/21/npr-
     funding-iran-nuclear-deal-ploughshares.

23   "Quincy Institute Responds to Soleimani's Assassination," press release, Quincy Institute for
     Responsible Statecraft, January 3, 2020, https://quincyinst.org/press/quincy-institute-responds-to-
     soleimanis-assassination/.

24   Adam Kredo, Give Iran Nukes, Says Quincy Institute's New Iran Expert, *Washington Free Beacon*,
     September 16, 2022. https://freebeacon.com/national-security/give-iran-nukes-says-quincy-insti-
     tutes-new-iran-expert/.

25   Building Open Societies: Soros Foundations Network 2002 Annual Report (New York: Open
     Society Institute, 2003), 21; download at https://www.opensocietyfoundations.org/publications/
     soros-foundations-network-2002-annual-report#publications_download.

26   WorldNetDaily, "Soros Supports Mullahs: The Left Embraces Yet Another Enemy," Free Republic,
     January 15, 2005, https://freerepublic.com/focus/f-news/1321295/posts.

27   Natalie Winters and Raheem Kassam, "WATCH: Biden Lauds Soros's Pro-Iran Efforts at Event
     Hosted by 'Death to America'-Linked Group," National Pulse, August 29, 2020, https://thenation-
     alpulse.com/2020/08/29/biden-soros-iran-regime-event/.

28   "Discussion Forum with Iranian UN Ambassador," Open Society Foundations, January 14, 2005,
     https://www.opensocietyfoundations.org/events/discussion-forum-iranian-un-ambassador.

29   "Statement on OSI Activities in Iran," press release, Open Society Foundations, May 21, 2007,
     https://www.opensocietyfoundations.org/newsroom/statement-osi-activities-iran.

30   See Octavian Dumitrescu, "The Intelligence and Security Services of Iran," World Security Net-
     work, November 10, 2020, https://www.worldsecuritynetwork.com/Iran/Dumitrescu-Octavian/
     The-Intelligence-and-Security-Services-of-Iran.

31   Robin Wright and William Branigin, "Ahmadinejad Met with Protests, Criticism at Columbia
     University," *Washington Post*, September 24, 2007, https://www.washingtonpost.com/archive/
     business/technology/2007/09/24/ahmadinejad-met-with-protests-criticism-at-columbia-univer-
     sity/14f8dd1e-096a-4dbf-9fde-fd79ecdf46a3/.

32   "Iran Touts Collaboration with Soros' Open Society Foundations," Misinformation Spreaders
     Gazette, quoting the *Free Beacon*, September 6, 2018, https://ibloga.blogspot.com/2018/09/iran-
     touts-collaboration-with-soros.html. This website quotes three paragraphs taken from the *Free
     Beacon*, then follows the quotation with a link that invites readers to "GO READ THE WHOLE
     THING." The link itself, however, leads only to a *Free Beacon* page tagging articles on George
     Soros (https://freebeacon.com/tag/george-soros/). The quoted article does not appear. See also
     Iran Gateway (@IranGateway), "1) @JZarif (Foreign Minister) was questioned at the Parliament
     (Majlis) on Sep 2nd. He faced questions on the loyalty of his team of negotiators given their dual
     citizenships (mostly American or European) and also his connection to George Soros." Twitter,
     September 5, 2018, 7:58 a.m., https://twitter.com/IranGateway/status/1037324081467719681.

ENDNOTES

33   Adam Edelman, Biden's comments downplaying China threat to U.S. fire up pols on both sides, NBC Ndews, May 2, 2020, https://www.nbcnews.com/politics/2020-election/biden-s-comments-downplaying-china-threat-u-s-fires-pols-n1001236.

34   Joseph R. Biden Jr., "China's Rise Isn't Our Demise," *New York Times*, September 7, 2011, https://www.nytimes.com/2011/09/08/opinion/chinas-rise-isnt-our-demise.html.

35   See Peter Schweizer, Red-Handed: How American Elites Get Rich Helping China Win (New York: HarperCollins, 2022).

36   Eli Lake, The Secret History of the Iran-Deal 'Echo Chamber', Bloomberg, https://www.bloomberg.com/opinion/articles/2016-05-24/the-secret-history-of-the-iran-deal-echo-chamber, and Ploughshares Fund, Annual Report, Dec 11,2015, https://www.ploughshares.org/content/annual-report-2015.

37   See "Robert Malley—George Soros Acolyte Joins Obama Regime," Pacific Pundit, February 25, 2014 admin Latest Ramblings, https://www.pacificpundit.com/2014/02/25/robert-malley-george-soros-acolyte-joins-obama-regime/.

38   It is listed among other Soros-funded organizations at "Organizations Funded by George Soros and His Open Society Foundations," Millennium Report, June 3, 2020, https://themillenniumreport.com/2020/06/organizations-funded-by-george-soros-and-his-open-society-foundations/.

39   See Dominic Green, "Here Comes Trouble: Biden's Anti-Israel Advisers," Jewish Chronicle, February 19, 2021, https://www.thejc.com/comment/analysis/here-comes-trouble-biden-s-anti-israel-advisers-1.511957.

40   Diana West, Who is Robert Malley? Feb. 1, 2011, https://dianawest.net/Home/tabid/36/EntryId/1668/Who-Is-Robert-Malley.aspx, And, Alex Safian, "Robert Malley and US Policy on Israel," CAMERA (Committee for Accuracy in Middle East Reporting and Analysis), March 11, 2015, https://www.camera.org/article/robert-malley-and-us-policy-on-israel/.

41   See Michael Pregent, "The Iran Deal Was a Bad Deal in 2015. It's an Even Worse One Now," *Newsweek*, April 12, 2021, https://www.*newsweek*.com/iran-deal-was-bad-deal-2015-its-even-worse-one-now-opinion-1582527.

42   Associated Press, "$1.7-Billion Payment to Iran Was All in Cash Due to Effectiveness of Sanctions, White House Says," Los Angeles Times, September 7, 2016, https://www.latimes.com/nation/nationnow/la-na-iran-payment-cash-20160907-snap-story.html.

43   See Rachel Ehrenfeld, "Investigate Obama's and Kerry's Unlawful Deals with Iran," American Center for Democracy, January 27, 2018, https://acdemocracy.org/investigate-obamas-and-kerrys-unlawful-deals-with-iran/.

44   George Phillips, Iran Deal: $150 Billion to Fund Obama's War, July 28, 2015, Gatestone Institute, https://www.gatestoneinstitute.org/6225/iran-150-billion-dollars.

45   Elise Labott, John Kerry: Some sanctions relief money for Iran will go to terrorism, CNN, January 21, 2016, https://www.cnn.com/2016/01/21/politics/john-kerry-money-iran-sanctions-terrorism/index.html.

46   Elise Labott, "John Kerry: Some Sanctions Relief Money for Iran Will Go to Terrorism," CNN, January 21, 2016, https://www.cnn.com/2016/01/21/politics/john-kerry-money-iran-sanctions-terrorism/index.html. This post has been since removed from CNN's website. However, you can read about Kerry's acknowledgement that some of the money "will end up in the hands of the IRGC or other entities, some of which are labeled terrorists. I'm not going to sit here and tell you that every component of that can be prevented," here- Rachel Ehrenfeld, Investigate Obama's and Kerry's Unlawful Deals with Iran, January 27, 2018, American Thinker. https://www.americanthinker.com/articles/2018/01/investigate_obamas_and_kerrys_unlawful_deals_with_iran.html.

ENDNOTES

47   Amir Taheri (@AmirTaheri4,) "Robert Malley, a protege of George Soros, as #JoeBiden's 'Iran man' may please 'New York Boys' faction. Soros wants 'moderates' to win power in Tehran. Since a meeting with Islamic President Khatami in Davos in 2004, Soros has tried to help Khomeinist 'moderates' come on top," Twitter, January 24, 2021, 11:46 a.m., https://twitter.com/amirtaheri4/status/1353398905011056640.

48   Taheri, "Robert Malley."

49   Adam Kredo, "White House Partner Asked Soros for $750K to Fund Pro-Iran Deal 'Echo Chamber,'" *Washington Free Beacon*, August 18, 2016, https://freebeacon.com/national-security/wh-partner-asked-soros-to-fund-echo-chamber/.

50   Avi Issacharoff, "Boosted by nuke deal, Iran ups funding to Hezbollah, Hamas," Times of Israel, September 21, 2015, https://www.timesofisrael.com/boosted-by-nuke-deal-iran-ups-funding-to-hezbollah-hamas/?utm_source=The+Counter-Terrorist-Financing+Farce&utm_campaign=The+Counter-Terrorist-Financing+Farce&utm_medium=email.

51   Majid Rafizadeh, "In first, Hezbollah confirms all financial support comes from Iran," Alarabiya News, June 25, 2016, https://english.alarabiya.net/features/2016/06/25/In-first-Hezbollah-s-Nasrallah-confirms-all-financial-support-comes-from-Iran.

52   See "Discussion Forum with Iranian UN Ambassador," Open Society Foundations, accessed July 14, 2022, https://www.opensocietyfoundations.org/events/discussion-forum-iranian-un-ambassador.

53   Jane Mayer, The Money Man: Can George Soros's millions insure the defeat of President Bush? The *New Yorker*, Oct. 18, 2004, Archived from the original on July 12, 2012. Retrieved May 27, 2012.none, https://web.archive.org/web/20120712065522/http://www.uni-muenster.de/PeaCon/global-texte/r-m/soros-TheNewYorker.htm.

54   Marc Santora, Soros Foundations Leaving Hungary Under Government Pressure, *New York Times*, May 15, 2018, https://www.nytimes.com/2018/05/15/world/europe/soros-philanthropy-hungary-viktor-orban.html, also see-George Soros, Rebuttal of the October 9 National Consultation in Hungary, November 20, 2017, https://www.georgesoros.com/rebuttal/.

55   Miles Yu, "Inside China: George Soros vs. China," *Washington Times*, January 28, 2016, https://www.washingtontimes.com/news/2016/jan/28/inside-china-george-soros-vs-china/.

56   George Soros, Soros on Soros, 118.

57   "An Evening with George Soros at Open Russia Club," Mikhail Khodorkovsky website, June 28, 2016, https://khodorkovsky.com/an-evening-with-george-soros-at-open-russia-club/.

58   An Evening with George Soros at Open Russia Club,"

59   An Evening with George Soros at Open Russia Club."

60   See "Hungary, Crypto Museum, accessed July 14, 2022, https://www.cryptomuseum.com/spy/hu.htm.

61   See "Bulgarian Agents Described as Ready to Do Moscow's Bidding," *New York Times*, March 23, 1983, https://www.nytimes.com/1983/03/23/world/bulgarian-agents-described-as-ready-to-do-moscow-s-bidding.html.

62   See Alexandra Grúňová, ed., The NKVD/KGB Activities and its Cooperation with other Secret Services in Central and Eastern Europe 1945–1989, accessed July 14, 2022, https://nsarchive.files.wordpress.com/2013/05/bul-nkvd-aj.pdf.

63   See "One-man Marshall Plan': Was Soros Wrong to Bet on Liberal Democracy?," Democracy Digest, July 23, 2018, https://www.demdigest.org/one-man-marshall-plan-was-soros-wrong-to-bet-on-liberal-democracy/.

64 See the Open Society Foundations Management Training Program Quarterly Performance Report for December 1–31, 1993, at https://pdf.usaid.gov/pdf_docs/PDABI206.pdf.

65 Judicial Watch: New Documents Show State Department and USAID Working with Soros Group to Channel Money to 'Mercenary Army' of Far-Left Activists in Albania, October 3, 2018, https://www.judicialwatch.org/judicial-watch-new-documents-show-state-department-and-usaid-working-with-soros-group-to-channel-money-to-mercenary-army-of-far-left-activists-in-albania/.

66 FOX News, GOP senators ask Tillerson to probe US funding of Soros groups abroad, March 15, 2017. https://www.foxnews.com/politics/gop-senators-ask-tillerson-to-probe-us-funding-of-soros-groups-abroad.

67 See Jacob Grandstaff, "Soros in Romania: Part 1," Capital Research Center, December 21, 2017, https://capitalresearch.org/article/george-soross-romanian-ghosts/; ; World Tribune Staff, "Soros groups in Romania, Colombia reportedly got U.S. funding," World Tribune, March 28, 2018, https://www.worldtribune.com/soros-groups-in-romania-colombia-reportedly-got-u-s-funding/.

68 Kellyanne Richardson, "Soros Brags About 'The Soros Empire Replacing The Soviet Empire" in Europe (Video)," DefiantAmerica.com, March 5, 2022, https://defiantamerica.com/soros-brags-about-the-soros-empire-replacing-the-soviet-empire-in-europe-video/.

69 Gloria Neumeier, Thank You, George Soros, (Letter to the Editor) November 10, 2018, The *New York Times*, https://www.nytimes.com/2018/11/10/opinion/letters/george-soros.html.

70 George Soros, George Soros Tells How he was Present at the "Velvet Revolution", YouTube, December 29, 2019, https://www.youtube.com/watch?v=xn-H_BAl8ho.

71 See "Rice, Saakashvili, and Soros," American Conservative, November 18, 2011, https://www.theamericanconservative.com/rice-saakashvili-and-soros/.

72 Newsmax, May 31, 2005, http://archive.newsmax.com/archives/articles/2005/5/31/164945.shtml. This article has since been removed from the website, but the quotation can still be found on Infogalactic, s.v. "Rose Revolution," https://infogalactic.com/info/Rose_Revolution#cite_note-42.

73 Connie Bruck, "The World According to George Soros," *New Yorker*, January 15, 1995, https://www.newyorker.com/magazine/1995/01/23/the-world-according-to-soros.

74 "The Open Society Foundations in Ukraine," Open Society Foundations, May 18, 2022, https://www.opensocietyfoundations.org/newsroom/the-open-society-foundations-in-ukraine.

75 See "Open Society in Ukraine," fact sheet, Open Society Foundations, accessed July 14, 2022, https://www.opensocietyfoundations.org/uploads/ec4ff2ac-e774-4e73-b6d5-5ba5f63c093f/fact-sheet-open-society-in-ukraine-eng-20200128.pdf.

76 "Ukraine ratifies EU association agreement," Deutsche Welle, Sept. 16, 2014. https://www.dw.com/en/ukraine-ratifies-eu-association-agreement/a-17925681.

77 "The Open Society Foundations in Ukraine."

78 "The Open Society Foundations in Ukraine."

79 See Josh Raab, "In Ukraine, A Battle of Words and Images," Time, July 8, 2014, In Ukraine, A Battle of Words and Images; Henry Foy, "New Europe 100—Changemakers in Central and Eastern Europe," Financial Times, November 14, 2016, https://www.ft.com/content/ece06f66-90a7-11e6-a72e-b428cb934b78; "StopFake receives an award from the National Democratic Institute," Kyiv Mohyla Foundation of America, November 23, 2017, https://www.kmfoundation.com/2017/9503.

80 James Bovard, "Team Biden dumps ditzy disinfo czar Nina Jankowicz—but its board remains a threat to free speech," *New York Post*, May 18, 2022, https://nypost.com/2022/05/18/team-biden-dumps-ditzy-disinfo-czar-nina-jankowicz-but-board-remains-threat/.

ENDNOTES

81   Lev Golinkin, "Meet the Head of Biden's New 'Disinformation Governing Board,'" Kontinent USA (originally on but removed from the Nation's website, at https://www.thenation.com/article/politics/meet-the-head-of-bidens-new-disinformation-governing-board/), May 16, 2022, https://newkontinent.org/meet-the-head-of-bidens-new-disinformation-governing-board/.

82   See "StopFake#117 with Nina Jankowicz," YouTube video, January 29, 2017, https://www.youtube.com/watch?v=mb_RrC2F5bM.

83   Golinkin, "Meet the Head of Biden's New 'Disinformation Governing Board.'"

84   Mark Thompson, "George Soros: I may invest $1 billion in Ukraine,"CNN, March 30, 2015, https://money.cnn.com/2015/03/30/investing/ukraine-soros-billion-russia/index.html.

85   Thompson, "George Soros."

86   "President awarded George Soros with the Order of Freedom," International Renaissance Foundation, November 12, 2015, https://www.irf.ua/en/prezident_ukraini_nagorodiv_dzhordzha_sorosa_ordenom_svobodi/.

87   John Solomon, "US Embassy pressed Ukraine to drop probe of George Soros group during 2016 election," The Hill, March 26, 2019, https://thehill.com/opinion/campaign/435906-us-embassy-pressed-ukraine-to-drop-probe-of-george-soros-group-during-2016/.

88   Solomon.

89   Solomon.

90   See Chuck Ross, "Firms Tied To Fusion GPS, Christopher Steele Were Paid $3.8 Million By Soros-Backed Group," Daily Caller, April 1, 2019, https://dailycaller.com/2019/04/01/fusion-gps-steele-soros-millions/; "Trump Intelligence Allegations, https://www.documentcloud.org/documents/3259984-Trump-Intelligence-Allegations.html.

91   "Address by the President of the Russian Federation," February 21, 2022, http://en.kremlin.ru/events/president/transcripts/67828.

92   See Rebecca Shabad and Shannon Pettypiece, "Biden says any Russian troop movement into Ukraine will be seen as an invasion," NBC News, January 20, 2022,, https://www.nbcnews.com/politics/white-house/harris-says-u-s-prepared-levy-serious-severe-costs-if-n1287760.

93   Steven Nelson, See-no-evil Biden says he's not at all concerned about Hunter 'conflicts', *New York Post*, September 19, 2022, https://nypost.com/2022/09/19/biden-says-hes-not-at-all-concerned-about-hunter-conflicts/, and Scott Pelley, President Joe Biden: The 2022 60 Minutes Interview, CBS, September 18, 2022, https://www.cbsnews.com/news/president-joe-biden-60-minutes-interview-transcript-2022-09-18/.

94   Matt Palumbo, "George Soros Speaks Out on Ukraine—But Here's the Real Reason Why." Dan Bongino Show, February 28, 2022, https://bongino.com/george-soros-speaks-out-on-ukraine-but-heres-the-real-reason-why.

95   Palumbo, "George Soros Speaks Out on Ukraine."

96   Remarks Delivered at the 2022 World Economic Forum in Davos, George Soros website, May 24, 2022, https://www.georgesoros.com/2022/05/24/remarks-delivered-at-the-2022-world-economic-forum-in-davos/.

97   Remarks Delivered at the 2022 World Economic Forum.

98   Gretchen Morgenson, "INTERNATIONAL BUSINESS; Soros's Quantum Fund Losses in Russia Put at $2 Billion," *New York Times*, August 27, 1998, https://www.nytimes.com/1998/08/27/business/international-business-soros-s-quantum-fund-losses-in-russia-put-at-2-billion.html.

99   Shaun Walker, "Russia bans two Soros foundations from disbursing grant," *Guardian*, November 30, 2015, https://www.theguardian.com/world/2015/nov/30/russia-bans-two-george-soros-foundations-from-giving-grants.

100 Mária Schmidt, "The Gravedigger of the Left," American \Center for Democracy, April 26, 2017, https://acdemocracy.org/george-soros-the-gravedigger-of-the-left/.

101 George Soros, "The Danger of Reagan's 'Imperial Circle,'" Financial Times, May 23, 1984, https://www.georgesoros.com/1984/05/23/the-danger-of-reagans-imperial-circle/.

102 Schmidt, "The Gravedigger of the Left." The full version was posted on April 25, 2017, in English, on About Hungary, and the original Hungarian, A Baloldal Sírásója, on Látószög., See: https://acdemocracy.org/george-soros-the-gravedigger-of-the-left/.

103 Schmidt.

104 Yu, "Inside China"; Kaufman, Soros, 218.

105 Bruck, "The World According to George Soros" (see chap. 1, n. 35).

106 Kaufman, Soros, 218.

107 Yu, "Inside China."

108 Mark DE LA Iglesia, "Time to Shut Down Dirty Money's 'London Laundromat,'" Open Society Foundations, May 23, 2022, https://www.opensocietyfoundations.org/voices/time-to-shut-down-dirty-money-s-london-laundromat.

6: SOROS'S ANTI-ISRAEL CRUSADE

1 Trump Advisor David Friedman: Criticism of Ad 'Abuse' of the Anti-Semitic Label, Jewish Insider, Nov. 8, 2016, https://jewishinsider.com/2016/11/trump-advisor-david-friedman-jewish-criticism-of-ad-abuse-of-the-anti-semitic-label/.

2 Soros, Soros on Soros, 240–42.

3 Connie Bruck, "The World According to George Soros," New Yorker, January 23, 1995, https://www.newyorker.com/magazine/1995/01/23/the-world-according-to-soros.

4 Soros, The Bubble of American Supremacy, 19–20.

5 Soros, 20.

6 Is it true that the Quran says to not take the Jews and Christians for friends? Al Islam, https://www.alislam.org/articles/is-it-true-that-quran-says-to-not-take-jews-christians-for-friends/.

7 Soros, 20–21.

8 See Rachel Ehrenfeld and Shawn Macombe, "Soros: The Man Who Would be Kingmaker, Part III," American Center for Democracy, October 29, 2004, https://acdemocracy.org/soros-the-man-who-would-be-kingmaker-part-iii/.

9 Uriel Heilman, "The Sound and the Fury," Jerusalem Post, November 27, 2003, http://www.urielheilman.com/soros.html.

10 Ira Stoll, New York Sun, December 4, 2003, quoted in Rachel Ehrenfeld, "Soros Is No Dreyfus," American Thinker, July 11, 2017, https://www.americanthinker.com/articles/2017/07/soros_is_no_dreyfus.html.

11 Awdah Awdah, Al-Ra'y, October 5, 1990, quoted in Yossef Bodansky, Target America: Terrorism in the U.S. Today (New York: SPI, 1993), 369–70.

12 Uriel Heilman, "The Sound and the Fury," Jerusalem Post, November 27, 2003, http://www.urielheilman.com/soros.html.

13 Ehrenfeld, "Soros Is No Dreyfus."

14 OSF, Open Society Foundations Condemn Israeli Attack on Civil Society Groups, August 19, 2022 https://www.opensocietyfoundations.org/newsroom/open-society-foundations-condemn-israeli-attack-on-civil-society-groups?amp;amp.

15 See Alexander H. Joffe and Gerald M. Steinberg, Bad Investment: The Philanthropy of George
    Soros and the Arab-Israeli Conflict, NGO Monitor Monograph Series, May 2013, https://www.
    ngo-monitor.org/soros.pdf.

16 Eli Lake, "A Soros Plan, a Marginalized Israel," Bloomberg, August 16, 2016, https://www.bloom-
    berg.com/opinion/articles/2016-08-16/how-george-soros-threatens-to-make-israel-a-pariah.

17 Lake, "A Soros Plan."

18 Lake, "A Soros Plan."

19 Stefan Kanfer, "Connoisseur of Chaos," City Journal (Winter 2017), https://www.city-journal.org/
    html/connoisseur-chaos-14954.html and NGO Monitor, I'lam, July 19, 2018, https://www.ngo-
    monitor.org/ngos/i_lam/.

20 Richard Goldstone, "Reconsidering the Goldstone Report on Israel and War Crimes," *Washington
    Post*, April 1, 2011, https://www.washingtonpost.com/opinions/reconsidering-the-goldstone-
    report-on-israel-and-war-crimes/2011/04/01/AFg111JC_story.html.

21 See Christian Datoc, "George Soros' 'Open Society Foundations' Named 2016's LEAST Transpar-
    ent Think Tank," Daily Caller, July 6, 2016, https://dailycaller.com/2016/07/06/george-soros-
    open-society-foundations-named-2016s-least-transparent-think-tank/.

22 See again Joffe and Steinberg, Bad Investment.

23 Eli Lake, "Soros Revealed as Funder of Liberal Jewish-American Lobby," *Washington Times*,
    September 24, 2010, https://www.washingtontimes.com/news/2010/sep/24/soros-funder-liberal-
    jewish-american-lobby/.

24 Armstrong Williams, "George Soros' Israel-Hatred Spills Out into the Open." Algemeiner, Septem-
    ber 28, 2016, https://www.algemeiner.com/2016/09/28/george-soros-israel-hatred-spills-out-into-
    the-open/.

25 "George Soros to Give $100 Million to Human Rights Watch," Human Rights Watch, September
    7, 2010, https://www.hrw.org/news/2010/09/07/george-soros-give-100-million-human-rights-
    watch.

26 Benjamin Weinthal, HRW accepts Saudi funds to not criticize repression of gays, The Jerusalem
    Post, March 5, 2020. https://www.jpost.com/Middle-East/Anti-Israel-HRW-accepts-Saudi-funds-
    to-not-criticize-repression-of-gays-619695.

27 Gerald Steinberg, "Selling Out to Soros," NGO Monitor, September 13, 2010, https://www.ngo-
    monitor.org/in-the-media/selling_out_to_soros/. The original NYP article is no longer accessible
    from the link in this article.

28 Steinberg, "Selling Out to Soros."

29 "Human Rights Watch (HRW)," NGO Monitor, June 28, 2022, https://www.ngo-monitor.org/
    ngos/human_rights_watch_hrw_/.

30 See "Leadership: Mark Malloch-Brown," Open Society Foundations, accessed July 14, 2022,
    https://www.opensocietyfoundations.org/who-we-are/leadership/mark-malloch-brown.

31 "Exposed: How the Left Is Stealing Your Church," D. James Kennedy Minis-
    tries website, accessed July 14, 2022, https://offers.djameskennedy.org/stealing-
    your-church/?utm_campaign=StealingYourChurch&utm_source=CW&utm_
    medium=DJKMwebsite20210914&utm_content=L2406&PN=41200622&doing_wp_cron=165
    7825449.3059179782867431640625.

32 John Aman, "Soros' Cash Helps 'Flip' Evangelicals Away from Israel," WND, September 29, 2021,
    https://www.wnd.com/2021/09/soros-cash-helps-flip-evangelicals-away-israel/.

33 Adam Eliyahu Berkowitz, "SOROS FUNDED GROUP TARGETING EVANGELICALS WITH ANTI-ISRAEL PROPAGANDA," Israel365 News, Jul 15, 2022, https://www.israel365news. com/199867/soros-funded-group-targeting-evangelicals-with-anti-israel-propaganda/; Aman, "Soros' Cash Helps 'Flip' Evangelicals Away from Israel."

34 Aman, "Soros' Cash Helps 'Flip' Evangelicals Away from Israel."

35 Rashida Talib, Financial Disclosure Report, Filing ID # 10022443, 5/16,/2018, Clerk of the House of Representatives, https://disclosures-clerk.house.gov/public_disc/financial-pdfs/2018/10022443.pdf.

36 Joe Schoffstall, "Rashida Tlaib Misrepresented Soros Stipend in Financial Disclosures," *Washington Free Beacon*, December 6, 2018, https://freebeacon.com/politics/rashida-tlaib-misrepresented-soros-stipend-financial-disclosures/. See also Rashida Tlaib's Financial Disclosure Report, filed May 16, 2018, https://disclosures-clerk.house.gov/public_disc/financial-pdfs/2018/10022443.pdf.

37 "Leadership in Government Fellowship: Gigi B. Sohn," Open Society Foundations, accessed July 15, 2022, https://www.opensocietyfoundations.org/grants/leadership-in-government-fellowship?fellow=gigi-b-sohn, See: Martyn Warwick, Will Rosenworcel finally move and push Gigi Sohn into the FCC seat?Aug. 5, 2022, https://www.telecomtv.com/content/access-evolution/will-rosenworcel-intervene-and-push-gigi-sohn-into-the-fcc-seat-45121/.

38 Schoffstall, "Rashida Tlaib Misrepresented Soros Stipend in Financial Disclosures"; see also her 2017 Form 990-PF at https://freebeacon.com/wp-content/uploads/2018/12/Open-Society-grant-to-Tlaib.pdf.

39 Rashida Tlaib, Financial Disclosure Report, p. 2.

40 Schoffstall, "Rashida Tlaib Misrepresented Soros Stipend in Financial Disclosures."

41 See "Leadership in Government Fellowship," Open Society Foundations, accessed July 15, 2022, https://www.opensocietyfoundations.org/grants/leadership-in-government-fellowship?eligibility=1.

42 Schoffstall, "Rashida Tlaib Misrepresented Soros Stipend in Financial Disclosures."

43 Joel Griffith, Rashida Tlaib Spouts Politically Correct Anti-Semitism for the 21st Century, Heritage Foundation, July 30, 2019, https://www.heritage.org/civil-society/commentary/rashida-tlaib-spouts-politically-correct-anti-semitism-the-21st-century.

44 Claude Thompson, Rashida Tlaib slams *New York Times* for 'dehumanizing our Palestinian people who just want to be free', Washington Examiner, May 5,2019. https://www.washingtonexaminer.com/news/rashida-tlaib-slams-new-york-times-for-dehumanizing-out-palestinian-people-who-just-want-to-be-free.

45 Joseph A. Wulfsohn, ADL prez accuses Tlaib of 'antisemitic dog whistling' for remarks ripping those profiting 'behind the curtain, https://www.foxnews.com/politics/adl-rashida-tlaib-antisemit-ic-dog-whistling.

46 Soros Justice Fellowships, 2005, https://www.opensocietyfoundations.org/grants/soros-justice-fellowships?fellow=michelle-alexander.

47 Rachel Ehrenfeld, "Soros, the NYT, and Anti-Israel Propaganda," American Center for Democracy, January 25, 2019, https://acdemocracy.org/soros-the-nyt-and-anti-israel-propaganda/.

48 See Michelle Alexander, "America, This Is Your Chance," *New York Times*, June 8, 2020, https://www.nytimes.com/2020/06/08/opinion/george-floyd-protests-race.html.

49 Institute for Contemporary Affairs, "American Non-Government Organizations Are Intertwined with PFLP Terror Group," Jerusalem Center for Public Affairs, December 6, 2018, https://jcpa.org/article/american-non-government-organizations-are-intertwined-with-pflp-terror-group/; Bureau of Counterterrorism, "Foreign Terrorist Organizations," accessed July 15, 2022. https://2009-2017.state.gov/j/ct/rls/other/des/123085.htm.

ENDNOTES

50 See "COUNCIL DECISION 2012/333/CFSP of 25 June 2012," Official Journal of the European Union, June 26, 2012, https://eur-lex.europa.eu/LexUriServ/LexUriServ.do?uri=OJ:L:2012:165:00 72:0074:EN:PDF.

51 See "Israeli legal group threatens to sue Australian charity for funding terror group," Times of Israel, October 14, 2012, https://www.timesofisrael.com/israeli-legal-threatens-to-sue-australian-charity-for-funding-terror-group/.

52 "Currently Listed Entities," Public Safety Canada, last modified June 25, 2021, https://www.publicsafety.gc.ca/cnt/ntnl-scrt/cntr-trrrsm/lstd-ntts/crrnt-lstd-ntts-en.aspx#2042.

53 "Implementation of the Measures including the Freezing of Assets against Terrorists and the Like," Ministry of Foreign Affairs of Japan, July 5, 2002, https://www.mofa.go.jp/announce/announce/2002/7/0705.html.

54 Arutz Sheva Staff, "Six 'Popular Front' Groups Declared Terrorist Organizations," 7 Israel National News, October 22, 2021, https://www.israelnationalnews.com/news/315538.

55 See Michelle Alexander, "Time to Break the Silence on Palestine," *New York Times*, January 19, 2019, https://www.nytimes.com/2019/01/19/opinion/sunday/martin-luther-king-palestine-israel.html.

56 Alan M. Dershowitz.

57 See Michael Steinberger, "George Soros." *New York Times* Magazine, July 17, 2018, https://www.nytimes.com/2018/07/17/magazine/george-soros-democrat-open-society.html.

58 Neon Nettle, George Soros Buys Up Lion's Share of *New York Times* Stock, woked.co › news › george-soros-buys-up-lions-share-of-new-york-times-stock, See- US Securities and Exchange Commission (SEC) filing of May 2021. https://www.sec.gov/Archives/edgar/data/1029160/000114036118023894/xslForm13F_X01/form13fInfoTable.xml.

59 Dan Gainor, "Why Is Soros Spending over $48 Million Funding Media Organizations?," Fox News, May 7, 2015, https://www.foxnews.com/opinion/why-is-soros-spending-over-48-million-funding-media-organizations.

60 Gainor, quoted in Rachel Ehrenfeld, "Soros, the NYT, and Anti-Israel Propaganda," American Thinker, January 25, 2019, https://www.americanthinker.com/blog/2019/01/soros_the_nyt_and_antiisrael_propaganda.html.

61 Gainor, "Why Is Soros Spending Over $48 Million Funding Media Organizations?"

62 Open Society Foundations, "The Soros Foundations Network," George Soros, February 1, 1994, https://www.georgesoros.com/1994/02/01/the-soros-foundations-network/.

63 Ehrenfeld, "Soros, the NYT, and Anti-Israel Propaganda."

64 Emma Bowman, George Soros: Open Societies Are Under Threat, NPR, October 26, 2019, https://www.npr.org/2019/10/26/773454708/george-soros-open-societies-are-under-threat.

65 OSF, AWARDED GRANTS, TIDES 2019, https://www.opensocietyfoundations.org/grants/past?filter_keyword=tides&filter_year=2019&page=2.

66 For example, see James Simpson, Black Lives Matter, Capital Research Center, Septemver21, 2016. https://capitalresearch.org/article/blm-roots/ ; and Hayden Ludwig, Tides' Legal Laundering (Full Series), Profiling the Tides Foundation, one of the Left's leading dark money groups, https://capitalresearch.org/?s=Tides.

67 "Tides Network," NGO Monitor, July 14, 2021, https://www.ngo-monitor.org/funder/tides-network/.

68 "Grassroots International (Boston)," NGO Monitor, February 10, 2022, https://www.ngo-monitor.org/ngos/grassroots_international_boston_/.

69   "The European-Funded NGO PFLP Network," NGO Monitor, November 14, 2016, updated November 15, 2016, https://www.ngo-monitor.org/reports/european-funded-ngo-pflp-network/.

70   "About," NGO Monitor, accessed July 15, 2022, https://www.ngo-monitor.org/about/.

71   Terrorists in Suits: The Ties Between NGOs Promoting BDS and Terrorist Organizations (State of Israel, Ministry of Strategic Affairs and Public Diplomacy, February 2019), https://www.gov.il/BlobFolder/generalpage/terrorists_in_suits/en/De-Legitimization%20Brochure.pdf. See also "Bisan Research & Development Center," NGO Monitor, October 27, 2021, https://www.ngo-monitor.org/ngos/bisan-research-development-center/.

72   Lea Bilke, Amb. Alan Baker, "Israel's Designation of Six Terrorism-Linked NGOs Was in Full Accordance with International Law," Jerusalem Center for Public Affairs, November 2, 2021, https://jcpa.org/israels-designation-of-six-terrorism-linked-ngos-was-in-full-accordance-with-international-law/.

73   Omri Weisman, American Non-Government Organizations Are Intertwined with PFLP Terror Group, Institute for Contemporary Affairs, No. 619, December 6, 2018, Jerusalem Center for Public Affairs, https://jcpa.org/article/american-non-government-organizations-are-intertwined-with-pflp-terror-group/.

74   Institute for Contemporary Affairs, "American Non-Government Organizations Are Intertwined with PFLP Terror Group."

75   Occam's Razor, "Dream Defenders: Defending the Dream of Anti-Israel Activism," Legal Insurrect, October 1, 2016, https://legalinsurrection.com/2016/10/dream-defenders-defending-the-dream-of-anti-israel-activism/.

76   Tides Foundation, The Dream Defenders Education Fund, https://www.tides.org/project/the-dream-defenders-education-fund/.

77   See Britannica, s.v. "Popular Front for the Liberation of Palestine," accessed July 15, 2022, https://www.britannica.com/topic/Popular-Front-for-the-Liberation-of-Palestine.

78   "NGO Campaigns for Ahed Tamimi, and Against the Rights of Children."

79   Reuters, "A History of Israel's Prisoner Swaps," Jerusalem Post, October 27, 2011, https://www.jpost.com/Diplomacy-and-Politics/A-history-of-Israels-prisoner-swaps.

80   Occam's Razor, "Dream Defenders."

81   Occam's Razor, "Dream Defenders."

82   Institute for Contemporary Affairs, "American Non-Government Organizations Are Intertwined with PFLP Terror Group."

83   Occam's Razor, "Dream Defenders." See "History: Rebellion," accessed July 15, 2022, https://dd-blackedouthistory.tumblr.com/.

84   Ehrenfeld, "Soros' Anti-Israel/BDS Funding." Not surprisingly, the link to the curriculum embedded in this article no longer works.

85   See Dream Defenders Fight PAC, "DD SunDDay School: A Rock and A Hard Place, Dr. Angela Davis," YouTube video, recorded live on October 4, 2020, posted October 15, 2020, https://www.youtube.com/watch?v=ETUP_bjnavo.

86   See "Angela Davis receives the Lenin Peace Prize (1979)," YouTube video, November 6, 2017, https://www.youtube.com/watch?v=FuhnJ1tKWJY.

87   See "Adalah," NGO Monitor, February 15, 2022, https://www.ngo-monitor.org/ngos/adalah/.

88   NGO Monitor, Adalah, February 2022, https://www.ngo-monitor.org/ngos/adalah/

89   Jonathan Schanznr and Kate Havard, Boycott, Divestment and Sanctions movement attracting groups with terrorist ties, The Hill, Mov. 2, 2016FLP.

90   See "Adalah's US-based "Justice Project: A Foray into BDS," NGO Monitor, August 24, 2018,
      https://www.ngo-monitor.org/reports/adalahs-us-based-justice-project-a-foray-into-bds/.

91   Ron Kampeas, "Soros Email Hack Reveals Plans to Fight 'Racist' Israeli Policies," Times of Israel,
      August 15, 2016, https://www.timesofisrael.com/soros-email-hack-reveals-plans-to-fight-racist-
      israeli-policies/.

92   See "Rockefeller Brothers Foundation," NGO Monitor, January 17, 2017, updated February 13,
      2017, https://www.ngo-monitor.org.il/funder/rbf/.

93   "Adalah's US-based "Justice Project."

94   See "Israel, Palestinian Leaders Should Guarantee Right of Return as Part of Comprehen-
      sive Refugee Solution," Human Rights Watch, December 21, 2000, https://www.hrw.org/
      news/2000/12/21/israel-palestinian-leaders-should-guarantee-right-return-part-comprehensive-
      refugee.

95   Gerald M. Steinberg and Maayan Rockland (the Begin-Sadat Center for Strategic Studies and
      Bar-Ilan University), "Palestinian Activists at Human Rights Watch," Mideast Security and Policy
      Studies 177, p. 5, https://besacenter.org/wp-content/uploads/2020/07/177-MONOGRAPH-
      Steinberg-and-Rockland-FINAL-1.pdf.

96   "Senior Palestinian Islamic Jihad and Hamas figures praise Iran's military support and threaten
      that in the next war the rocket fire from the Gaza Strip will reach all the cities in Israel and the
      "resistance axis" will coordinate its actions on all fronts." The Meir Amit Intelligence and Terrorism
      Information Center, June 1, 2019. https://www.terrorism-info.org.il/en/senior-palestinian-islamic-
      jihad-hamas-figures-praise-irans-military-support-threaten-next-war-rocket-fire-gaza-strip-will-
      reach-cities-israel-res/.

97   See "Terror-linked and boycott promoting NGOs behind potential ICC investigation," NGO
      Monitor, December 24, 2019, updated March 4, 2021, https://www.ngo-monitor.org/reports/
      terror-linked-and-boycott-promoting-ngos-behind-potential-icc-investigation/.

98   See "Analysis: Israel Designates 6 PFLP-linked NGOs as Terrorist Organizations," NGO Monitor,
      October 24, 2021, https://www.ngo-monitor.org/reports/analysis-israel-designates-6-pflp-linked-
      ngos-as-terrorist-organizations/.

99   Nadine Epstein, Soros: A Small Sacrifice for Netanyahu, Moment Magazine, March-April, 2019,
      https://momentmag.com/soros-a-small-sacrifice-for-netanyahu/.

100   Soros, Soros on Soros, 114.

101   See "Summary of the PFLP's NGO Network," NGO Monitor, October 20, 2021, https://www.
      ngo-monitor.org/reports/summary-pflps-ngo-network/.

102   See Rachel Ehrenfeld, "Paying for Terrorism," Wall Street Journal, October 23, 2002, https://www.
      wsj.com/articles/SB1035323843647433831; and Ehrenfeld, "Trump Cutting Palestinian Funds
      for Terror," American Center for Democracy, September 17, 2018, https://acdemocracy.org/
      trump-cut-palestinian-funds-for-terror/.

103   See Paul Shindman, "How Much Did the Palestinian Authority Spend in Terror Salaries in 2020?,"
      World Israel News, February 22, 2021, https://worldisraelnews.com/how-much-did-the-palestin-
      ian-authority-spend-in-terror-salaries-in-2020/.

104   "WATCH: Palestinians Lose $165 Million in US Aid over Terror Stipends," World Israel News,
      October 13, 2018, https://worldisraelnews.com/watch-palestinians-lose-165-million-in-us-aid-
      over-terror-stipends/.

105   https://acdemocracy.org/trump-cut-palestinian-funds-for-terror/#prettyPhoto/0/.

106 David Brunnstrom, "Trump cuts more than $200 million in U.S. aid to Palestinians," Reuters, August 24, 2018, https://www.reuters.com/article/us-usa-palestinians/trump-cuts-more-than-200-million-in-u-s-aid-to-palestinians-idUSKCN1L923C.

107 Ehrenfeld, "Trump Cutting Palestinian Funds for Terror."

108 World Israel News Staff, "Palestinians Call Israeli Law Against Pay-for-Slay 'Blackmail'," World Israel News, July 18, 2018, https://worldisraelnews.com/palestinians-call-israeli-law-against-pay-for-slay-blackmail/,

109 Shindman, "How Much Did the Palestinian Authority Spend in Terror Salaries in 2020?" See also World Israel News Staff, "Palestinians Vow to Continue Terror Funding Despite Sanctions," World Israel News, July 4, 2018, https://worldisraelnews.com/pa-says-despite-sanctions-we-will-never-stop-funding-terror/.

110 Shindman, "How Much Did the Palestinian Authority Spend in Terror Salaries in 2020?"

111 Adam Kredo, "Watchdog Sues Biden Admin over Funding for Palestinian Government," *Washington Free Beacon*, January 17, 2022, https://freebeacon.com/biden-administration/watchdog-sues-biden-admin-over-funding-for-palestinian-government/.

112 Kredo, "Watchdog Sues Biden Admin over Funding for Palestinian Government"; Laura Kelly, "GOP Lawmakers Block Biden Assistance to Palestinians." The Hill, April 9, 2021, https://thehill.com/policy/international/547417-gop-lawmakers-block-biden-assistance-to-palestinians/.

113 Deborah Brand, "In Ramallah, U.S. Lawmakers Slam Abbas over Terrorist Pay-for-Slay," Breitbart, July 14, 2021, https://www.breitbart.com/middle-east/2021/07/14/in-ramallah-members-of-congress-slam-abbas-over-pay-for-slay/.

114 Ryan Heath, "Blinken Announces $110M in New Gaza Funding. Now Comes the Hard Part," Politico, May 25, 2021, https://www.politico.com/news/2021/05/25/blinken-gaza-funding-490824.

115 Lauren Marcus, "What Did Abbas tell Blinken about Russia, Ukraine and Israel?," World Israel News, March 28, 2022, https://worldisraelnews.com/what-did-abbas-tell-blinken-about-russia-ukraine-and-israel/amp/.

116 Amnesty International, "Q&A: ISRAEL'S APARTHEID AGAINST PALESTINIANS: CRUEL SYSTEM OF DOMINATION AND CRIME AGAINST HUMANITY," accessed July 15, 2022, https://www.amnesty.org/en/latest/research/2022/02/qa-israels-apartheid-against-palestinians-cruel-system-of-domination-and-crime-against-humanity/.

117 The International Legal Forum (@The_ILF), "You may have heard that @amnesty @AmnestyUK is about to release a baseless report, filled with malicious lies, gross distortions of truth and fabrications of law, accusing #Israel of 'apartheid'," Twitter, January 31, 2022, https://twitter.com/The_ILF/status/1488161728458366987.

118 Zachary Keyser, "Amnesty Denounces S-G's Tweet That Alluded Israel Assassinated Arafat," Jerusalem Post, April 6, 2021, https://www.jpost.com/arab-israeli-conflict/amnesty-denounces-s-gs-tweet-that-alluded-israel-assassinated-arafat-665357.

119 Lazar Berman, "Israel Blasts Amnesty UK for 'Antisemitic' Report Accusing It of Apartheid," Times of Israel, January 31, 2022, https://www.timesofisrael.com/lapid-attacks-delusional-amnesty-uk-ahead-of-report-accusing-israel-of-apartheid/.

120 See "Dr. Agnes Callamard, former Special Rapporteur (2016–2021)," United Nations, accessed July 15, 2022, https://www.ohchr.org/en/special-procedures/sr-executions/dr-agnes-callamard-former-special-rapporteur-2016-2021.

ENDNOTES

121 Tyler Durden, "UN Investigation Finds US Soleimani Killing 'Unlawful' as There Was 'No Evidence' of Imminent Threat," Ron Paul Institute, July 8, 2020, http://www.ronpaulinstitute.org/archives/featured-articles/2020/july/08/un-investigation-finds-us-soleimani-killing-unlawful-as-there-was-no-evidence-of-imminent-threat/.

122 Berman, "Israel Blasts Amnesty UK for 'Antisemitic' Report Accusing It of Apartheid,"

123 "MFA Press Release: Amnesty UK Expected to Publish a False, Biased, and Antisemitic Report Tomorrow," Ministry of Foreign Affairs, January 1, 2022, https://www.gov.il/en/departments/news/amnesty-uk-expected-to-publish-biased-antiemitic-report-31-jan-2022.

124 "MFA Press Release."

125 See "Analysis: Israel Designates 6 PFLP-linked NGOs as Terrorist Organizations."

126 See The New Arab Staff, "Amnesty, HRW Slam Israel for Declaring Six Palestinian NGOs 'Terrorist Orgs'," New Arab, October 22, 2021, https://english.alaraby.co.uk/news/amnesty-hrw-slam-israel-outlawing-six-palestinian-ngos.

127 Judah Ari Gross, "Israel Disputes US Claim It Wasn't Told of Plan to Outlaw Rights Groups," Times of Israel, October 23, 2021, https://www.timesofisrael.com/israel-disputes-us-claim-it-wasnt-told-of-plan-to-outlaw-rights-groups/.

128 Terrorists In Suits–The Ties Between NGOs promoting BDS and Terrorist Organizations, Ministry of Strategic Affairs and Public Diplomacy (MSA), February 2019, https://www.gov.il/BlobFolder/generalpage/terrorists_in_suits/en/De-Legitimization%20Brochure.pdf.

129 "PCHR: Palestinian Centre for Human Rights," Arab.org, accessed July 15, 2022, https://arab.org/directory/palestinian-center-human-rights/.

130 "Human Rights and International Humanitarian Law Secretariat," NGO Monitor, September 18, 2017 (updated on October 30, 2017), https://www.ngo-monitor.org/reports/human-rights-international-humanitarian-law-secretariat/.

131 Alex Kane, "Gaza-based human rights worker prevented from entering U.S. (Updated)," Mondoweiss, October 8, 2012, https://mondoweiss.net/2012/10/gaza-based-human-rights-worker-denied-entry-to-u-s/.

132 "PCHR's Role in the ICC 'Investigation',," NGO Monitor, September 23, 2020, https://www.ngo-monitor.org/reports/pchrs-role-icc-investigation/.

133 "Palestinian Centre for Human Right's Links to the PFLP Terror Group," NGO Monitor, January 27, 2020, https://www.ngo-monitor.org/reports/palestinian-centre-for-human-rights-links-to-the-pflp-terror-group/.

134 See Wikipedia, s.v. "Revolutionary Cells (German group)," accessed July 15, 2022, https://en.wikipedia.org/wiki/Revolutionary_Cells_(German_group).

135 See "WATCH: Former Director of Mossad Recounts Operation Entebbe," United with Israel, July 5, 2021, https://unitedwithisrael.org/watch-former-director-of-mossad-recounts-operation-entebbe/.

136 Aaron Reich, "On This Day: Israeli Minister Rehavam Ze'evi Assassinated by Terrorists 20 Years Ago," Jerusalem Post, October 17, 2021, https://www.jpost.com/arab-israeli-conflict/on-this-day-israeli-minister-rehavam-zeevi-assassinated-by-terrorists-20-years-ago-682206.

137 See "Palestinian Center for Human Rights (PCHR)," NGO Monitor, June 21, 2022, https://www.ngo-monitor.org/ngos/palestinian_center_for_human_rights_pchr_/.

138 See the Palestinian Centre for Human Rights' funding webpage at https://pchrgaza.org/en/funding/.

139 PCHR Annual Report 2017, p. 4, https://pchrgaza.org/en/wp-content/uploads/2018/06/annual-report-english2017.pdf#page=4.

140 Harriet Sherwood, "Israel Labels Palestinian Human Rights Groups as Terrorist Organisations," *Guardian*, October 22, 2021, https://www.theguardian.com/world/2021/oct/22/israel-labels-palestinian-human-rights-groups-terrorist-organisations/.

141 Sharon Wrobel, "Israeli Foreign Ministry Argues Banned Palestinian Groups Are 'Main Source' of PFLP Funds," Algemeiner, October 25, 2021, https://www.algemeiner.com/2021/10/25/israeli-foreign-ministry-argues-banned-palestinian-groups-are-main-source-of-pflp-funds/.

142 Deborah Brand, "Israel Denies Biden Administration Claims It Was Not Informed of Palestinian Rights Group Terror Ties," Breitbart, October 25, 2021, https://www.breitbart.com/middle-east/2021/10/25/israel-denies-biden-administration-claims-it-was-not-informed-of-palestinian-rights-group-terror-ties/.

143 "Summary of the PFLP's NGO Network."

144 Adam Kredo and Matthew Foldi, "DOCUMENT: Here's Why Israel Designated Six Palestinian Charities as Terror Groups," *Washington Free Beacon*, December 6, 2021, https://freebeacon.com/national-security/document-heres-why-israel-designated-six-palestinian-charities-terror-groups/.

145 Israel/Palestine: Designation of Palestinian Rights Groups as Terrorists, HRW, Oct 4, 2021. https://www.hrw.org/news/2021/10/22/israel/palestine-designation-palestinian-rights-groups-terrorists.

146 B'Tselem's response to MoD Gantz's declaration of Palestinian human rights organizations as terrorist organizations, Oct, 20, 2021, https://www.btselem.org/press_releases/20211024_response_to_declaration_of_palestinian_human_rights_ngos_as_terrorist_organizations_by_israeli_mod_gantz.

147 Aaron Boxerman, "Israeli 'Terror' Designation of Palestinian NGOs Sparks Furious Int'l Backlash," Times of Israel, October 22, 2021, https://www.timesofisrael.com/israeli-terror-designation-of-palestinian-ngos-sparks-furious-backlash/.

148 Ben Samuels, "Progressive Democrats Push Resolution Against Israel's NGO Terror Designations," Haaretz, October 28, 2021, https://www.haaretz.com/us-news/2021-10-28/ty-article/.premium/progressives-push-resolution-against-israels-ngo-terror-designations/0000017f-dc7f-db22-a17f-fcffb4e60000.

149 United Nations, "Bachelet Describes 'Disastrous' Human Rights Situation across Occupied Palestinian Territory," UN News, December 7, 2021, https://news.un.org/en/story/2021/12/1107352.

150 Aryeh Savir, "'Shame on You!' Israel's Envoy Rips Up Human Rights Council Report at UN," United with Israel, October 31, 2021.

151 Savir, "'Shame on You!"

152 The United Nations Independent International Commission of Inquiry on the Occupied Palestinian Territory, including East Jerusalem, and in Israel, https://www.ohchr.org/en/hr-bodies/hrc/co-israel/index.

153 Algemeiner Staff, Erdan: UN Report Condemning Israel 'Has No Place' in Human Rights Body, The Algemeiner, Oct. 29, 2021. https://www.algemeiner.com/2021/10/29/israels-erdan-un-report-condemning-israel-has-no-place-in-human-rights-body/.

154 Savir, "'Shame on You!"

155 Deborah Brand, "Israel's U.N. Envoy Rips Up Human Rights Council Report over 'Obsessive Bias," Breitbart, October 31, 2021, https://www.breitbart.com/middle-east/2021/10/31/israels-un-envoy-rips-up-human-rights-council-report-at-un-over-obsessive-bias/.

156 Ben Zion Gad, "'Israeli Apartheid' Top Human Rights Issue of 2021—HRW," Jerusalem Post, December 21, 2021, https://www.jpost.com/international/article-689307.

ENDNOTES

157 Kenneth Roth (@KenRoth), "The top human rights news in 2021 included . . . ," Twitter, December 19, 2021, https://twitter.com/KenRoth/status/1472573828224147465?ref_src=twsrc%5Etfw %7Ctwcamp%5Etweetembed%7Ctwterm%5E1472573828224147465%7Ctwgr%5E%7Ctwcon %5Es1_&ref_url=https%3A%2F%2Fwww.jpost.com%2Finternational%2Farticle-689307.

158 Gad, "'Israeli Apartheid'."

159 "Ken Roth's Immoral Anti-Israel Obsession and the Gaza War," NGO Monitor, September 4, 2014, https://www.ngo-monitor.org/reports/ken_roth_s_immoral_anti_israel_obsession_and_the_ gaza_war_/.

160 Kenneth Roth (@KenRoth), "Germans rally against anti-Semitism that flared in Europe in response to Israel's conduct in Gaza war. Merkel joins," Twitter, September 15, 2014, 7:54 a.m., https://twitter.com/KenRoth/status/511496648695226368.

161 Robert L. Bernstein, Rights Watchdog, Lost in the Mideast, The New York Times, Oct. 19, 2009, https://www.nytimes.com/2009/10/20/opinion/20bernstein.html.

162 Aina J. Khan, Kenneth Roth, 'Godfather' of Human Rights Work, to Step Down, The New York Times, May 1, 2022, https://www.nytimes.com/2022/04/26/world/americas/kenneth-roth-human-rights-watch.html.

163 Tova Lazaroff, Kenneth Roth to resign from Human Rights Watch after 30 years at the helm, The Jerusalem Post, April 26, 2022.

164 See Patrick Goodenough, "More Skewed Focus on Israel, As UN Rights Council Creates First Open-Ended Commission of Inquiry," cnsnews, May 28, 2021, https://cnsnews.com/article/international/patrick-goodenough/more-skewed-focus-israel-un-rights-council-creates-first.

165 Austin Ruse, "UN Secretary General Nominates Abortion Advocate for Top Human Rights Post," C-Fam, July 24, 2008, https://c-fam.org/un-secretary-general-nominates-abortion-advocate-for-top-human-rights-post/.

166 Iron Dome Air Defence Missile System, Army Technology, https://www.army-technology.com/ projects/iron-dome/.

167 Anat Kurz and Shlomo Brom, eds., The Lessons of Operation Protective Edge (Tel Aviv: The Institute for National Security Studies, 2014), 39, https://www.inss.org.il/wp-content/uploads/sites/2/ systemfiles/SystemFiles/ZukEtanENG_final.pdf.

168 See Louis René Beres, "Putting Israel's Self-Defense in Context," U.S. News, July 30, 2014, https:// www.usnews.com/opinion/articles/2014/07/30/why-israels-response-to-hamas-isnt-disproportionate.

169 Patrick Goodenough, "UN Human Rights Council Defends Selection of Outspoken Israel Critic to Head Israel Inquiry," cnsnews, February 17, 2022, https://cnsnews.com/index.php/article/international/patrick-goodenough/un-human-rights-council-defends-selection-outspoken-israel.

170 See Patrick Goodenough, "Lawmakers to Blinken: Stop the UN's Unprecedented Permanent Inquiry Targeting Israel," January 27, 2022, https://cnsnews.com/article/international/patrick-goodenough/lawmakers-blinken-stop-uns-unprecedented-permanent-inquiry.

171 See Reuters, "Blinken discusses Palestinian Authority reform with Mahmoud Abbas," January 31, 2022, https://www.reuters.com/world/middle-east/blinken-spoke-palestinian-president-abbas-monday-state-dept-2022-01-31/.

172 Daniel Greenfield, "Biden's Israel Ambassador Tells BDS Group He Wants Jews Out of Jerusalem," Front Page Mag, March 23, 2022, https://www.frontpagemag.com/fpm/2022/03/bidens-israel-ambassador-tells-bds-group-he-wants-daniel-greenfield/.

173 Tovah Lazaroff and Gil Hoffman, "Nides: Israeli Settlement Growth Infuriates Me, Calls It 'Stupid Things'," Jerusalem Post, March 16, 2016, https://www.jpost.com/israel-news/article-701410.

174 DRL Strengthening Human Rights and Accountability in Israel and the West Bank and Gaza, U.S. Department of State, Feb. 11, 2022, https://www.state.gov/drl-strengthening-human-rights-and-accountability-in-israel-and-the-west-bank-and-gaza/.

175 Secretary Antony Blinken (@SecBlinken), "Spoke today with @HRW's @KenRoth and @Amnesty's @AgnesCallamard on human rights challenges, including in Ukraine, Russia, China, and the Middle East. Human rights are central to U.S. foreign policy. We support the important work of human rights defenders," Twitter, March 16, 2022, 5:14 p.m., https://twitter.com/SecBlinken/status/1504219464488960000?s=20&t=gINMcsRLEqrWIRz_rPkeIw.

7: SOROS IS NO DREYFUS

1   Rabbi Dov Fischer is western regional vice president of Coalition for Jewish Values., It's a mitzvah, not anti-Semitism, to attack George Soros' dangerous DA campaigns, Mew York Post, Feb 1, 2022. https://nypost.com/2022/02/01/its-a-mitzvah-not-anti-semitism-to-attack-george-soros-da-campaigns/.

2   Mario Calvo-Platero, The Great Anticipator, La Repubblica, August 11, 2020 https://www.george-soros.com/2020/08/11/the-great-anticipator/.

3   Robert Slater, Soros: The Life, Times & Trading Secrets of the World's Greatest Investor (New York: Irwin, 1996), n.p.

4   "George Soros," Geni, accessed July 18, 2022. https://www.geni.com/people/George-Soros/6000000017823750593; Tivadar Soros, Masquerade: Dancing Around Death in Nazi-Occupied Hungary, edited and translated from Esperanto by Humphrey Tonkin (New York: Arcade, 1965), 220, https://archive.org/details/masquerade00tiva/page/n7/mode/2up.

5   Michael Kranish, "'I'm proud of my enemies:' Excerpts from a Post interview with George Soros," Washington Post, June 9, 2018, https://www.washingtonpost.com/politics/im-proud-of-my-enemies-excerpts-from-a-post-interview-with-george-soros/2018/06/08/23c1cb4e-6b33-11e8-bea7-c8eb28bc52b1_story.html.

6   Soros, Soros on Soros, 242–43.

7   Connie Bruck, "The World According to Soros," New Yorker, January 15, 1995, https://www.newyorker.com/magazine/1995/01/23/the-world-according-to-soros.

8   Soros, Soros on Soro, 242.

9   "George Soros," New York Times Magazine, July 17, 2018, https://www.nytimes.com/2018/07/17/magazine/george-soros-democrat-open-society.html.

10 Bruck, "The World According to Soros."

11 Bruck.

12 Rudy W. Giuliani (@RudyGiuliani), "Soros has funded many enemies to the State of Israel," Twitter, December 24, 2019, 1:40 p.m., https://twitter.com/RudyGiuliani/status/1209559585545052160?ref_src=twsrc%5Etfw.

13 Lev Golinkin, "Rudy Giuliani's anti-Soros tirade exposes three uncomfortable truths," CNN, December 24, 2019, https://www.cnn.com/2019/12/24/opinions/rudy-giuliani-george-soros-anti-semitism-golinkin/index.html. Brandon Gage, "Rudy Giuliani Throws Antisemitic, Racist Tantrum Over Black Lives Matter," HillReporter.com. July 7, 2021, https://hillreporter.com/rudy-giuliani-throws-antisemitic-racist-tantrum-over-black-lives-matter-106267.

14 Yaron Steinbuch, Black Lives Matter co-founder describes herself as 'trained Marxist', New York Post, June 25, 2020, https://nypost.com/2020/06/25/blm-co-founder-describes-herself-as-trained-marxist/.

15   Charles Creitz, "Giuliani Calls on Trump to Declare Black Lives Matter a Domestic Terror Organization," Fox News, August 17, 2020, https://www.foxnews.com/us/giuliani-trump-black-lives-matter-domestic-terrorism.

16   JTA and Sam Sokol, "Giuliani Doubles Down on Jewish Soros Comments, Saying the Philanthropist Uses Judaism as 'a Shield and a Sword,'" Haaretz, December 4, 2020, https://www.haaretz.com/us-news/2020-12-04/ty-article/giuliani-doubles-down-on-soros-comments-uses-judaism-as-a-shield-and-a-sword/0000017f-db45-db5a-a57f-db6fe21d0000.

17   Julia Manchester, "Youngkin under Fire for invoking George Soros in School Board Debate," Hill, October 22, 2021, https://thehill.com/homenews/campaign/578080-youngkin-under-fire-for-invoking-george-soros-in-school-board-debate/.

18   World Israel News Staff, "Criticizing Progressive Jewish Billionaire Is Not Antisemitic, Rabbi Explains Why," World Israel News, October 22, 2021, https://worldisraelnews.com/criticizing-progressive-jewish-billionaire-is-not-antisemitic-Rabbi-explains-why/.

19   @marcorubio, Aug, 7, 2022. https://twitter.com/marcorubio/status/1556238074828320768.

20   Jacob Ogles, "Critics label Marco Rubio's tweet on George Soros-backed prosecutors as anti-Semitic," Florida Politics, Aug 8, 2022. https://floridapolitics.com/archives/545023-critics-label-marco-rubios-tweet-on-george-soros-backed-prosecutors-as-anti-semitic/.

21   JTA and Josefin Dolsten, "Republican Sen. Cotton Accuses Soros-Funded Think Tank of Fostering Anti-Semitism," Haaretz, January 9, 2020, https://www.haaretz.com/us-news/2020-01-09/ty-article/republican-sen-cotton-accuses-soros-funded-think-tank-of-fostering-anti-semitism/0000017f-e815-da9b-a1ff-ec7f82930000.

22   Trita Parsi, How Israel could imperil Biden efforts on Iran , YouTube, January 28, 2021, https://quincyinst.org/2021/01/28/trita-parsi-how-israel-could-imperil-biden-efforts-on-iran/.

23   Sean Durns, Eric Rozenman , J Street Echoes Iran's Best Friend in Washington, CAMERA, October 21, 2015, https://www.camera.org/article/j-street-echoes-iran-s-best-friend-in-washington/.

24   Armin Rosen, Washington's Weirdest Think Tank, Tablet Magazine, April 27, 2021, https://www.tabletmag.com/sections/news/articles/quincy-trita-parsi-soros-koch-armin-rosen.

25   Alexander Soros, he Hate That Is Consuming Us, The New York Times, Oct 24, 2018, https://www.nytimes.com/2018/10/24/opinion/george-soros-mailbox-bomb.html ADL, The Antisemitism Lurking Behind George Soros Conspiracy Theories, November 11, 2018, https://www.adl.org/blog/the-antisemitism-lurking-behind-george-soros-conspiracy-theories, Also, Lili Bayer and Larry Cohler-Esses, Evil Soros: Dog Whistling Anti-Semitism In Viktor Orbán's Hungary, Forward, May 30, 2017, and Peter Walker, Farage criticised for using antisemitic themes to criticise Soros, The Guardian, May 12, 2019, https://www.theguardian.com/politics/2019/may/12/farage-criticised-for-using-antisemitic-themes-to-criticise-soros; Also: AP, Soros spokesperson blames toxic politics for bomb scare, Times of Israel, Oct. 23, 2018, https://www.timesofisrael.com/liveblog_entry/soros-spokesperson-blames-toxic-politics-for-bomb-scare/.

26   Jennifer Rankin, "EU Takes Hungary to ECJ over Crackdown 'Aimed at George Soros,'" Guardian, December 7, 2017, https://www.theguardian.com/world/2017/dec/07/eu-hungary-court-crackdown-george-soros.

27   Brooke Singman, "Soros-Funded University Closer to Shutting Down after Hungary Approves New Rules," Fox News, April 4, 2017, https://www.foxnews.com/world/soros-funded-university-closer-to-shutting-down-after-hungary-approves-new-rules.

28   Associated Press, "EU Court Rules Against Hungary over Law That Targeted Soros-Affiliated University," October 6, 2020, https://www.theguardian.com/law/2020/oct/06/top-eu-court-rules-against-hungary-on-soros-university.

29   Assosiated Press, Demonization of Soros Recalls Old Anti-Semitic Conspiracies, VOA, May 15, 2017, https://www.voanews.com/a/soros-anti-semitic-conspiracies/3851563.html.

30   Cristina Maza, Viktor Orbán's Election Win: Everything You Need to Know About Anti-Soros Hysteria and Authoritarianism in Hungary, *Newsweek*, April 9, 2018, https://www.*newsweek*.com/viktor-orbans-election-win-everything-you-need-know-about-anti-soros-hysteria-877415.

31   Jemimah Steinfeld, Hungary elections 2022: What does another Orban term mean for freedoms?, Index on Censorship, April 1, 2022, https://www.indexoncensorship.org/2022/04/hungary-elections-2022-what-does-another-orban-term-mean-for-freedoms/.

32   Jack Montgomery, "Four More Years: Hungary's Orban Declares Victory over 'International Left, Soros Empire, Mainstream Media' Breitbart, April 4, 2022, https://www.breitbart.com/europe/2022/04/04/four-more-years-hungarys-orban-declares-victory-over-international-left-soros-empire-mainstream-media/.

33   Mark Shiffer, The Dreyfus Affair, Anti-Semitism, and Zionism, The Times of Israel, Oct 1, 2020. https://blogs.timesofisrael.com/the-dreyfus-affair-anti-semitism-and-zionism/.

8: CALLING THE TUNE

1   Tristan Justice, "Soros-Funded 'Disinformation' Group Paid Nearly $1 Million More to Creators of Steele Dossier Disinformation Operation," Federalist, November 30, 2021, https://thefederalist.com/2021/11/30/soros-funded-disinformation-group-paid-nearly-1-million-more-to-creators-of-steele-dossier-disinformation-operation/.

2   Chuck Ross, "Firms Tied to Fusion GPS, Christopher Steele Were Paid $3.8 Million by Soros-Backed Group," Daily Caller, April 1, 2019, https://dailycaller.com/2019/04/01/fusion-gps-steele-soros-millions/.

3   J. Christian Adams, "Leaked Documents Reveal Expansive Soros Funding to Manipulate Federal Elections," PJ Media, November 7, 2016, https://pjmedia.com/jchristianadams/2016/11/07/leaked-documents-reveal-expansive-soros-funding-to-manipulate-federal-elections-n123917.

4   See radamson, "Soros-Funded Media Matters Attacks Conservatives," Human Events, October 29, 2007, https://archive.humanevents.com/2007/10/29/sorosfunded-media-matters-attacks-conservatives/; the *Washington Post* (@washingtonpost), "How mega-donors helped Clinton raise over $1 billion," Twitter, October 23, 2016, 8:26 p.m., https://twitter.com/washingtonpost/status/790363710804094976; Rachel Ehrenfeld and Shawn Macomber, "The Soros-Kerry Nexus," American Center for Democracy, October 19, 2004, https://acdemocracy.org/the-soros-kerry-nexus/; Mihailo S. Zekic, "George Soros and Barack Obama, Philadelphia Trumpet, April 2021, https://www.thetrumpet.com/23622-george-soros-and-barack-obama; Andrea Morris, "Billionaire George Soros Gives Whopping $50M to Help Biden and Other Dems Win US Elections," CBN News, July 28, 2020, https://www1.cbn.com/cbnnews/politics/2020/july/billionaire-george-soros-gives-whopping-50m-to-help-biden-and-other-dems-win-us-elections; Texans Jack & Dodie, "Soros, the Billionaire Funding BLM, Biden-Harris, Mayors and DAs Revealed," Clever Journeys, September 23, 2020, https://cleverjourneys.com/2020/09/23/soros-the-billionaire-funding-blm-biden-harris-mayors-and-das-revealed/; Joe Schoffstall, "Soros Pours Record $50 Million Into 2020 Election," *Washington Free Beacon*, July 27, 2020, https://freebeacon.com/elections/soros-pours-record-50-million-into-2020-election/.

5   Gregory Zuckerman and Julia Chung, "Billionaire George Soros Lost Nearly $1 Billion in Weeks After Trump Election," *Wall Street Journal*, updated January 23, 2017, https://www.wsj.com/articles/billionaire-george-soros-lost-nearly-1-billion-in-weeks-after-trump-election-1484227167.

6   Sam Meredith, "Soros Says China's Xi Is the 'Most Dangerous' Opponent of Those Who Believe in Open Society," CNBC, January 24 2019, updated Fri, January 25 2019, https://www.cnbc.com/2019/01/24/davos-soros-says-chinas-xi-most-dangerous-opponent-of-open-society.html; Katia Porzecanski, "George Soros Says Trump Administration Is 'Danger to the World'." Bloomberg, January 25, 2018, https://www.bloomberg.com/news/articles/2018-01-25/george-soros-says-trump-administration-is-danger-to-the-world#xj4y7vzkg.

7   Bruck, "The World According to George Soros," emphasis in original.

8   "The Restriction of Political Campaign Intervention by Section 501(c)(3) Tax-Exempt Organizations," IRS website, accessed July 20, 2022, https://www.irs.gov/charities-non-profits/charitable-organizations/the-restriction-of-political-campaign-intervention-by-section-501c3-tax-exempt-organizations.

9   See Rachel Ehrenfeld and Shawn Macomber, "Soros: The Man Who Would Be Kingmaker, Part I," American Center for Democracy, October 28, 2004, https://acdemocracy.org/the-man-who-would-be-kingmaker-part-i/.

10 Bruck, "The World According to George Soros."

11 See "Joe Biden Calls for Defunding the Police," YouTube video, 3:05, posted by GOP War Room, July 8, 2020, https://www.youtube.com/watch?v=ppoUCQLSXFE.

12 See the fifty-second clip of this interview on "Harris: 'I Applaud Eric Garcetti' for Defunding the Los Angeles Police," YouTube video, post by GOP War Room, June 9, 2020, https://www.breitbart.com/middle-east/2022/08/07/nearly-600-missiles-fired-at-israel-first-rocket-sirens-in-jerusalem/https://www.youtube.com/watch?v=nOmP6f02HHg.

13 Joshua Rhett Miller, "Bail Fund Backed by Kamala Harris Freed Minneapolis Man Charged with Murder," *New York Post*, September 8, 2021, https://nypost.com/2021/09/08/bail-fund-backed-by-kamala-harris-freed-man-charged-with-murder/.

14 See Internet Archive, accessed July 20, 2022, https://web.archive.org/web/20210903234111/https:/twitter.com/MNFreedomFund/status/1433917004084350984.

15 See Parker Thayer and Hayden Ludwig, "Breaking: Arabella's Left-Wing Activist Network Raked in $1.7 Billion in 2020—a 'Dark Money' Blowout," Capital Research Center, November 22, 2021, https://capitalresearch.org/article/breaking-arabellas-left-wing-activist-network-raked-in-1-7-billion-in-2020-a-dark-money-blowout/?blm_aid=45982721.

16 See "The Future of the Social Sector," Arabella Advisors, accessed July 20, 2022, https://www.arabellaadvisors.com/the-future-of-the-social-sector/.

17 Thayer and Ludwig, "Breaking."

18 Scott Walter, "Inside the Left's Web of 'Dark Money,'" *Wall Street Journal*, October 22, 2020, https://www.wsj.com/articles/inside-the-lefts-web-of-dark-money-11603408114.

19 Hayden Ludwig, "New Ethics Complaint: Soros-Funded Arabella Front Helped Democrats Break Congressional Ethics Rules," Capital Research Fund, January 25, 2022, https://capitalresearch.org/article/new-ethics-complaint-soros-funded-arabella-front-helped-democrats-break-congressional-ethics-rules/.

20 "Types of Organizations Exempt under Section 501(c)(4)," IRS, accessed July 20, 2022, https://www.irs.gov/charities-non-profits/other-non-profits/types-of-organizations-exempt-under-section-501c4.

21 Scott Bland, "Liberal 'Dark-Money' Behemoth Funneled More Than $400M in 2020," Politico, November 17, 2021, https://www.politico.com/news/2021/11/17/dark-money-sixteen-thirty-fund-522781.

22 Ludwig, "New Ethics Complaint."

ENDNOTES

23 Ludwig, "New Ethics Complaint."

24 Eliyohu Mintz, "George Soros' Quiet Overhaul of the U.S. Justice System," Eliyohu Mintz: My Thoughts on Education (blog), August 30, 2016, http://eliyohumintz.net/george-soros-quiet-overhaul-of-the-u-s-justice-system-2/.

25 Lee Brown, "Judge Jackson's Refusal to Define 'Woman' Threatens Women's Rights Movement, Ex-Olympian Warns," New York Post, March 24, 2022, https://nypost.com/2022/03/24/supreme-court-nominee-judge-ketanji-brown-wont-define-woman/.

26 See "Demand Justice," Influence Watch, accessed July 20, 2022, https://www.influencewatch.org/non-profit/demand-justice/.

27 See "Vera and Donald Blinken Open Society Archives," https://www.osaarchivum.org/blog/.

28 Discover the Network, Organizations Funded Directly by George Soros and his Open Society Foundations—The Millennium Report, March 21, 2017, https://themillenniumreport.com/2017/03/organizations-funded-directly-by-george-soros-and-his-open-society-foundations/.

29 Alex Safian, "Robert Malley and US Policy on Israel," CAMERA, March 11, 2015, https://www.camera.org/article/robert-malley-and-us-policy-on-israel/; Michael Pregent, "The Iran Deal Was a Bad Deal in 2015. It's an Even Worse One Now | Opinion," Newsweek, April 12, 2021, https://www.newsweek.com/iran-deal-was-bad-deal-2015-its-even-worse-one-now-opinion-1582527.

30 See John Solomon, "George Soros's Secret 2016 Access to State Exposes 'Big Money' Hypocrisy of Democrats," The Hill, August 7, 2019, https://thehill.com/opinion/white-house/456619-george-soross-secret-2016-access-to-state-exposes-big-money-hypocrisy-of-democrats/; Chris Kanthan, "US Staged a Coup in Ukraine—Here's Why and How," Nation of Change, August 15, 2018, https://www.nationofchange.org/2018/08/15/how-and-why-the-us-staged-a-coup-in-ukraine/; George Soros, "Keep the Spirit of the Maidan Alive," Open Society Voices, April 7, 2014, https://www.opensocietyfoundations.org/voices/keep-spirit-maidan-alive.

31 Key Global Health Positions and Officials in the U.S. Government, Global Health Policy, July 26, 2022. https://www.kff.org/global-health-policy/fact-sheet/key-u-s-government-agency-positions-and-officials-in-global-health-policy-related-areas/.

32 "Nominations" September 22, 2021, p. 56, https://www.foreign.senate.gov/imo/media/doc/09%2022%202021%20--%20Nominations%20--%20Nides%20Cohen%20Telles%20Udall%20Margon.pdf; Tovah Lazaroff, "Margon Rejects Pro-BDS Charge at Hearing for Top US Human Rights Post," Jerusalem Post, September 23, 2021, https://www.jpost.com/bds-threat/margon-reject-pro-bds-charge-at-hearing-for-top-us-human-rights-post-680146. See also Sarah Margon (@sarahmargon), "Airbnb to remove listings in Israeli settlements of occupied West Bank. Thanks @Airbnb for showing some good leadership here. Other companies should follow suit," Twitter, November 19, 1:06 p.m., https://twitter.com/sarahmargon/status/1064595675936108544; Peter Beinart, "I No Longer Believe in a Jewish State," New York Times, July 8, 2020, https://www.nytimes.com/2020/07/08/opinion/israel-annexation-two-state-solution.html.

33 Lauren Marcus, "Biden Pick to Key State Department position Another Long-Time Israel Critic," Jewish Voice, April 23, 2021, https://thejewishvoice.com/2021/04/biden-pick-to-key-state-department-position-another-long-time-israel-critic/.

34 U.S. Department of State, "DRL Strengthening Human Rights and Accountability in Israel and the West Bank and Gaza," state.gov, February 11, 2022, https://www.state.gov/drl-strengthening-human-rights-and-accountability-in-israel-and-the-west-bank-and-gaza/.

ENDNOTES

35 Adam Kredo, "How the Biden Administration Is Funding the Effort to Delegitimize Israel," *Washington Free Beacon*, March 10, 2022, https://freebeacon.com/biden-administration/how-the-biden-administration-is-funding-effort-to-delegitimize-israel/.

36 Allum Bokhari, "Biden Pushes Soros-Linked Far Left Radical Alvaro Bedoya for FTC Commissioner," Breitbart, November 12, 2021, https://www.breitbart.com/tech/2021/11/12/biden-pushes-soros-linked-far-left-radical-alvaro-bedoya-for-ftc-commissioner/.

37 See the Gigi Sohn webpage at http://gigisohn.com/about/; and the "Net Neutrality" page on the Daily Dot, accessed July 20, 2022, https://www.dailydot.com/tags/net-neutrality/.

38 See Joseph Vazquez, "Biden's FCC Nominee Is Heavily Connected to George Soros," mrc-NewsBusters, November 15, 2021, https://www.newsbusters.org/blogs/business/joseph-vazquez/2021/11/15/bidens-fcc-nominee-heavily-connected-george-soros.

39 "Coalition: FCC Nominee Gigi Sohn Needs a Second Hearing over Locast & Ethics Issues," Americans for Tax Reforms, January 28, 2022, https://www.atr.org/coalition-fcc-nominee-gigi-sohn-needs-a-second-hearing-over-locast-ethics-issues/.

40 Martyn Warwick, Will Rosenworcel finally move and push Gigi Sohn into the FCC seat?Telecom TV, Aug. 5, 2022. https://www.telecomtv.com/content/access-evolution/will-rosenworcel-intervene-and-push-gigi-sohn-into-the-fcc-seat-45121/.

41 The Editorial Board, "A Media Censor for the FCC?" *Wall Street Journal*, November 8, 2021, https://www.wsj.com/articles/a-media-censor-for-the-fcc-gigi-sohn-joe-biden-nominee-11636408804.

42 "Public Knowledge," Influence Watch, accessed July 20, 2022, https://www.influencewatch.org/non-profit/public-knowledge/.

43 See "Awarded Grants," Open Society Foundations, accessed July 20, 2022, https://www.opensocietyfoundations.org/grants/past?filter_keyword=Public+Knowledge.

44 Editorial Board, "Gigi Sohn's Strange Bedfellows," *Wall Street Journal*, December 6, 2021, https://www.wsj.com/articles/gigi-sohns-strange-bedfellows-newsmax-media-oan-fox-confirmation-censorship-net-neutraility-11638722334.

45 See "Leadership in Government Fellowship: Gigi Sohn," Open Society Foundations, accessed July 20, 2022, https://www.opensocietyfoundations.org/grants/leadership-in-government-fellowship?fellow=gigi-b-sohn; "Leadrhip in Government Fellowship, Open Society Foundations, accessed July 20, 2022, https://www.opensocietyfoundations.org/grants/leadership-in-government-fellowship?filter_year=2019&filter_past_year=2017&past=1.

46 Newsbusters, "Biden's FCC Nominee Is Heavily Connected to George Soros," NOQReport, November 15, 2021, https://noqreport.com/2021/11/15/bidens-fcc-nominee-is-heavily-connected-to-george-soros/.

47 Editorial Board, "A Media Censor for the FCC?"

48 Adam Eliyahu Berkowitz, "Biden Appoints Anti-Israel Muslim to Top Intelligence Position," Israel365 News, January 25, 2021, https://www.israel365news.com/164438/biden-appoints-anti-israel-muslim-to-top-us-intelligence-position/.

49 Adam Eliyahu Berkowitz, "Biden Hires Anti-Israel 'Soros Agent' to Key Position," Israel365 News, May 5, 2021, https://www.israel365news.com/190139/biden-hires-anti-israel-soros-agent-to-key-position/.

50 See "Ur M. Jaddou, Director, U.S. Citizenship and Immigration Services," U.S. Citizenship and Immigration Services, last updated August 3, 2021, https://www.uscis.gov/about-us/organization/leadership/ur-m-jaddou-director-us-citizenship-and-immigration-services; "America's Voice," Influence Watch, accessed July 21, 2022. https://www.influencewatch.org/non-profit/americas-voice/.

51   "Awarded Grants," America's Voice 2016–2019, Open Society Foundations, https://www.opensociety-foundations.org/grants/past?filter_keyword=america%27s%20voice&filter_year=2016%2C2017%2C2018%2C2019&page=2.

52   "America's Voice," Influence Watch.

53   See "Executive Branch Personnel Public Financial Disclosure Report (OGE Form 278e): Tyler Moran," U.S. Office of Government Ethics, accessed July 21, 2022, http://dailysignal.s3.amazonaws.com/WH%20Disclosure%20-%20Tyler-Moran.pdf; see "Who We Are," Immigration Hub, accessed July 21, 2022, https://theimmigrationhub.org/about-us; "Emerson Collective," Influence Watch, accessed July 21, 2022, https://www.influencewatch.org/non-profit/emerson-collective/.

54   See "About Us," You Are Home, accessed July 21, 2022, https://www.wearehome.us/about.

55   See "About Us," National Immigration Law Center, accessed July 21, 2022, https://www.nilc.org/about-us/our-supporters/.

56   "New Battleground Poll: Relentless Efforts to Deport Dreamers Jeopardizes Vote for President Trump," Immigration Hub, June 19, 2020, https://theimmigrationhub.org/new-battleground-poll-relentless-efforts-to-deport-dreamers-jeopardizes-trumpvote.

57   See Executive Branch Personnel Public Financial Disclosure Report (OGE Form 278e): Esther Olavarria," U.S. Office of Government Ethics, accessed July 21, 2022, http://dailysignal.s3.amazonaws.com/WH%20Disclosure-esther-olavarria.pdf.

58   Center for American Progress (CAP), Capital Search Center, https://capitalresearch.org/tag/center-for-american-progress-cap-cap-action-fund/.

59   See Executive Branch Personnel Public Financial Disclosure Report (OGE Form 278e): Ruiz, Emma N," U.S. Office of Government Ethics, accessed July 21, 2022, http://dailysignal.s3.amazonaws.com/WH%20Disclosure%20Emmy%20Ruiz.pdf.

60   See "Alumnus/Alumna of the Month: Vanita Gupta '01," NYU Law, accessed July 21, 2022. https://www.law.nyu.edu/alumni/almo/pastalmos/20032004almos/vanitaguptajanuary.

61   Lynn L. Bergeson and Carla N. Hutton, "DOJ and EPA Announce New Enforcement Strategy to Advance Environmental Justice," National Law Review 12, no. 126 (May 6, 2022): https://www.natlawreview.com/article/doj-and-epa-announce-new-enforcement-strategy-to-advance-environmental-justice; see also "FACT SHEET: President Biden Takes Executive Actions to Tackle the Climate Crisis at Home and Abroad, Create Jobs, and Restore Scientific Integrity Across Federal Government," White House, January 27, 2021, https://www.whitehouse.gov/briefing-room/statements-releases/2021/01/27/fact-sheet-president-biden-takes-executive-actions-to-tackle-the-climate-crisis-at-home-and-abroad-create-jobs-and-restore-scientific-integrity-across-federal-government/.

62   See Bridget Johnson, "DHS Standing Up Disinformation Governance Board Led by Information Warfare Expert," Homeland Security Today.US, April 27, 2022, https://www.hstoday.us/federal-pages/dhs/dhs-standing-up-disinformation-governance-board-led-by-information-warfare-expert/.

63   See "Jennifer Daskal: Founding Editor," Just Security (blog), accessed July 21, 2022, https://www.justsecurity.org/author/daskaljennifer/; "About Us," Just Security, accessed July 21, 2022, https://www.justsecurity.org/about-us/.

64   See "Awarded Grants: New York University," 2017, 2019, https://www.opensocietyfoundations.org/grants/past?filter_keyword=Just+Security.

65   Lev Golinkin, "Meet the Head of Biden's New 'Disinformation Governing Board,'" Kontinent USA (formerly on the Nation website), May 16, 2022, https://newkontinent.org/meet-the-head-of-bidens-new-disinformation-governing-board/.

66   Post Editorial Board, Good riddance to the 'Ministry of Truth' and Nina Jankowicz, *New York Post*, May 18, 2022. https://nypost.com/2022/05/18/good-riddance-to-the-ministry-of-truth-nina-jankowicz/.

67   Sam Stein and Natasha Korecki, "The Most Influential Think Tank of the Biden Era Has a New Leader," Politico, June 30, 2021, https://www.politico.com/news/2021/06/30/center-for-american-progress-new-leader-497167.

9: JUST A TALENTED HUNGARIAN?

1   George Soros, US Democracy Under Concerted Attack.

2   George Soros, Why I Support Reform Prosecutors, *Wall Street Journal*, July 31, 2022. https://www.georgesoros.com/2022/07/31/why-i-support-reform-prosecutors/.

3   Hungarian Prime Minister Viktor Orban Delivers Remarks at CPAC Conference in Texas, Aug 4, 2022, C-SPAN. https://www.c-span.org/video/?522151-2/hungarian-prime-minister-viktor-orban-delivers-remarks-cpac-conference-texas.

4   John Downing, Hungary's Viktor Orban is Vladimir Putin's Trojan horse as conflict worsens, Independent.ie, Feb. 19, 2022. https://www.independent.ie/opinion/comment/hungarys-viktor-orban-is-vladimir-putins-trojan-horse-as-conflict-worsens-41361581.html.

5   Hungarian Spectrum, Vitor Orban, Russa's Trojan Horse in Europe, Oct. 27, 2020. https://hungarianspectrum.org/2020/10/27/viktor-orban-russias-trojan-horse-in-europe/.

6   Ruth Ben-Gihat, CPAC 2022 features Viktor Orban, Donald Trump—a celebration of autocracy, MSNBC, Aug. 5, 2022. https://www.msnbc.com/opinion/msnbc-opinion/cpac-2022-features-orban-trump-illiberalism-texas-n1297750.

7   Rachel Ehrenfeld, "ObamaCare's Medical Marijuana," Forbes, August 13, 2009, https://www.forbes.com/2009/08/13/george-soros-marijuana-legalization-opinions-contributors-rachel-ehrenfeld.html?sh=728607fb2b72,].

EPILOGUE

1   PRESIDENTIAL PROCLAMATION ON MARIJUANA POSSESSION, The U.S. Department of Justice, November 2, 2022. https://www.justice.gov/pardon/presidential-proclamation-marijuana-possession.

2   Christina Wilkie, Biden pardons thousands of people convicted of marijuana possession, orders review of federal pot laws, CNBC, October 6, 2022, https://www.cnbc.com/2022/10/06/biden-to-pardon-all-prior-federal-offenses-of-simple-marijuana-possession-.html.

3   FAIR Analysis: 5.5 Million Illegal Aliens Have Crossed our Borders Since Biden Took Office—How is Secretary Mayorkas Still Employed?, October 25, 2022, https://www.fairus.org/press-releases/border-security/fair-analysis-55-million-illegal-aliens-have-crossed-our-borders.

4   ("Who Are the Biggest Donors?" OpenSecrets. Accessed November 8, 2022. https://www.opensecrets.org/elections-overview/biggest-donors.

ENDNOTES

INDEX

INDEX

THC, 58, 60
The Story, 75, 172
Thompson, Bernie. (D-MS), 83
Tiananmen Square, 139
Tides Center, 29, 71, 154
Tides Foundation, 71, 150, 151, 152
Tides Inc., 71–72
Tides Network, 71
Tides Two Rivers Fund, 71
"Time to Break the Silence on
    Palestine," 149
Time Magazine, 107
Tinder, 72
Tlaib, Rashida, 147, 148
tobacco smoke, 54
Tobias, Andrew, 14
Torrez, Raul, 85
Traboulsi, Samir, 16
transitional justice, 62
Tranparify, xiii
transgenderism, 11, 21
Transparency International Ukraine, 132
Travelers' Aid of New York, 107
Trayvon, Martin, 63, 152
Treaty of Versailles, 141
Trocaire, 156
Trotsky, Leon, 32
Trump administration, 117, 156,
    157, 168, 188
Trump, Donald, 4, 10, 23, 28, 75, 85, 122,
    123, 135, 156, 157, 173, 178, 179, 182,
    183, 186, 187
Trump-Russia collusion, 134, 178
Turkey, 32
Turner, Carlton E., 55
Twitter, 43, 71, 159, 166, 187
Tymas, Whytney, 77, 79

U

Uganda, 161
Ukraine, 10, 110, 115 116, 117, 131–136,
    169, 185, 190
Ukraine's Odessa region, 135
Ukraine's Order of Freedom, 134
Ukroboronprom, 135
UN high commissioner for human
    rights, 167
UN Watch, 167
UN Women, 156
Underwriting Democracy, 20
undocumented migrants, 3, 114
undocumented immigrants, 105, 109
UNDP, 156
Unended Quest, 2, 26, 27
UNICEF, 156
United Nations, 33, 57, 107, 127, 139, 145,
    146, 154, 155, 156, 158, 159, 163, 164,
    165, 166, 167
United Nations Human Rights Council
    (UNHRC), 146, 164, 165, 167
United Nations Relief and Works Agency
    (UNRWA), 158
United for Progress PAC, 22
United States, 6, 15, 20, 22, 23, 32, 34,
    35, 37, 39, 46, 65, 78, 86, 104, 108,
    109, 110, 113, 123, 134, 135, 149,
    164, 175, 192
United States Agency for International
    Development (USAID), 120, 129,
    130, 131, 158
United States Naval Academy, 128
universal jurisdiction, 20
UNT Dallas Foundation, 110
Urban Institute, 107, 108
US Citizenship and Immigration
    Services, 188
US Constitution, 2, 3, 98

INDEX

Yanukovych, Viktor, 132
Yesh Din, 146
Yivo Institute for Jewish Research, 23
Young Lords, 153
Youngkin, Glenn, 173
Yu, Miles, 128, 138, 139
Yushchenko, Viktor, 132

Z

Zalishchuk, Svitlana, 135
Zapatistas, 153
Zarif, Javad, 124, 127
Zeevi, Rehavam, 162
Zelenskyy, Volodymyr, 134
Zhao wing, 139
Zimmerman, George, 63
Zionism, 99, 140, 165,
Ziyang, Zhao, 138
Zola, Emile, 176